TOWARDS MANAGED PRIMARY CARE

Towards Managed Primary Care

The Role and Experience of Primary Care Organizations

JUDITH SMITH
University of Birmingham, UK

NICK GOODWIN
London School of Hygiene and Tropical Medicine, UK

ASHGATE

Published by
Ashgate Publishing Limited
Gower House
Croft Road
Aldershot
Hampshire GU11 3HR
England

Ashgate Publishing Company
Suite 420
101 Cherry Street
Burlington, VT 05401-4405
USA

Ashgate website: http://www.ashgate.com

British Library Cataloguing in Publication Data
Smith, Judith, 1964-
    Towards managed primary care : the role and experience of
    primary care organizations
    1. Health services administration - England 2. Primary care
    (Medicine) - England
    I. Title II. Goodwin, Nick
    362'1'068'0942

Library of Congress Cataloging-in-Publication Data
Smith, Judith, 1964-
    Towards managed primary care : the role and experience of primary
    care organizations / by Judith Smith and Nick Goodwin.
        p. cm.
    Includes bibliographical references and index.
    ISBN 0-7546-4227-5
    1. Primary health care--Great Britain. 2. National health services
    --Great Britain--Administration. 3. Health services administration
    --Great Britain. I. Goodwin, Nick. II. Title.
    [DNLM: 1. Primary Health Care--organization & administration
    --Great Britain. 2. State Medicine--organization & administration
    --Great Britain. W 84.6 S653t 2005]

RA395.G6S55 2005
362.1'0941--dc22

                                                                    2005024895

ISBN 0 7546 4227 5

Printed and bound in Great Britain by Antony Rowe Ltd, Chippenham, Wiltshire.

Contents

List of Figures

List of Tables

List of Boxes

Acknowledgements

The research on which this book is based was the result of the hard work of a team from the University of Birmingham, and we owe them particular thanks for their insights, contribution, and support. Special thanks are due to Emma Regen who project managed and led much of the research but was unable to author this book due to wider commitments, Chris Ham who supervised the study, Jonathan Shapiro, Hugh McLeod, James Raftery, Darren Baines, and Myrte Elbers who were part of the core research team, and Tracey Gray, Alison Hall, Kate Wood, Ralph Smith and Carey Hendron who provided valuable administrative and technical support.

Alan Glanz at the Department of Health's Policy Research Programme funded and guided the research with his usual wisdom and discretion, and the members of our project advisory group offered sound and constructive advice at all stages. Particular thanks are due to the many people in primary care groups and trusts who gave willingly of their time to take part in research fieldwork, especially at a time of organizational change within the NHS. We would also like to thank those who commented on the book, in particular Jackie Cumming, Bob Wells and Beverley Sibthorpe for their views from 'down under', Nick Mays for sageful comments, and finally to Martin Roland and Sally Wyke for their encouraging and expert remarks as the book's critical readers.

In writing this book, Judith wishes to thank Edward Peck at HSMC for enabling her to have the time and space to prepare the manuscript, Shirley Smith and the Cartwright-Rowleys for lending their homes and desks for a much-needed bolt-hole, and most of all, Tony, Richard, and Kathryn for putting up with the absence of their wife/mother, all in the cause of primary managed care.

Nick wishes to thank his work colleagues at the Health Services Research Unit and the NHS SDO R&D Programme for their support as the book neared completion. Nick would particularly like to thank Deidre Byrne for providing her expertise in helping to prepare the camera ready copy. To all his friends and family, but especially to Lourdes, there are further thanks for putting up with an absent friend over many weekends and for occasionally providing a sanctuary in which to think and to write.

List of Abbreviations

AHP	Allied Health Professional
CHI	Commission for Health Improvement
CHP	Community Health Partnership
CPPIH	Commission for Patient and Public Involvement in Health
DHSS	Department of Health and Social Security
EUR	Euro
FHSA	Family Health Services Authority
FPC	Family Practitioner Committee
GMS	General Medical Services
GP	General Practitioner
HMO	Health Maintenance Organization
HSMC	Health Services Management Centre
IM&T	Information Management and Technology
IPA	Independent Practitioner Association
IT	Information Technology
LHB	Local Health Board
LHCC	Local Health Care Co-operative
LIFT	Local Improvement Financial Trust
NatPaCT	National Primary and Care Trust Development Programme
nGMS	New General Medical Services
NHS	National Health Service
NHSE	National Health Service Executive
NSF	National Service Framework
PACT	Prescribing Analysis Cost Data
PALS	Patient Advice and Liaison Service
PCG	Primary Care Group
PCO	Primary Care Organization
PCT	Primary Care Trust
PDS	Personal Dental Service
PEC	Professional Executive Committee
PHO	Primary Health Organization
PMS	Personal Medical Service
TPP	Total Purchasing Pilot
WHO	World Health Organization

Chapter 1

Introduction

The Scope of this Book

This book tells the story of the primary care trust (PCT) that, over the period 2002-2005, became the main local public health, funding and commissioning body within the NHS in England. As its name suggests, the PCT has its roots in primary care, being responsible for the planning, delivery and quality assurance of primary care and community health services, and seeking to involve primary care professionals closely in its health improvement, decision-making, resource allocation, and service management activities.

PCTs have their origins in the emergence in the UK in the early 1990s of what have been termed 'primary care organizations' (PCOs). These bodies sought to increase the influence of primary care professionals, and in particular general practitioners (GPs), in health planning and resource allocation, and in the health system more generally. PCOs emerged as a response to the introduction of GP fundholding, an NHS scheme that enabled individual GP practices to take on a budget on behalf of their patients to purchase elective health services from hospitals and community service providers and improve services within their own practices. GP fundholders gradually started to group together into new organizations in the mid-1990s, and in parallel, GPs who chose not to engage in fundholding formed 'commissioning groups' or 'locality forums' that worked alongside local health authorities in planning and advising on local health services.

It has been a long and eventful journey since the tentative emergence of PCOs in the early 1990s, but PCTs in England now represent the main local health organization alongside acute hospitals and mental health trusts. The origins of PCOs, and the rationale for their development, both within the NHS and in the international context is explored. In particular, the experience of the NHS is seeking to organize and manage the two most ambitious incarnations of the PCO, the primary care group (PCG) and the primary care trust (PCT) is examined by drawing on evidence from a major three-year evaluation of these organizations, funded by the Department of Health Policy Research Programme and carried out by the Health Services Management Centre at the University of Birmingham.

Primary Health Care as the Central Function in a Health System

Before we consider how this book addresses the development and impact of PCG/Ts it is important to explore why it was that primary health care came to assume such a prominent place within the English health system, and what reasons existed for increasing the managed nature of the primary care sector. To answer these questions, one must look back to the point at which primary health care took its place as a serious player in health policy and management following the International Conference on Primary Care held in Alma Ata in 1978 (WHO, 1978). This conference developed an international vision of 'Health for All' by the year 2000 and reaffirmed primary care as the central mechanism to achieve this since:

> It [primary health care] forms an integral part of both the country's health system of which it is the central function and the main focus of the overall social and economic development of the community. It is the first level of contact of individuals, the family and the community with the national health system, bringing health care as close as possible to where people live and work and constitutes the first element of a continuing health care process (WHO, 1978, p. 1).

In making the case that primary care was the central function of a health system, the WHO conference was setting the scene for subsequent analysis of health systems and their outcomes, analysis that would underline the crucial importance of effective primary care to the overall health of a population. Perhaps the most influential of such analysts is Barbara Starfield, whose work has demonstrated clearly the benefits of a strong primary care orientation in a health system. Based on her extensive research, Starfield demonstrated how a primary care-led system not only improved health outcomes, but also lowered overall health care costs (Starfield, 1998). By ranking the primary care orientation of 12 western industrialized nations, she concluded that:

> ...countries with a strong primary care base to their health system achieve better outcomes, and at lower costs, than countries in which the primary care base is weaker (Starfield, 1998, p. 401).

In Starfield's analysis, features which were consistently associated with good/ excellent primary care included the comprehensiveness and family orientation of primary care practices, within a wider system in which governments regulated the distribution of healthcare resources via taxation or national insurance. Thanks to its historical basis on a system of primary care practices with gate-keeping and care co-ordinating roles, the UK ranked strongest in terms of its primary care orientation (Starfield, 1998). As a result, in 1997, only Spain had a lower per-capita expenditure on healthcare whilst the UK ranked in the top-third for health outcomes (Starfield, 1998).

Recognition of this link between strong primary care and improved health outcomes was re-emphasized in 1988 with the publication of the White Paper 'Promoting Better Health' (Department of Health and Social Security, 1988).

'Promoting Better Health' represented two things. Firstly, official recognition by government and policy makers that primary care was a potential force for change in relation to improving people's health. Secondly, the first step towards a more managed approach to primary care development in the UK, announcing the government's intention to use a series of targets and payments as a way of incentivizing GPs to achieve health objectives specified by policy makers and managers. This White Paper paved the way for the GP Contract of 1990 with its new system of targets, incentives and payments designed to facilitate much higher levels of practice-based chronic disease management, health promotion, health screening, immunizations and vaccinations, and an overall extension of the range of services delivered at practice level. In this way, 'Promoting Better Health' and the new 1990 GP Contract sought to introduce a greater degree of management into primary care, legitimizing the role of the Family Health Services Authority as a body enabled to develop and improve primary care through a process of applying the new GP contract and providing support to practices in reaching new objectives and targets. This was in sharp contrast to former Family Practitioner Committees that carried out a mainly administrative function in processing the financial claims of GPs, dentists, pharmacists and opticians. The scene was now set for a new era of 'managed' primary care and the eventual creation of primary care organizations (Peckham and Exworthy, 2003).

The Move Towards Managed Primary Care

The detail of how primary care in the UK became increasingly managed or 'corporate' (Smith and Walshe, 2004) over the period 1988 to 2004 is set out in Chapters 3 and 8 of this book. The reasons for this increasing desire on the part of policy makers to draw primary care more into the mainstream of NHS management can be identified as follows:

- to improve health outcomes;
- to manage demand and control costs;
- to engage primary care practitioners in commissioning;
- to enable greater integration of health services;
- to develop services in community and primary care settings; and
- to enable greater scrutiny of primary care services.

To Improve Health Outcomes

The increasing recognition of the importance of primary care as a vehicle for improving health outcomes has been outlined above. The mounting body of international evidence in this regard (Starfield, 1994; Starfield, 1998, Macinko et al, 2003; Schoen et al, 2004) is strongly supported by the experience of the UK health care system, where commentators agree that primary care became a more significant player in the NHS during the 1990s (Peckham and Exworthy, 2003; Ham,

2004). The ability of NHS primary care to be used as a means of improving health outcomes is enabled by two key factors. Firstly, the use of the 'registered list' as the basis of general practice, that is the registration of 99 per cent of the population with a named general practitioner who is paid a capitation fee for being responsible for the health and care of that population (Peckham and Exworthy, 2003). Secondly, the existence of a strong gatekeeping function in the NHS meaning that people cannot refer themselves directly to specialist care. This function was seen by Starfield (1998) as crucial to effective primary care delivery. These two factors taken together bear witness to a primary care system that provides a sound basis for a range of public health interventions, such as vaccinations and immunizations, child health surveillance, and health screening. As such, the identification of the improvement of the health of the local population as a core function of PCG/Ts (NHS Executive, 1998a) is a logical development in the trajectory of primary care being increasingly viewed as a the forum for developing people's well-being, in line with the original Alma Ata understanding of primary care (WHO, 1978).

To Manage Demand and Control Costs

A further consequence of the strong gatekeeping function in UK primary care is the capacity for a strong degree of demand management and cost control within the health care system. In contrast with a country such as France, that enables patients to refer themselves directly to specialists for outpatient consultations, the UK has a built-in system of demand management whereby the NHS has vested in GPs the role of determining the pattern and scale of usage of secondary care services. This gatekeeping function has been in place since the creation of the NHS in 1948, and has been credited with the relatively low overall costs of the NHS in relation to international comparisons (Ham, 2004). The central role played by primary care in determining levels and patterns of referrals to diagnostic services and to secondary care is undoubtedly one of the main reasons for the policy interest, from the late 1980s onwards, in drawing primary care more clearly into the mainstream of NHS management. Hence, the potential for using primary care as part of a policy to change patterns of service delivery towards a more primary care-focus (NHS Executive, 1994) was a key factor in the moves from the 1990s towards more managed primary care.

To Engage Primary Care Practitioners in Commissioning

Given that primary care is the main locus for referrals to secondary care in the UK, the Conservative Government in 1989 determined that GPs should be given the opportunity to hold budgets for this referred care, both in terms of community and some hospital services (Department of Health and Social Security, 1989). The rationale for this was both to improve patient choice of providers and to develop more responsive hospital services within an internal market (Thatcher, 1993). There was also a desire to use GPs more explicitly as a route for controlling health care costs and managing demand. Margaret Thatcher notes in her memoirs:

> Giving GPs budgets of their own also promised to make it possible for the first time to put reasonable limits on their spending…the more closely we examined the concept of having GPs shop around for the best quality and value treatment for their patients, the more fruitful the idea seemed (Thatcher, 1993, p. 615).

This move to give budgets to GPs for services to which they referred their patients represented the first move towards engaging primary care practitioners in the purchasing or commissioning of health care, a move that is explored in detail in Chapters 3 and 11.

To Enable Greater Integration of Health Services

A key UK health policy imperative during the 1990s was that of seeking to develop more integrated health services and in particular of finding ways of bridging what was often seen as the inappropriate divide between primary and secondary care and between health and social care services (Goodwin and Shapiro, 2001). New 'intermediate care' services at the interface of primary and secondary care were becoming more prevalent. For example, there was a trend towards the development of stroke rehabilitation teams, community-based mental health care, and intensive home nursing services aimed at avoiding hospital admission. There was a desire on the part of policy makers and managers to extend such services across the NHS and to find ways of incentivizing the development of a greater range of community-based services that dovetailed with primary care and hospital provision (Department of Health and Social Security, 1988; NHS Executive, 1994). The wish for this integration to be shaped and developed by primary care was made clear in the articulation in 1994 of a policy of a 'primary care-led NHS' (NHS Executive, 1994).

The role of primary care in leading and bringing about improved NHS service integration has, since 2000, increasingly been seen through the lens of managed care from the United States. Within managed care, an organization typically has a capitated budget for providing care for a particular group of patients, and a brief to try and do this in as integrated and cost-effective manner as possible. Managed care organizations in the United States are based on the premise of providing as much care as possible in the home or community, and in using hospital care as a support to the main community services (Robinson and Steiner, 1998). Once again, this is evidence of the need for effective local primary care organizations capable of holding a budget and designing and delivering high quality integrated care.

To Develop Services in Community and Primary Care Settings

Allied to the concept in the 1990s of developing a greater range of integrated services across the traditional boundaries of primary and secondary care was an imperative to extend the provision of services within primary care itself. This was seen as a prerequisite to being able to have a broader range of care outside hospitals, something that was being encouraged as part of overall trends towards care that was less reliant on inpatient hospital stays (Ham et al, 1998). 'Promoting Better Health' (Department of Health and Social Security, 1988) was the first major policy initiative in this regard, seeking to incentivize GPs and their teams to deliver chronic disease management care (previously the domain of hospital outpatient services) and health promotion within practices. One of the areas in which GP fundholding and its spin-off developments (GP commissioning, GP multifunds, total purchasing projects – see Chapter 3) had an impact on health care was in focusing on the development of additional services within primary care settings (Smith et al, 2004). The reasons for this desire on the part of primary care budget-holders and commissioners to develop primary care included: an interest in improving services of immediate relevance to their own practices; a wish to avoid referrals to hospital by means of offering new services in local settings; a recognition that patients prefer not to go to hospital in most cases; and the relatively straightforward nature of such developments in comparison with persuading acute hospitals to reshape care (LeGrand et al, 1998; McClelland et al, 2001; Smith et al, 2004).

To Enable Greater Scrutiny of Primary Care Services

The importance of ensuring proper scrutiny and performance management of health services, from both a clinical and financial/managerial perspective, has been a prime policy preoccupation in the UK, in particular since 1997. The announcement of a policy of clinical governance in 1997 (Department of Health, 1997a) appeared at first to apply only to hospital services, but subsequent guidance (Department of Health, 1998a) clarified that fact that clinical governance would indeed apply to primary care and community-based services, with a requirement that systems be put in place to develop agreed standards for care and its management, monitor those standards, and take action to address shortfalls. In order to develop this more structured and rigorous approach to the management and assurance of quality within primary care, there was a need for overarching structures. The parallel development of PCG/Ts in the English NHS was the structural solution provided by the government in respect of providing governance and accountability arrangements that would hold practices to account for their clinical as well as managerial activities. So it was that PCG/Ts became the local governing body for the quality and management of primary care and community health services – their role in managing the performance of local services is explored in more depth in Chapter 8.

Issues Raised by the Development of More Managed Primary Care

The desire on the part of the NHS to have a more managed primary care system raises some crucial questions about organizational development and in particular how to bring about a cultural sea-change in primary care away from a relatively autonomous practice-based system towards one more focused on local primary care organizations with responsibility for the care and health of a population. Practical challenges for the NHS (and for any other health system seeking to develop more managed primary care) include:

- understanding the context of and creating the appropriate conditions for primary care organizations;
- getting it right – the organization and management of primary care organizations;
- making it happen – bringing about change in primary care organizations; and
- looking to the future – implications for research and practice.

These four core challenges are used as the basis for the discussion and analysis of research evidence on PCG/Ts within this book. The selection of these four core areas of context, organization, change, and the future is based on the premise that the development of effective primary care organizations requires that each of these issues is properly understood and addressed by those clinicians and managers charged with delivering managed primary care.

Overview of the Book

The main focus of this book is on the practical experience of developing and managing PCTs and on the lessons that can be drawn from this for future policy relating to the management and evaluation of organizations in primary care in the UK and elsewhere.

Exploring the Context of Primary Care Groups and Trusts

In the first three chapters, this book considers the context and conditions within which primary care organizations have developed in a number of countries. What is revealed is how the English system has been the most vigorous implementer of the PCO approach and that, as a result, there have been particular difficulties faced by practitioners in managing, and researchers in evaluating, such a complex and innovative process.

In assessing the international context of PCO development, Chapter 2 focuses on a comparison of the experience in the four countries of the UK together with an assessment of PCO innovations in, the USA, Netherlands, Sweden, New Zealand, and Australia. The increasingly divergent nature of health policy across the four UK nations is drawn out, with a focus on how, post-devolution in 1999, the degree to which primary care organizations have been used as a vehicle for service development and health commissioning has varied extensively. For example Scotland has abandoned the quasi-market in favour of a system based on vertical integration across acute and primary care, whilst England has retained a clearly market-based system with PCOs as the main local planning and funding body, and a return in 2005 to a policy of practice-led commissioning (Department of Health, 2004a). The trend towards more managed primary care in the USA (through managed care), the Netherlands (through local PCOs and transmural care), Sweden (with a range of regional experiments), New Zealand (through strong independent practitioner associations), and Australia (through professionally-led divisions of general practice) is explored as part of an overall consideration of the move towards a greater focus on primary care and its role in health systems. Comparisons are made of these different experiences, and overall themes and messages distilled.

Chapter 3 focuses on the English experience of developing PCOs, tracking their emergence from 1991 (with GP fundholding), through its extensions and alternatives in the 1990s, to the Labour Government's policy of implementing a national network of PCGs, followed by a move to PCTs, over the period 1999-2005. In examining each of the phases of development of PCOs in the English NHS, there is a particular focus on highlighting the main lessons to have emerged from major policy evaluation studies, and in developing a set of core themes that define the overall experience of moving towards an arguably more primary care-based health system, at least in terms of organizational form and function. The chapter concludes by setting out a policy and management agenda for PCTs in England, noting the importance of recent contextual developments such as the establishment of foundation hospital trusts, the introduction of a new 'payment by results' financial regime marking a clear return to the use of market forces to shape health services, and the encouragement of integration of roles between health and local government (Department of Health, 2004a).

Chapter 4 represents a consideration of the experience of designing and carrying out policy evaluation studies of PCOs, with a focus on how such research projects can be made robust enough to deal with the complexities of PCOs and in particular the rapidly changing policy context within which PCOs inevitably have to operate. The process of designing and carrying out the HSMC national evaluation of PCG/Ts is used as an example of the issues faced by researchers seeking to carry out rigorous and yet relevant research in a health system where organizational change takes place with almost frightening regularity. The selection of appropriate research methods is explored, as is the importance of understanding the interplay between the context of PCOs and the mechanisms used by those seeking to use PCOs as a vehicle for change (Pawson and Tilley, 1997; Goodwin et al, 2000). The chapter concludes with an exploration of the politics of evaluation, tackling issues such as how researchers respond to changes in the policy context and ways in which research can influence policy and practice, and the relationship between researchers and funders.

The Organization and Management of Primary Care Groups and Trusts

In this section of the book, practical management challenges common to all PCOs are examined, including the development of appropriate organizational and governance arrangements, the role and engagement of GPs, nurses and allied health professionals in operating PCOs, and the management of performance.

Chapter 5 represents an assessment of the organizational arrangements and structures put in place by PCG/Ts, including an evaluation of good practice that can be distilled for future management and research in PCOs. Issues considered in this chapter include the range of structural options for shaping a PCO, the relationship between clinical and managerial leadership, the dynamics of different professional groups and disciplines within the governing bodies of PCOs, the costs of running effective PCOs, and the ways in which proper accountability arrangements can be assured – both in relation to PCO staff and local users and communities.

This theme of how to engage local professionals and other staff in the strategic and operational development of PCOs is further developed in Chapters 6 and 7. In Chapter 6, an overview is given of the experience of GPs within PCOs, focusing on their role at board, professional executive, and 'grassroots' level. This includes an examination of the degree to which GPs have influenced the direction of PCOs and the ways in which GPs in PCOs link with the 'constituents' back in practices. Similarly, in Chapter 7, the role and engagement of nurses and allied health professionals is explored, with some sobering conclusions reached regarding the dissonance between the apparent enthusiasm of such groups for the work and aims of PCOs, yet their relatively under-developed capacity to have effective influence at senior and strategic levels.

The section on the organization and management of PCG/Ts concludes with Chapter 8, this being a consideration of the issue of performance management in PCG/Ts. An examination of what constitutes 'good performance' in a PCG/T is given, followed by an account of the experience of developing targets and performance measures for these NHS organizations. The practical reality of managing PCG/T performance is explored in relation to the assessment of performance of individual clinicians, the development of performance of practices and clinical teams, the management of locality performance, and the overall assessment and performance management of PCG/Ts as whole organizations. The chapter concludes with a consideration of the relationship between a PCO and its supervisory tier and the rest of a health system, with lessons being provided in relation to how performance can be appropriately measured, developed and improved.

Bringing about Change in Primary Care Organizations

The final section of the book focuses on how PCOs can become vehicles for change within a health system, developing local health services and improving the health of the populations for whom they assume responsibility. Chapter 9 explores the public health role of PCG/Ts and considers to what degree there has been success in achieving health improvement objectives. A detailed exploration is made of the relationship between English PCOs and their local authority (municipal authority), including the dynamic between health and social care provision, developing a broader view of health beyond the traditional NHS biomedical model, and examining the role of the PCT as the key link between the local NHS and the local authority. The chapter concludes with a consideration of the ways in which PCG/Ts have tried to develop partnerships with the local community, distilling a set of facilitating and inhibiting factors in relation to this often problematic area of health services management (where PCOs have faced similar hurdles to those encountered by hospitals and other providers before them).

Chapter 10 examines how PCOs have developed and improved primary care services. It examines the lessons related to what facilitated or inhibited effective primary care development, drawing on the relatively extensive evidence base in this area of PCO evaluations, at least in comparison with health improvement and commissioning (Smith et al, 2004). Primary care development is examined within three core areas: practice service development; the management and development of prescribing; and the introduction of clinical governance within primary care.

The most controversial and problematic area of activity for PCG/Ts, is that of how to make a reality of the commissioning function. As Chapter 2 reveals, English PCTs remain the only PCO internationally to have taken on fully this type of responsibility. In Chapter 11, an assessment is made of the experience of PCG/Ts in developing the commissioning function and in bringing about changes to clinical services in intermediate and secondary care. The importance of understanding the different levels at which commissioning takes place is emphasized, as is the importance of securing effective clinical engagement, developing adequate management capacity, effective relationships with other elements of the local health system, and robust budget-holding and accountability processes. The chapter concludes with an examination of how recent changes to the English NHS policy context, both in relation to commissioners and providers, might influence the future role of PCOs in the commissioning of health and health services.

In Chapter 12, the vital importance of ensuring effective clinical engagement in PCG/Ts is returned to, with an overall assessment of how PCOs can sustain such engagement in the longer term. The nature and motivation of professionals to work within 'managed' systems is examined and a warning is sounded about the risk of PCOs becoming overly bureaucratic and 'statutory', hence risking the loss of the clinical ownership that has marked out those PCOs with highest levels of clinical engagement such as GP fundholding, New Zealand Independent Practitioner Associations (IPAs) and GP commissioning groups. Lessons are drawn out as to how effective clinical engagement can be nurtured, including how this can take place at practice, locality and overall PCO level.

Looking to the Future – Implications for Research and Practice

The book's conclusions are set out in two chapters, one (Chapter 13) that focuses on the evaluation of progress made by PCG/Ts (implications for research) and the other (Chapter 14) that concentrates on lessons for future policy and practice in developing PCOs in the UK and the international context, with an emphasis on what facilitates and inhibits such developments. The concluding chapters take the lessons as distilled in all preceding chapters and draw them together into an overall set of messages about how PCOs can be researched and developed, with an emphasis on using the available research evidence as the basis for robust and practically-oriented lessons. The book's overriding conclusion is that primary care has become increasingly more important within many health systems, and as part of this, the governments of many countries, including the UK, have sought to manage primary care more closely and effectively. The development of PCOs has been a crucial part of this policy direction, and this book tells one part of the story of PCO development, seeking to draw from that story messages of relevance to others embarked on traveling or researching such journeys.

Chapter 2

Developing Primary Care Organizations: The International Context

In Europe and other Western countries there is considerable agreement among national policy-makers that primary care should be re-engineered to become central to a well-designed health care system (Saltman et al, 2004). The growth of the primary care organization (PCO) has become an international phenomenon and has been used as a strategy to tackle a series of key challenges facing healthcare systems including appropriateness, efficiency and equity in service provision. PCOs are tackling a range of common problems, including variations in the patterns and levels of prescribing in primary care, rising demand for unplanned admissions to hospitals and lengthening waiting lists (Mays et al, 2001).

The allocation of health care budgets on a capitation basis is a key mechanism that helps PCOs co-ordinate the delivery of care to enrolled populations. This approach is the basis of the 'managed care' model of service delivery that is characterized by the vertical integration of service delivery between primary, secondary and tertiary care (Robinson and Steiner, 1998). Furthermore, PCOs have developed to expand the scope of care provision into a range of entirely new care services (such as health promotional activities, screening and immunizations) and/or to substitute for hospital-based services (such as the provision of minor surgery or the development of diagnostic treatment centres) (Wensing et al, 1998; Groenewegen et al, 2000).

Despite these trends, divergent reform processes are apparent in different countries which reveal a degree of uncertainty as to the best way forward. This chapter seeks to provide an overview of these international trends by examining how and why countries are adopting the PCO as a key strategy in health system reform since the different experiences of PCO development raise important generic issues and lessons for the effective development and management of primary care organizations generally.

Primary Care in the Four UK Countries

During the 1990s the NHS in the UK experimented with a range of differing primary care configurations with the dual aim of engendering leverage (and hence better quality) over hospital providers and re-investing in primary care. By 1997, a 'mosaic' of diverse primary care organizations had been created reflecting a plurality of purchasing agencies (Mays and Dixon, 1996; Smith et al, 1998). As a consequence, primary health care professionals within the UK system had been taken on a rapid journey away from a situation of working in isolated and small general practices, to working in large multi-disciplinary teams with ever growing responsibilities for tasks such as commissioning hospital services, tackling service integration and health improvement (Goodwin, 2001).

In the mid 1990s, policy makers began to embrace the so-called 'third way' manifest in reinforcing and rationalizing parts of the Conservative market reforms, such as primary care-led services, and encouraging the devolution of resources to primary care organizations but under a more controlled system of regulatory mechanisms (Greer, 2001). The New Labour Government elected in 1997 was committed to ending the internal market system yet the role of the PCO wielding devolved resources to influence primary and secondary care services was reaffirmed. Devolution of a different kind emerged in 1999 as the UK's constituent nations gained a degree of political autonomy. Whilst the UK had often been seen as a paradox of four nations within one country (Exworthy, 2001) political devolution has led to explicit variations in health policy reform and the nature of primary care innovations.

The NHS and Primary Care in England

The direction of health care in England emerged from the NHS White Paper 'The New NHS: Modern, Dependable' (Department of Health, 1997). Initially, the paper heralded the abolition of the internal market in favour of a greater focus on national quality standards. However, the centre-piece to the strategy from a primary care perspective was the creation of PCGs designed to cover 'natural communities' of about 100,000 people. Initially a ten-year programme of development, it was envisaged that these primary care organizations would eventually reach PCT status whereby they would be devolved budgets to deliver primary and community care services; commission (purchase) secondary care services; and be responsible for improving health and tackling inequalities.

In reality, further NHS reforms and political expediency pushed the development of PCTs to the forefront of care planning and delivery in the English NHS within just three years. By April 2004, 304 PCTs in England had been established with full delegated budgetary responsibility for 75 per cent of hospital and community health services. Hence, the primary care organization in England was placed at the vanguard of care provision since it has responsibility both for the planning, co-ordination, provision and/or commissioning of a comprehensive range of services for local populations. Many commentators suggest that the primary care organization in England, and primary care managerialism, will remain key elements in health policy for some time (Peckham and Exworthy, 2003) yet further reforms of their function are likely in the future, particularly with the rise of Foundation Hospitals and consumer choice as political goals, and the introduction of a policy of practice-based commissioning in April 2005. The full story of the genesis of English PCTs is described in Chapter 3.

The NHS and Primary Care in Scotland

Since devolution, the Scottish Parliament has had full legislative power for health care and *NHS Scotland* has undergone a series of major structural changes. Following policy recommendations in their 1997 White Paper *Designed to Care* (Secretary of State for Scotland, 1997) the approach taken has been to deconstruct the internal market system of purchasers (Health Boards and fundholders) and providers (NHS trusts) to be replaced over time by a system of 15 unified Health Boards. These Boards represent a single corporate entity for health care, most containing one acute and one primary care trust acting as operating divisions, and with responsibility for strategic planning, governance and performance management for their population (NHS Confederation, 2004a).

In terms of primary care, fundholding (repealed as part of the abolition of the purchaser-provider split) was replaced by 79 Local Healthcare Co-operatives (LHCCs). These co-operatives acted as voluntary networks of GP practices with responsibility for delivering services for their local community. However, unlike PCTs in England, they were not budget-holding and commissioning authorities, but received their funding from their local primary care trust and operated to the priorities set out by Local Health Plans. The primary care trusts themselves are responsible for primary, community and mental health services and cover populations of between 25,000 and 150,000 (Exworthy and Peckham, 2003).

The removal of primary care-based purchasing in Scotland has thus been replaced with a 'closed' system emphasizing partnership working. During 2003, LHCCs evolved into Community Health Partnerships (CHPs) with an enhanced role in service planning and delivery. CHPs are able to take on greater responsibility for the deployment of resources by NHS Boards and act as a focus to integrate primary, secondary and specialist services. Moreover, they are expected to play a role in integrating care provision with local authorities; play a pivotal role in delivering health improvement to their local communities; and engage in a dialogue with local people through public partnership forums (NHS Confederation, 2003a).

The NHS and Primary Care in Wales

The process of political devolution has been slower in Wales and, unlike Scotland, the Welsh Assembly has no law-making powers despite being responsible for structural changes to health care systems (Hazell and Jervis, 1998). At the time of devolution, the NHS Wales Department included a system of five Health Authorities, 16 NHS Trusts and the fledgling creation of a range of voluntary Local Health Groups, the Welsh equivalent of English Primary Care Groups but with no devolved powers to purchase or commission services.

Since April 2003, the five Health Authorities in Wales have been replaced by 22 Local Health Boards (LHBs) each of which is coterminous with its associated unitary authority. The aims of the LHBs are to provide a more locally sensitive and democratic health service by devolving responsibility for commissioning and improving health to a more local scale (NHS Confederation, 2003b). Like PCTs in England, each LHB has its own board and management team and its main roles are similar – securing and providing primary and community care services; securing secondary care; improving the health of local communities; and engaging with local partners and the public. In the short term, however, as LHBs develop their organizational and managerial capabilities, a 'Business Services Centre' has taken responsibility for contracting with GPs and secondary care hospitals. However, the longer term idea is to create PCT-like organizations that receive 75 per cent of the overall NHS Wales budget to commission services directly. Unlike PCTs in England, provision of community services remains a function for the NHS Trusts.

The NHS and Primary Care in Northern Ireland

Political devolution in Northern Ireland has been a fraught process. Following the development of new proposals for the future organization of health and social services in Northern Ireland in 1998, the Northern Ireland Assembly has been continually suspended and re-established. This has led to a policy vacuum in which firm decisions have been difficult to make in a system lacking political consensus (Greer, 2001).

Initially, the Northern Ireland Assembly discussed two potential models for health and social care. The first was an English-style internal market led by primary care organizations; the second a Scottish-style regional planning system merging purchasers and providers (Greer, 2001). The 1999 production of 'Fit for the Future' (Department of Health and Social Security, 1999) presented the preferred vision of primary care co-operatives with responsibility for assessing health and social care needs, developing local plans for improving health and well-being, and taking a central role in the commissioning of services from providers. A number of primary care commissioning group pilots were established to test the new approach whilst existing fundholding arrangements were retained (McCay and Donnelly, 2000).

This plurality in primary care-based organizations was replaced in April 2002 with the creation of 15 Local Health and Social Care Groups. These groups have responsibility for planning the delivery of primary and secondary care. Like former PCGs in England and LHBs in Wales, these groups are subcommittees of their local Health and Social Services Board and comprise multi-agency representation including representatives from acute hospital trusts. GPs, though invited, are generally not participating in protest at the abolition of fundholding. It is hoped that these groups will assume responsibility for the commissioning of services involving delegated budgets in the longer term (NHS Confederation, 2003c).

The UK: One Country, Four Health Care Systems

The impact of political devolution in the UK has led to significant variations in health care delivery. In England, the direct decentralization of budgets to PCTs to provide and commission services reveals an approach that has retained a dual belief in the potential for primary care organizations to plan, co-ordinate and integrate services but also to use budgets and contracts to influence secondary care provision. In Wales and Northern Ireland, fledgling primary care organizations have planning and health improvement as their main objectives. Though budgets to commission services may be devolved to them in the longer term, they are more strategically aligned with local authorities, in the case of Wales, and more vertically integrated with providers and planners, in the case of Northern Ireland. In Scotland, Community Heath Partnerships act as the forum for developing service integration and care strategies, but do not receive formal budgets under a system that is more centrally managed and controlled. What is apparent across these countries is consensus in the efficacy of the primary care organization as a mechanism to plan and co-ordinate service provision, but a difference in opinion as to their role in purchasing services directly.

The International Trend to Develop Primary Care Organizations

As the UK develops its health and social care systems based around primary care organizations, policy makers and managers may be able to draw lessons from the extensive experience of the process in other countries. Common features in many Western health care systems include the development of capitated primary care networks, the devolution of financial and clinical responsibilities, and the development of public-private partnerships (Goodwin, 1999). This section examines this trend across a range of different systems – the business model in the USA, the social insurance models of Australia and the Netherlands, and the tax-based systems in Sweden and New Zealand.

Primary Care in the USA

The USA employs a business model to health care provision through the use of private health insurance and does not have a strong tradition in the management and integration of primary care services (Robinson, 2003). The notion of restricting choice through gatekeeping, or employing prescribed care pathway protocols, is regarded as contrary to this business ethic (Starfield, 1994). Consequently, free primary care is available only to the over 65s and to those on very low incomes through the Medicare and Medicaid insurance schemes that between them cover 22 per cent of the population.

Managed care in the USA has been promoted to control rising health care costs (Table 2.1) and overcome a growing cohort of uninsured and under-insured people. In its original philosophy, managed care was a not-for-profit system whereby high quality comprehensive benefits would be provided in a system that emphasized integration, health promotion and education, and cost-effectiveness. The strategy was for insurers to select and manage providers on the basis of quality and to engender compliance with the use of managed care techniques such as disease management protocols, care pathways, utilization review, and contractual incentives and penalties

(Robinson and Steiner, 1998; Smith, 1998). Before the emergence of managed care and HMOs there was no formal system of primary care in the USA. However, under most HMO schemes, patients are allocated a primary care physician who becomes responsible for their care and through whom appraisals and referrals to secondary care are made.

Table 2.1 Main contributors of medical cost inflation in the USA

- Fee-for-service payment means providers have the incentive to over-treat patients to realize greater income
- Medicare and Medicaid are 'frozen' into the fee-for-service indemnity model due to the political power of the medical profession
- Lack of costs sharing (user charges) and employer-led contributions means patients are not concerned or aware of the costs of what they receive
- Employer contributions to health insurance are tax free without limits creating an incentive for employees to take compensation in the form of medical cover rather than cash
- Absence of utilization management and quality controls

Source: Enthoven (1999).

The level of management in primary care varies depending on the type of managed care system employed. For example, under a 'preferred provider' arrangement, an insurer selects providers and negotiates prices, usually on some form of discounted fee-for-service arrangement. A primitive system of utilization management is usually employed in which, for example, primary care physicians would need to seek approval before referring patients for non-emergency operations. Primary care physicians under this arrangement usually remain in solo or small group practices dealing with the insurer on a non-exclusive basis (Robinson and Steiner, 1998). The approach lacks any formal integration and only a limited degree of 'management'.

The most popular and growing form of managed care organization in the USA is the Independent Practitioner Association (IPA). Within primary care, they comprise a combination of practices within an association which contracts as a single body with insurance agencies. In this model, primary care physicians are able to share risks, manage resources, integrate primary care networks and undertake utilization review. However, such activities remain limited because these for-profit corporate organizations are primarily seen as a method to protect self-interests and grow monopolies. In Boston, for example, 1100 primary care physicians covering 1.5 million patients have developed Partners Community Health Incorporated as an organization that works collectively on behalf of primary care physicians to negotiate prices with insurers, create networks, and manage capital facilities. There is very little medical management (Shapiro and Goodwin, 2001). This type of model grew in the USA from 1.5 million enrolees in 1980 to 14.7 million in 1992 and accounted for about 40 per cent of all managed care enrolees in the USA (Miller and Luft, 1994; Gabel, 1997).

The 'purest' model of the managed care organization is encapsulated in the staff-model of Kaiser Permanente, an integrated purchaser-provider system in which physicians and hospital providers work exclusively within a 'closed' system providing comprehensive care packages to the insured. There are 8.2 million members, mostly located in California (Robinson, 2003). The Kaiser model has attracted great interest from abroad due to its low hospital utilization rates. Comparisons with Kaiser and the UK NHS reveal that acute bed days for the eleven leading causes of bed use were 3.5 times lower (Ham et al, 2003). Significantly, all studies point to the higher level of integration, active patient management, use of intermediate care, and medical leadership as key contributory factors (Feacham et al, 2002; Willis, 2002; Ham et al, 2003). As Shapiro (2003) points out, Kaiser Permanente is unlike any other managed care approach in the USA as primary care physicians work in multi-disciplinary groups in a not-for-profit culture that reduces any distinction between primary and secondary care, or generalist and specialist, thus helping to integrate care in primary and community settings.

The managed care model in the USA has come under increasing pressure from the medical profession, whose clinical freedoms and profits are compromised, and also from patients, who have seen their right of entitlement to care and freedom of choice eroded. As Robinson (2001) has observed, a managed care backlash is underway that has forced insurers to compete for enrolees on the basis of choice leading to a renewed rise in premiums to the point where most managed care organizations are not performing that much better than unmanaged plans.

Primary Care in the Netherlands

Like other European countries, in the early 1990s the Netherlands introduced a system of budgets to encourage competition, engender effectiveness and raise quality (Schut, 1995). As a social health insurance-based system, rather than create competition between providers patients were given the opportunity to choose between 24 competing insurance agents or 'sickness funds'. These sickness funds receive risk-adjusted capitation payments from the Central Fund, and work with providers to develop a range of coverage and benefits within their scheme, including contracting with primary care providers. However, their effectiveness in developing comprehensive networks of providers and using utilization review techniques to create efficiency and reduce costs in hospital provision has been mixed (Schut and Van Dorslaer, 1999).

Primary care in the Netherlands is well developed and largely provided by independent GPs working mostly in solo practices with an average list size of 2300 patients (Busse, 2002). Under the terms of the Dutch Health Insurance Act, patients must register with a GP who is then responsible for their primary care needs. GPs are paid on a flat capitation basis, regardless of patient profiles, and services are provided free at the point of delivery with few co-payments. Patients with private health insurance can choose any GP, pay a fee for service, and claim back the costs from their insurance company. The GP acts as gatekeeper in the system and also tend to 'specialize' in common and minor diseases and in care for patients with chronic illnesses. The impact of gatekeeping, specialization and capitated payments is a low referral rate (in only 6 per cent of contacts) and a strikingly low rate of prescribed drugs that are provided in only slightly more than half of all diagnoses compared to a 75 to 95 per cent in other European countries (Busse, 2002).

Primary care in the Netherlands, however, remains poorly integrated with secondary care since GPs have no hospital privileges and no leverage over secondary care provision. Moreover, there is a shortage of GPs in parts of the larger urban areas. In recent years, however, GPs have developed so-called locum groups of eight to ten members to provide out-of-hours services and substitute for each other in cases of illness or holiday. Indeed, the number of group practices and health centres staffed by multi-professional groups, including GPs, nurses, physiotherapists and social workers, has been increasingly rapidly (Van der Linden et al, 2001; Busse 2002). One of the reasons for the growing popularity of larger organizations of primary care providers has been growing public dissatisfaction with rising waiting lists and the lack of integrated provision and co-ordination of care, with associated variations in quality, due to competing sickness funds (Lieverdink, 2001).

A good example of the development of the primary care organization in the Netherlands is the creation, in January 2001, of the Almere Health Care Group that provides a comprehensive and integrated package of primary, outpatient and residential care provision for 140,000 people. The integrated primary and community care system salaries employees directly and encourages team working between GPs, pharmacists, physiotherapists and other health and social care staff. A system of five primary health care centres, each covering between 20,000-30,000 patients, provides a comprehensive range of primary care services in a single location. A common services organization facilitates the working of the Group and a management team promotes and contracts its services to sickness funds as well as performance manages the system. The aim of the primary care organization is to provide services of a better quality as patients demand more integrated and comprehensive care that is locally accessible (Almere Health Care Group, 2004).

Group working of this sort in the Netherlands remains the exception and Government policies remain concentrated on the use of sickness funds to provide leverage in the system. The July 2001 reform plan 'Vraag aan Bod' ('Enquiry for a Solution') emphasized the need to restructure the insurance system to improve equity and coverage and proposed one unified insurance scheme to be managed by a competing system of sickness funds and private health insurers (Ministry of Health, Welfare and Sport, 2001; Sheldon 2001).

Primary Care in Sweden

County councils in Sweden have the responsibility to provide health and social care with the majority of funding coming from county council taxes with supplementary grants from the national government. Primary care is provided predominantly by salaried public doctors and most hospitals are publicly-owned and have independent management status. Patients do not have to enrol with a primary care practice but have freedom to choose between primary care centres or outpatient hospital departments – about 50 per cent of first contacts are undertaken in hospitals. It is the county councils' responsibility to manage health care services and they must purchase both primary and secondary health care services, or ask an agent to do this on their behalf (Leon and Rico, 2002).

Primary care providers in public facilities are generally employed by, and receive a monthly salary from, the county councils. This includes GPs, who must work in two or more partner groupings, and other professionals licensed to work in the same primary health care centres including district nurses, physiotherapists, midwives, and psychologists. District nurses in these centres tend to play a specialist role, often carrying out first-contact assessments, whilst 87 per cent of GPs in Sweden provide out of hours care on a rota system. There have been some variances. For example, in order to promote innovation and service development, some councils have introduced the use of capitation funding to health centres and target-based payments for preventative services. These primary care centres are responsible to a population with a defined geographical boundary and patients become registered (Adamiak and Karlberg, 2003). Some primary care doctors operate privately and under contract with their council on a fee-for-service basis. The Swedish system also employs user charges for most medical services. Each county council may set its own levels within a national ceiling. Consultation fees with a public health physician (EUR 11-15 in 2000) are set lower than for a specialist in hospital (EUR 16-27) to encourage use of primary care services.

Following the launch of internal market reforms in 1989, a purchaser-provider model in health care developed incrementally to the extent that three-quarters of county councils employed a purchaser-provider model by 1999 (Leon and Rico, 2002). Purchasing systems vary by council between devolved purchasing to localities and central single council-led agencies. The internal market opened up the potential for primary care professionals to be involved in local purchasing boards, thereby expanding their level of influence over other levels of care. However, whilst some counties have piloted the decentralization of budgets to the primary care level, GPs and hospitals have been more likely to work co-operatively to jointly co-ordinate between the levels of care (Olesen et al, 1998). This latter trend reflects a fear of rising activity, costs and inequalities that might result from competition (Harrison and Calltorp, 2000). As in the UK, promoting integration and co-operation became key activities during the second part of the 1990s and many local purchasing agents were integrated back into unified county agencies. Indeed, county councils themselves have promoted mergers and joint purchasing agreements between themselves (Leon and Rico, 2002).

However, more recently there has been a renewed emphasis on the use of private providers in the system following the election in 1998 of a liberal coalition government. This has been promoted in the name of increased public choice, but has raised fears that greater contracted-out provision will push expenditures upwards and also favour the well-off where private physicians and private companies will situate. In Stockholm, a county council has already pioneered privatization through 'selling' a general hospital to a private company and is also promoting private-like primary health care co-operatives. These changes in emphasis bear a striking resemblance to consumerist policies being advanced in England that are promoting provider pluralism and extending the independence of providers through its Foundation Hospital initiative (Woods, 2001). A key political debate in Sweden is the extent to which such structural changes have been undertaken purely for the sake of effectiveness and efficiency whilst there is seemingly political agreement that the role of primary care and family doctors should be enhanced to help use resources effectively and to increase co-ordination between providers (Adamiak and Karlberg, 2003).

Primary Care in New Zealand

New Zealand's healthcare system is financed predominantly from taxation and covers all residents in the country. Whilst public hospital and outpatient services are free, most people must meet some of the costs of primary health care and make a co-payment for pharmaceuticals. Out-of-pocket expenses account for nearly 16 per cent of health care expenditure and primary care is charged to users on a fee-for-service basis. Within this user fee system for primary care there are significant subsidies for low and middle income earners and 'high users'. *Community* or *High User* card holder get reduced co-payments whilst a *Free Child Health Scheme* that was introduced in 1996 subsidizes GP consultations to those under six years old (Healy, 2002).

Primary health care in New Zealand has been influenced heavily by a series of political reforms. From 1993-1999, a purchaser-provider split was developed in which four regional health authorities, and then one central Health Funding Authority, purchased services from 23 autonomous Crown-owned enterprises (similar to NHS trusts). However, a change to a Liberal/Alliance government in 1999 mostly eliminated the purchaser-provider split. The New Zealand Health and Disability Act (2000) disestablished the Health Funding Authority in favour of 21 District Health Boards covering geographically-defined populations with responsibilities for managing public hospitals, community health services and public health programmes (Davis and Ashton, 2001).

Since the latest reforms, primary health care is beginning to be provided more comprehensively through capitation funding to general practice groups (French et al, 2001). Nevertheless, general practitioners predominantly work privately with two-thirds working in group practices though far fewer (about 6 per cent) work in multi-professional community health centres. Patients are free to choose their GP and are free to see more than one GP, although in practice continuity of care is high. GPs can set their own fee rates for consultations, though most receive their income retrospectively through the Government subsidy rates for concession cardholders and children. Some 15 per cent of GPs, mostly in low income areas, are paid via capitation-based contracts. All GPs are required to provide after-hours coverage and co-operatives are commonplace (Healy, 2002).

The primary care organization in New Zealand dates back to the early 1990s with the spontaneous development of Independent Practice Associations. These limited liability companies arose in response to a perceived threat from government to GP contracts and reimbursement arrangements (Malcolm and Powell, 1996; Malcolm et al, 1999). These were formed to enable greater power in negotiations with payers and varied in size – the largest being Pegasus, a group of 330 GPs in Christchurch. Interestingly, the New Zealand Government embraced these developments through the 1991 Health and Disability Services Act in which GPs were actively encouraged to form Independent Practitioner Associations to take responsibility for managing the budget for a range of primary and ambulatory care expenditure such as prescriptions, diagnostic tests and community care services (Mays et al, 2001). The incentive, like fundholding in the UK, was that practices could retain any savings. By 1999, over 80 per cent of GPs were part of an IPA and there role had developed to address clinical quality and cost-effectiveness through the integration of primary, social and secondary care services, particularly for the management of chronic conditions (Healy, 2002).

In the late 1990s, plans for a number of primary care-led Integrated Care Organization pilots were encouraged to further integrate service delivery but also to have a role in subcontracting with hospital providers (Ashton, 1998). These could take two forms: first, a collaborative provider model based on vertical integration, and second, an independent management model to purchase and co-ordinate services from providers. However, fears of increasing administrative costs and service inequities saw the pilot scheme shelved following the November 1999 election of a new Liberal/Alliance government (Cumming, 2000; Mays et al, 2001).

Since 2001, a new policy of not-for-profit Primary Health Organizations (PHOs) has been instituted designed to build on the IPA legacy and as part of a new national Primary Health Care Strategy. PHOs have responsibility for managing capitation funds for enrolled patients using a devolved budget from their District Health Board. Users are encouraged to register with a GP practice within their local PHO who then becomes responsible for managing their care and is paid a capitation fee for the enrolled patient. The aim is to both improve the quality of primary health care and access for low-income groups. The latter is a particular problem in New Zealand where those living on low incomes in disadvantaged areas have low levels of access to primary health care (Davis and Ashton, 2001). Hence, PHOs offer an organizational structure that is similar to English PCTs but with a specific emphasis on integration of care and health improvement and without the funding and purchasing role in relation to secondary and tertiary care.

The continual growth of primary care organizations in New Zealand has had the combined effect of superimposing a more corporate structure on general practice with increased scope for collaborative partnerships. Robinson (2003) describes how a greater emphasis has been placed on methods to integrate services across primary, secondary and community care in the fields of diabetes management and older people's care. In some cases, this has led to reduced hospital admissions (Mays et al, 2001). Nevertheless, despite these innovations, significant user co-payments in primary care and rising out-of-pocket expenditures during the 1990s have led to a growing concern with equity and access (Schoen et al, 2000).

Primary Care in Australia

Public health care in Australia has been provided on a universal access basis since the 1983 introduction of Medicare. The scheme is financed through general taxation and everyone is entitled to benefits regardless of income or whether they hold private health insurance. Medicare itself covers treatment in public hospitals (at no cost to the patient); specialist services (usually with a patient co-payment) outside hospital or in private hospitals; GP consultations; and referred costs (diagnostics and pharmaceuticals). Other primary care-based services are excluded.

Primary care in Australia is provided predominantly by independent general practitioners on a fee-for-service basis. Under Medicare, all Australians are entitled to a rebate which is 100 per cent of a 'schedule fee' set by the Government (known as The Commonwealth Medicare Benefit Schedule). However, doctors are able to charge their own fees and patients pay any gap between the fee charged and the rebate out of their own pockets. Currently, around 70 to 75 per cent of GP transactions in Australia are at the schedule fee, a process known as 'bulk billing', with no patient contribution (Swerrison and Duckett, 2002).

Recent reforms have introduced some limited access under Medicare to primary health care services provided by nurses and allied health professionals. Moreover, in rural areas and the outer fringes of large cities where there are workforce shortages, GP practices can apply for grants which enable them to employ practice nurses on a sessional basis. This assists doctors in activities related to chronic disease management and prevention programmes, especially smoking cessation.

Over the last decade, reform of general practice has been undertaken due to concerns about rising costs led by a fee-for-service system that encourages unnecessary consultations and follow-up treatments. Moreover, quality and access is variable as private physicians are overly concentrated in affluent urban locations whilst remote rural areas struggle to attract GPs. There were no requirements, and few opportunities, for GPs to participate in local health planning processes and response to community needs has been poor. Over the past decade, a series of general practice reforms have been introduced to manage primary care activities more directly:

- the creation of 120 Divisions of General Practice which are professionally-led and regionally-based voluntary associations of GPs that co-ordinate primary care ranging in size from just 8 to as many as 300 GPs depending on geographic location. The Divisions are funded by the Commonwealth Government to support general practice and GPs with the aim of improving quality and health outcomes for local communities. A performance framework for Divisions is being introduced to tackle variations in capacity to deliver the agenda;

- a Practice Incentive Programme to improve quality and accountability of GP services such as paying for after-hours care, immunizations and prescribing reviews;
- a Rural Incentives Programme to provide payments for GPs to relocate to rural and remote communities and outer-urban areas; and
- the development of a quality framework for general practice including changes to the fee schedule that encourages participation in care assessment, care planning and case conferencing.

The reform strategy in Australia has increased recognition of the need to expand the role of nursing and other AHPs in the management of chronic disease. As a result, there has been a trend towards larger and more multi-professional practices heralding a subtle shift away from a predominantly small-business, professional ownership model. Indeed, a small number of the Divisions themselves are developing managed care characteristics – such as the collation of data and the development of practice-support programmes – in order to develop innovative disease management strategies that address community needs. Networks of care between the Divisions are also emerging, such as in the virtual pooling of budgets and resources to tackle after hours care.

Despite such innovations, a mixed model of primary care has developed including larger corporate business structures that involve GPs in vertically-integrated organizations that include pathology and diagnostic services, private hospitals and other health and social care services. These services are contained in a one-stop approach to general practice within which GPs are encouraged, or required, to refer (White and Collyer, 1998; White, 2000; Swerrison and Duckett, 2002). According to O'Connor and Peterson (2002), these corporate developments resemble the IPA HMO models in the USA and so might not be so much concerned with providing integrated and extended services but with establishing medical monopolies. However, it appears that fears of corporatization in the primary care sector have been unfounded due to both the lack of commercial opportunities to make profits and the introduction of the Divisions which have promoted GPs and practices as the leaders of the public health agenda.

Summarizing the International Evidence: Key Themes and Issues for the Management of Primary Care Organizations

The development of the PCO has become an international phenomenon. What is striking is how international policy reforms seem to cross-fertilize these approaches between nations. Hence, the development of primary care purchasing in the quasi-markets of the UK, New Zealand and Sweden have similar policy roots (Ham et al, 1990). So too has been the trend towards the adoption of managed care techniques and the creation of managed care organizations to administer them (Rosleff and Lister, 1995). Whilst the trend in most countries that experimented with internal markets has been to backtrack from competition-based policies (Light, 2001), the role and legitimacy of the PCO as the vehicle for service integration and co-ordination has endured. Indeed, such organizations are beginning to take a much wider role internationally in developing a public health role and tackling health inequalities.

The international evidence suggests that PCOs face a number of fundamental managerial challenges. Of particularly relevance has been difficulty in engaging and integrating GPs into 'managed' systems of primary care. The tension between professional autonomy and managerialism has seen GPs become disengaged in centrally mandated PCOs, most notably in Northern Ireland where GPs are refusing to play any active part in Local Health and Social Care Groups. The same problems also exist in the corporate and vertically-integrated PCO models developed in the USA, Australia and New Zealand. Not only does primary 'managed' care challenge the GPs' autonomy it also threatens to encroach on their professional territory by imposing multi-professional team working and developing non-medical roles, especially nurse-led roles, into their bread and butter activities such as prescribing and immunization (O'Connor and Peterson, 2002). A key challenge for the future is how PCO managers can develop and sustain meaningful engagement of primary care professionals, an issue examined more closely in Chapters 6 and 12.

The experience of PCOs internationally appears to show consensus on their ability to integrate and co-ordinate primary and community care services in helping to improve quality, access and the cost-effectiveness of provision. This process appears most successful in corporate PCOs where this is achieved through vertical integration within a 'closed' system such as the Kaiser Permanente model in the USA. There is far less consensus, however, on the effectiveness of the role of the PCO as a purchaser/commissioner of care. In Sweden and New Zealand, the development of PCOs as commissioners appears to have been a fleeting strategy and recent reforms have centralized such functions. In the UK, devolution has led to variation in the degree to which budgetary and commissioning responsibilities are held by PCOs. Indeed, it appears that English PCTs are unique in having direct devolved responsibility for this task. The strategy in England to encourage choice, provider pluralism and semi-independent Foundation Hospitals means that making a reality of the commissioning function is a most pressing managerial challenge and a critical issue on which the English NHS system may succeed or fail. However, English PCTs have struggled to get to grips with the commissioning agenda revealing an urgent need to develop a new managerial cadre in this field (Smith and Goodwin, 2002). The management of commissioning is given specific attention in Chapter 11.

A final key development in the current international trend towards PCOs is the growing role they are playing in developing public health strategies and creating partnerships with social care services and other non-health care providers. In the UK and New Zealand, PCOs have begun to strategically align themselves with local authorities whilst in the USA, Australia and The Netherlands corporate and business strategies has seen a degree of 'forward integration' into the provision of long-term care. The role of PCOs in implementing public health strategies and developing new

Chapter 3

Developing Primary Care Groups and Trusts: The English Context

Primary care trusts represent the key agency responsible for securing health care services and improving health status in England. Their creation has been the culmination of a series of health sector reforms that for nearly two decades have promoted the role of primary care and primary care organizations. This chapter sets out an overview of the development of primary care groups and trusts in England, located within the context of broader political and NHS strategic developments. An assessment is made of the key lessons to be drawn from the experience of forming and operating these primary care organizations, using the published research as a basis for drawing such conclusions.

The 1980s: From Autonomous Administered Primary Care to the New GP Contract

Until the mid-1980s, NHS primary care was subject to relatively little policy and management interest, with changes to the terms and conditions of GPs, the development of NHS-owned health centres, an expansion in community nursing, and the emergence of group general practice being the main service developments of any note (Loudon et al, 1998). The focus of primary care provision was the general practice unit, and for GPs, their main contact with health service managers was via their interactions with the local family practitioner committee (FPC), this being the public body charged with administering the contract that each GP held with the NHS.

The late 1980s saw the advent of the first real attempts by government to put primary care at the heart of health policy. The White Paper 'Promoting Better Health' (DHSS, 1988) heralded a new and more managed approach to NHS primary care, whereby financial incentives would be used by the government to encourage GPs to achieve specific health targets as determined by policy makers. The resulting GP Contract (Department of Health, 1990) duly required GPs to meet targets related to issues such as cervical screening, childhood vaccinations and immunisations, the management of chronic diseases, and the provision of health promotion services. The new national GP contract was managed locally by a family health services authority (FHSA), these bodies having been established in 1990 as part of the introduction of general management into the NHS.

The Early To Mid-1990s: The Emergence of Primary Care Organizations

In 1991, the Conservative Government introduced its market reforms of the NHS, these measures having been announced in a white paper 'Working for Patients' in 1989 (Department of Health and Social Security, 1989). The 1991 reforms contained within their design two models of purchasing or commissioning. The first, based on health authorities, centred on the population and its health needs. The second, based on general practice, focused on patients and how services to patients could be improved by allocating a budget or fund to family doctors in individual practices (GP fundholding). Population-centred and patient-focused purchasing, as these models have been termed (Ham, 1996), evolved into a range of approaches, particularly as health authorities sought to involve general practitioners in decisions on the use of their budgets. The development of GP fundholding is viewed by commentators as having been something of an afterthought by the then Secretary of State for Health, Kenneth Clarke (Timmins, 1995; Dixon, 1998). It is suggested that Clarke wanted to offer patients an alternative purchaser of care to a health authority (Dixon, 1998). Other motivations for the introduction of fundholding included the offering of financial incentives to GPs to manage costs in the face of rising levels of prescribing and 'unnecessary' referrals; the promotion of choice to patients and an extension of the ability of primary care to develop new and more accessible services; thus gaining leverage over hospitals to improve quality and efficiency.

In parallel to the steps taken by health authorities to work more closely with GPs, GP fundholders in some places took the initiative to come together in networks that became known as multifunds, often as a way of enabling smaller practices to participate in the fundholding scheme but also to create organizations that could pool resources to avoid competition, share financial risks, and develop a stronger corporate strategy in their local health economy. At the same time, other GPs collaborated in the establishment of fundholding consortia. The simultaneous move by health authorities to make their work sensitive to GPs and by some GPs to purchase services at a level higher than the individual practice indicated that managers and doctors both recognized the need to combine aspects of population-centred and patient-focused purchasing. And while in the early phases of the 1991 reforms, the debate was often framed in terms of the superiority of one or other of the original models of commissioning, over time there was a keener appreciation that the more interesting and important question was how to bring together the most positive aspects of different approaches, recognizing that there were strengths and weaknesses in each. What the totality of these new models of commissioning signalled was the emergence of a new entity within the NHS – the primary care organization.

This debate was made more complex by the Government's decision in autumn 1994 to develop a 'primary care-led NHS' (Department of Health, 1994). One of the consequences of this initiative was an extension to the model of GP fundholding, including the 'total purchasing pilot' scheme in which GPs were able to commission potentially all services for their patients. Another consequence was that health authorities renewed their efforts to involve GPs in purchasing, for example through the development of locality commissioning arrangements, practice-sensitive purchasing initiatives and GP commissioning groups. The effect was to increase still further the variety of commissioning models, including hybrids that explicitly combined features of the two original approaches (illustrated in Figure 3.1 below). Unlike in 1991, when the government resisted calls for research into the implementation of NHS reforms, the primary care-led NHS policy initiative was accompanied by a commitment to evaluate the most significant of these hybrids, the total purchasing pilot projects.

Primary care-led purchasing and commissioning evolved rapidly and in ways that were only partly anticipated by the architects of the NHS reforms. While the original impetus came from government, many of the most important innovations resulted from managers and doctors using the flexibility built into the design of the reforms to establish arrangements appropriate to different circumstances. It was in this way that total purchasing emerged in areas like Bromsgrove and Berkshire in advance of government endorsement of this approach in 1994. Within the total purchasing pilot scheme (announced in 1994 and implemented in 1996), volunteer fundholding practices, either alone or in groups, were delegated a budget by their local health authority to purchase potentially all of the hospital and community health services for their populations. The rationale for the 87 total purchasing pilot schemes seemed to be that fundholding GPs would continue to innovate and would develop new and more sensitive ways of meeting patients' needs than their parent health authorities (Mays and Mulligan, in LeGrand et al, 1998).

As a result of these various primary care-led innovations, not only was there a high degree of purchaser plurality in health care (Mays and Dixon, 1996), but also there were variations between districts in the coverage and mix of different approaches (Dowling, 2000). Not only this, but also the models of commissioning described in Figure 3.1 were rarely self-contained, with general practitioners often involved in commissioning through more than one route, and health authorities developing a range of approaches in different parts of the areas they covered.

The extent of commissioning plurality in the 1990s is illustrated by research carried out in 1997 that identified over 20 models of primary care organizations in England, with some health authority areas having as many as eight models within their boundaries (Smith et al, 1998). This diversity of primary care organizations within the NHS in the 1990s made it difficult for researchers to assess what was inevitably a rapidly changing picture (see Chapter 4). Notwithstanding this difficulty, a large number of evaluative studies were conducted and, as the extensive review of the NHS internal market conducted by LeGrand and colleagues (LeGrand et al, 1998) shows, many of these studies were of fundholding.

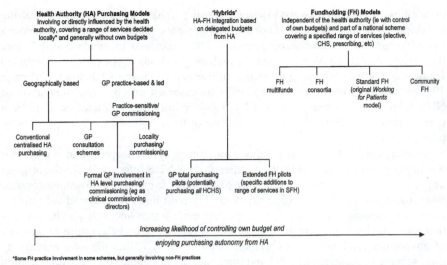

Figure 3.1 A typology of commissioning organizations in the NHS in 1996

Source: Mays, N. and Dixon, J. (1996), p. 15.

Learning from the Experience of Fundholding

A comprehensive review of the research evidence related to GP fundholding noted that although fundholding received the most attention in both popular debate and academic research (Goodwin, 1998), much of the literature came in the form of writer opinion, anecdote and individual case studies, with a lack of overall rigorous evaluation of the fundholding scheme as a whole. Two particular criticisms levelled by Goodwin were the very limited research into the impact of fundholding on patient care, and the very few studies that compared the performance of fundholders with that of non-fundholders or other purchasers. In concluding his review of the evidence related to fundholding, Goodwin identified the following common messages (Goodwin, 1998):

- prescribing costs rose more slowly in fundholding practices compared with non-fundholding practices initially, but this differential appeared to have been short-lived;
- comparative rates of referral from fundholding and non-fundholding practices showed no significant differences;
- fundholding practices developed more practice-based care services than non-fundholding practices;
- providers were more responsive to the demands of fundholders compared to non-fundholders;
- fundholding had attracted a high administrative workload and high transaction costs for both purchasers and providers;

- a two-tier system in access to care had been institutionalized; one for the patients of fundholders and one for non-fundholders; and
- there had been little change in the level of patient choice.

Goodwin (1998) noted that no overall consensus had been reached at the time as to whether fundholding had been a positive or negative experience and concluded that the real issue raised by the experience of fundholding was:

> how problematic it has proved for general practice to use fundholding at its innovative best. The issue to address…is how best to enfranchise general practice to take an active and innovative part within the health system (Goodwin in LeGrand et al, 1998, p.68).

Subsequent retrospective analysis of the fundholding experience has backed up the initial evidence by showing how fundholders achieved quicker admission for their patients in comparison to non-fundholders helping to reduce waiting times for patients in their own practices (Dowling, 2000; Propper et al, 2002). Moreover, a study by Dusheiko et al (2003) suggested that fundholders did, in fact, reduce referral rates to secondary care quite considerably – a finding suggesting that budget-conscious GPs were either being more judicious in their referral behaviour, or referring to a range of primary care-based alternatives. However, as research by Croxson et al (2001) uncovered, much of the differential seems to have been the result of fundholders 'gaming' the system by increasing referral patterns in the year before they became fundholders in order to gain a larger budget (since their initial budgets were determined by historical patterns of referral that year). The real impact of fundholding on the cost and quality of care and the ability of GPs to use budgets effectively has never reached any degree of consensus.

Learning from the Experience of Total Purchasing

The most systematic evaluation of primary care organizations in the 1990s was the three-year national evaluation study of total purchasing led by Mays and colleagues (Mays et al, 2001). These researchers noted how considerable variation existed between individual total purchasing projects, pointing out that: 'The scheme has been implemented without a central blueprint and with minimal guidance, partly because of strong conviction from the centre that GPs had great potential to improve the efficiency of services through their purchasing and that they should be allowed as much flexibility in implementation as suited local circumstances' (Mays and Mulligan in LeGrand et al, 1998, p 85). Mays and Mulligan note that this 'hands-off' approach by policy makers presented considerable difficulties in making an assessment as to the success or otherwise of total purchasing projects, given the lack of a national set of objectives for the scheme. Mays and colleagues' conclusions about the experience of total experience can be summarized as follows:

- the overall impact of TPPs was variable;
- achievements tended to be small-scale, local and incremental;

- pilots increased the costs of running the local health system;
- some were able to alter their patients' emergency use of hospital services by providing alternative forms of care; and
- the larger the size and scope of the pilot, the more time was needed to establish management systems before progress could be made against objectives (Mays et al, 2001, p. 277).

The evaluators of the TPP experiment went on to point out that these relatively modest achievements looked more substantial when considered within the constrained policy context of the time. TPPs were time-limited pilot projects that relied on health authority goodwill to have control over their own budgets, and were relatively small-scale schemes with limited bargaining power and management capacity in relation to providers. In addition, during the lifetime of the pilots, national policy shifted away from fundholding and its derivatives towards the primary care and group model of the New Labour government (Mays et al, 2001).

Perhaps the enduring legacy of TPPs is that they enabled the Labour government to hold faith with the primary care-led commissioning approach which had originated under the Conservative administration. As Mays and colleagues note:

> Despite their limitations, TPPs did enough to continue the momentum begun within standard fundholding to shift the balance of influence in the NHS from the hospital towards other parts of the wider health system (Mays et al, 2001, p. 277).

Learning from the Experience of GP Commissioning

A mapping exercise carried out in 1997 of approaches to commissioning in England (Smith et al, 1998) identified that 84 per cent of health authorities had between two and four models of commissioning in operation within their boundaries (in addition to fundholding and total purchasing). In comparison with fundholding and total purchasing however, there were fewer studies of these other primary care-based models of commissioning. Two of the most frequently found models of commissioning were locality and general practitioner (GP) commissioning groups. Mulligan has defined GP and locality commissioning in terms of their origins, namely bottom-up and top-down (in LeGrand et al, 1998):

GP commissioning Where groups of non-fundholding practices (although over time fundholders also began to join in) came together to propose service changes and developments to the health authority on behalf of their patients, which the health authority incorporated into its contracts.

Locality commissioning Where the health authority brought together all the practices in a geographic area to form a group charged with eliciting the view of all the GPs in the locality and channelling these constructively into the health authority's purchasing process.

Mulligan further points out that these two approaches to commissioning had much in common, both being collective, non-budget-holding alternatives to fundholding, working with or through the agency of the health authority on behalf of a sub-population of the authority. Likewise, both aimed to make health authority purchasing more sensitive to local variations in needs and patients' views, using GPs' views as the main conduit for gaining this local perspective. A review of the evidence related to GP and locality commissioning (Mulligan, 1998) suggested the following key conclusions:

- estimates for transaction costs were lower than under GP fundholding, but these estimates did not include negotiation time and other costs;
- there had been improvement in services, but probably not to the same extent as those claimed for fundholding;
- there appeared to be greater scope for promoting equity compared to fundholding;
- there was some limited evidence of peer-accountability to GPs; and
- many schemes had shown an improvement in GP-health authority relations.

Mulligan noted that much of the success of locality and GP commissioning schemes depended on local context and the attitude of the health authority. She concluded that these groups seemed better placed to make an impact than GP fundholding and could, when allowed to be selective in approach, make a difference to the quality of services. They were however deemed by Mulligan to be less successful in terms of negotiating with providers, and their true costs were not assessed. Her overall conclusion related to GP and locality commissioning groups was strikingly similar to that of Goodwin in relation to fundholding:

> What is clear is that the concept of GPs being involved in the commissioning process (in whatever form) is now so embedded in the NHS that the uncertainty has moved from whether they should be involved to finding ways of extending current approaches to GPs who currently have little or no involvement (Mulligan, 1998 in LeGrand et al, p. 83).

Conclusions from Research into Primary Care Organizations Before 1997

Reviews of the evidence on primary care innovations within the NHS internal market emphasized the importance of devolving purchasing to GP-led groups. This was a logical conclusion given the messages gleaned from their examination of evidence related to fundholding, total purchasing and locality/GP commissioning (LeGrand et al, 1998). In order to improve the effectiveness of primary care-led purchasing, reviews likewise encouraged improvements in the incentive structures for trusts and purchasers. For example, the review by LeGrand et al (1998) suggested that financial rewards and penalties within the system needed to be made more explicit and enforceable whilst simultaneously encouraging innovation and quality – an approach appealing to what LeGrand coined both the 'knightly and knavish' qualities of professionals in the system. In terms of warnings, this team cautioned against the imposition of yet stronger central government constraints through a performance framework for primary care-led commissioning.

The research group carrying out the national mapping of models of commissioning (Smith et al, 1998) set out from its observations more detailed advice to the new government about the challenges that would be faced in the development of future primary care organizations (Table 3.1).

Table 3.1 Advice about the development of primary care organizations, based on national mapping exercise

- The need to extend involvement beyond a small number of enthusiastic GPs, and to engage other health professionals within primary care teams.
- The importance of finding ways of involving patients and local people in the decision making processes of primary care organizations.
- The crucial nature of developing partnership arrangements with social services, local authorities, community health councils and NHS trusts.
- The need to support primary care organizations with an appropriate investment in management skills and reimbursement of GPs for the time given to management.
- The importance of developing an equitable formula for the allocation of resources to and within primary care organizations and to ensure that budgets were based on need.
- The vital need for arrangements in primary care organizations for managing risk to avoid budgets being blown off course by variations in demand and utilization.
- The importance of ensuring a framework for commissioning that would lead to greater consistency in the areas addressed by primary care organizations.
- The need to develop mechanisms within primary care organizations for the development and management of primary care provision.

Source: Smith et al (1998).

What these two studies emphasise is that by 1997, the principle of involving GPs in NHS commissioning had gained widespread acceptance in both policy and practice. The value of harnessing the views and enthusiasm of GPs in terms of seeking to influence the planning and purchasing of care for their patients seemed to have been established as a proper way of shaping service provision. Both groups of researchers suggested that there was a need to extend this GP involvement beyond the 'enthusiastic few' to the mainstream of general practice, and indeed to the wider primary care community including social care, nurses, and allied health professionals.

The studies were far more equivocal about the extent to which NHS market reforms, including primary care-led approaches to commissioning, had had any significant impact on the nature or quality of service provision within primary or secondary care. It was suggested that the reforms had led to greater changes in terms of NHS structure and culture (i.e. new arrangements that strengthened primary care as co-commissioners with health authorities of services from NHS trusts) than in respect of reshaped or higher quality clinical services.

A further message from research in this period was the need for a more consistent framework of objectives for commissioning by primary care-led bodies, moving beyond the very varied and local approaches seen within fundholding and its alternatives. This was suggested to be a way of assuring greater equity within commissioning, but was also seen as having the potential to stifle local innovation by practitioners keen to run and own 'their' organizations.

1997-2002: Towards A Single National Model of Primary Care Organization, The Primary Care Group and Primary Care Trust

The principle of general practitioner involvement in commissioning had become widely accepted during the 1990s. Debate about the relative strengths and weaknesses of the different models of primary care organization continued to be waged both before and immediately after the 1997 general election (LeGrand et al, 1998). In May 1997, the incoming Labour government inherited this diverse 'mosaic' of commissioning models and set about determining policy for the future of NHS commissioning 'beyond fundholding' (Smith et al, 1997).

In June 1997, Alan Milburn, the Minister of State for Health, announced plans to pilot new approaches to commissioning health services. The intention was to establish a programme of GP commissioning pilots, based around a number of separate projects and approaches. The programme followed on from the announcement in May 1997 by the Secretary of State of plans to abolish the internal market and to begin a debate on models of commissioning for the future (EL [97]33, NHS Executive, 1997a). Forty projects were subsequently identified in the English regions and these were given approval to take part in a two-year pilot programme with effect from April 1998.

The government's guidance on GP Commissioning Groups (EL [97]37, NHS Executive, 1997b) set out the overall intention of the pilot programme as being: '...to build on the best of existing good practice, and to develop and pilot new approaches which will achieve the Government's objectives of fairness in meeting local needs for high quality health care.' A number of possible approaches were identified in the guidance, including larger groupings of GPs and other primary care professionals, partnership between health authorities and commissioning groups, and a spectrum of approaches to the commissioning group role, covering in particular advisory models to complement those with delegated budgets. In reality, the pilot programme largely drew in previously existing commissioning groups, thus enabling such projects to receive formal central government funding for the first time, something they had been denied under a Conservative government that clearly favoured fundholding based approaches.

Ironically, the pilots took place under fundholding regulations and held a cash-limited prescribing budget as a group of GP practices. Support costs were made available to the pilots based on bids submitted from sites, covering general management, prescribing advice, IT, and financial management support. A full national evaluation of the pilots was commissioned from the Health Services Management Centre at the University of Birmingham in 1997. Given that by early 1998 it was quite clear that the Labour government intended all of England to be covered by a network of primary care groups (PCGs) by April 1999 (Department of Health, 1997), the principal focus of the GP commissioning evaluation quickly shifted to one of identifying lessons for the development and implementation of PCGs.

The findings from this national evaluation of GP commissioning pilots revealed a number of important messages for PCGs and primary care organizations more generally. The pilots, in their role as shadow PCGs, saw themselves as having had a head start in many aspects of PCG working. They had had to establish their boards and other internal management arrangements, determine the source of their management and professional support, manage a prescribing budget, and commission elements of health care on behalf of their local population (the overall messages are summarized in Table 3.2).

Table 3.2 Lessons from GP commissioning pilots for primary care groups

- PCGs would tend to focus on issues of structure and process in their early days, as they established themselves as effective organizations.
- PCGs would need to determine arrangements for carrying out both strategic and operational work, and this might entail structures of a greater complexity than simply the PCG board.
- The time commitment for clinical staff was considerable and the impact on practices and trusts would need to be assessed and kept under review.
- High quality dedicated management support would be a vital prerequisite to PCG working.
- Prescribing would be a key focus for PCGs and its management would demonstrate many of the tensions and opportunities inherent in the implementation of clinical governance.
- IM&T was more complex and time-consuming than PCGs might at first imagine and would require significant attention by groups.
- Nurses were enthusiastic about involvement in PCGs, but groups would need to determine ways of ensuring that they were able to participate in decision making on an equal basis with GPs.
- The health authority/PCG dynamic was of particular importance to the effective development and functioning of the PCG.
- User and public involvement presented a real challenge for PCGs and was likely to remain a good intention unless there was clear guidance and support for groups about models of good practice in this area.
- Commissioning was likely to focus on needs assessment, quality issues and the prioritisation of resources. PCGs were likely to be more interested in health improvement rather than a traditional contracting agenda.
- There were many personal and organizational development needs to be addressed by PCGs, including work on team-building and effective board working.

Source: Regen et al (1999).

Primary Care Groups

In December 1997, the Labour Government set out its ten year vision for the NHS in a white paper 'The New NHS. Modern, Dependable' (Department of Health, 1997). The white paper re-emphasized the importance of involving clinicians in shaping primary care organizations and leading changes to services, and clearly identified GPs and community nurses as the leaders of the new PCGs and PCTs. In this way, the government was underlining its commitment to 'going with the grain' of a more organized approach to the delivery and management of primary care (Department of Health, 1997). The 'New NHS' also introduced a national focus to the development of primary care organizations, making membership of a PCG compulsory for all GPs, in contrast with the previous voluntary nature of primary care led commissioning bodies.

Following the 1997 white paper the previous diversity of arrangements for involving GPs in commissioning was to be rationalized into four models of commissioning, a stepped approach that would allow groups to develop and extend their range of influence and their degree of independence over time. The four models are set out in Table 3.3 below.

Table 3.3 Levels of PCG/Ts as set out in the 1997 NHS White Paper

Level one - primary care group. A group of GPs and community nurses acting as an advisory group to the health authority.

Level two - primary care group. A group of GPs and community nurses with devolved responsibility for the commissioning of approximately 90 per cent of services for their population, acting as a sub-committee of the health authority.

Level three - primary care trust. A free-standing trust of GPs and community nurses, commissioning services for local populations, and accountable to the local health authority.

Level four - primary care trust. A free-standing trust of GPs and community nurses, commissioning services for local populations and managing community services provision (such as district nursing and health visiting), accountable to the local health authority.

Source: Department of Health (1997).

The government defined three core functions for PCGs (NHSE, 1998) these being:

- to improve the health of the population in the PCG;
- to develop primary and community health services within the PCG; and
- to commission secondary and tertiary services for the population in the PCG.

A national network of 481 PCGs was established in England on 1st April 1999. A great deal of time and energy went into the setting up of management arrangements and support functions for these primary care organizations, as reported in early studies of the emerging PCGs (Audit Commission, 1999; Audit Commission, 2000; Smith et al, 2000; Wilkin et al, 2000). But even as they sought to establish themselves as new organizations, PCGs were aware of further impending organizational change. PCGs were considered to be the first steps of a staged process resulting in the eventual transition to primary care trust (PCT) status (see Table 3.3 above).

Primary Care Trusts

Primary care trusts were initially intended to be free-standing statutory bodies with additional freedoms and opportunities to develop integrated services that were more responsive to the needs of patients (Department of Health, 1997). In 1999, they were charged with the same functions as PCGs, but had a significantly larger range of responsibilities (NHSE, 1999). Accordingly, PCTs received a unified budget that typically represented approximately 70 to 80 per cent of the health care budget for the local population. The vast majority of early PCTs chose to operate at level four (as opposed to level three) acting as both the commissioners of care and as the providers of all, or parts of, the community health services formerly provided by community health trusts. The first 17 PCTs went 'live' from April 2000, followed by a further 23 groups in October 2000.

The impetus to move from PCG to PCT was increased following the publication of the NHS Plan (Department of Health, 2000) in which the government announced its intention that all PCGs would become PCTs by April 2004. In April 2001, a further 124 PCTs were established, bringing the total to 164. In July 2001, the pace of change was given yet further impetus when 'Shifting the Balance of Power' was published (Department of Health, 2001a), announcing the move of all PCGs to PCT status by April 2002, the abolition of all health authorities, the creation of 28 new strategic health authorities. It was now clear to primary care that the phased developmental ten-year approach as announced in 1997 had now been translated into a blueprint for wholesale organizational change, and the establishment of PCTs in all areas of England within a total of three years (1999-2002).

Learning from the Experience of Primary Care Groups and Early Primary Care Trusts

The Department of Health Policy Research Programme commissioned two major projects to evaluate the implementation, development and impact of primary care groups and trusts in England. One of these studies, an in-depth exploration of 12 case study PCG/Ts, grew out of the national evaluation of GP commissioning pilots, and was carried out by the Health Services Management Centre at the University of Birmingham over the period 1998-2001. The other, the National Tracker Study of 71 primary care groups and trusts, was led by the National Primary Care Research and Development Centre at the University of Manchester in collaboration with the King's Fund over the period 1999-2002. The two studies revealed strikingly similar and consistent messages about the experience of developing primary care organizations.

The HSMC study, in reporting its final conclusions in 2001, set out a number of overall lessons in relation to the progress made by PCG/Ts (Regen et al, 2001):

- PCG/Ts reported a significant number of service changes related to primary care, community health services and intermediate care.
- Clinical governance was a key lever for bringing about change in primary care.
- The health improvement planning process was an important driver of change.
- Lack of sufficient management capacity was a key barrier to progress.
- Using the commissioning process to bring about change in secondary care services was a particular challenge.
- Relationships between PCG/Ts and the health authority were highly variable.
- The development of strategic partnerships with local NHS providers and social services required further attention.
- The involvement of service users and the public in PCG/T planning and service development was relatively under-developed.
- 'Grass root' GPs reported low levels of direct involvement in PCG/T activities and decision-making, although they were strongly engaged in primary care development, prescribing and clinical governance agendas.
- Nurses were enthusiastic participants in PCG board and sub-group working, but questions remained about their influence at a strategic level.
- Externally imposed change (the transition from PCG to PCT) dominated the agenda, affecting PCGs' ability to perform their core functions.
- The transition to PCT status required a renewed emphasis on internal organizational development.

The issues set out above echo the key lessons from the National Tracker Survey of PCG/Ts. In their 2001 report, the survey's authors noted:

> In their first two years PCG/Ts have made substantial progress in developing and extending primary care provision and establishing processes to support quality improvement. Progress has been slower in developing their commissioning role, building partnerships and improving population health. Access to information to support core functions remains a serious obstacle to progress (Wilkin et al, 2001, p. ES6).

In parallel to these two academic studies, the UK Government's Audit Commission tracked the progress of primary care groups, publishing reports in 1999 and 2000. The commission concluded its study by recommending that PCG/Ts should have scope to pursue local as well as national priorities; set measurable milestones against which achievement is monitored; secure GP 'ownership' of plans by devolving more local planning and decisions to practices; have the resources to reward practices that achieve clinical governance targets and make economical use of resources; collaborate to make efficient use of staff and health authority support; involve patients, carers and the public more meaningfully in decision-making; and have systems to ensure the probity and cost-effectiveness of their services (Audit Commission, 2000, p. 67).

The Experience of Primary Care Trusts

Emerging PCTs were reported to be developing as fundamentally more bureaucratic and complex organizations than PCGs. Key individuals within PCTs identified a need for greater clarity with respect to their roles and responsibilities, a factor compounded by a lack of central guidance (Regen et al, 2001). The emerging relationship between PCT board and professional executive committee was characterised by some tensions and had required careful facilitation. Likewise, the ability to involve professionals directly in the formation of service objectives was seen as an essential but challenging part of the process. A key characteristic of PCT management was the retention of a locality structure to promote ownership of the overall organization by its constituents and to devolve tasks to promote local sensitivity. In addition, good relationships and understanding between health authorities and PCTs were seen as crucial in order for progress to be made. In particular, the release of management resources and the transfer of staff from health authorities were identified as key areas for negotiation by PCTs (Regen et al, 2001).

The final report of the National Tracker Survey of PCG/Ts (Wilkin et al, 2002) concluded that PCG/Ts had continued to build on their early achievements in establishing infrastructure and capacity for the improvement of services. These researchers cited specific PCG/T achievements as being improvements in access to care, an extension in the range of services made available in primary care, and work to raise quality standards. The same report pointed to 'signs of a gap between expectations and the capacity of PCTs to deliver change in the short-term' (Wilkin et al, 2002, p. ES1) and noted the tension facing PCTs in respect of the need to meet national policy demands and targets whilst addressing local issues and priorities.

Key Lessons from the Research into Primary Care Organizations

An assessment of the published research into emerging models of primary care organization in England (GP fundholding, GP and locality commissioning, total purchasing, GP commissioning pilots, primary care groups and trusts) reveals a number of key messages of relevance to the development of all such organizations seeking to draw together primary care professionals and other stakeholders in a manner that facilitates a more corporate and coherent arrangement for improving health, managing primary care services and commissioning secondary care:

- It takes at least two years to establish a fully functioning new primary care organization and to emerge from the inevitable turmoil of organizational change.
- The provision of adequate levels of management and organizational support is crucial if PCOs are to properly discharge their functions, but the level, quality

and depth of management expertise varies markedly.

- The effective engagement of GPs in the strategic aims and objectives of a primary care organization is crucial, but is particularly challenging in larger and more complex PCOs where there is a tension between professional autonomy and managerialism.
- Other professionals, and nurses in particular, are enthusiastic participants in the development of PCOs, but struggle to gain influence at a strategic level in comparison with medical and managerial colleagues.
- The involvement of service users and the public in the operation of PCOs is challenging and, for many, problematic.
- The development of strategic partnerships with local authorities, social services and other NHS providers is an important but time-consuming activity for PCOs.
- PCOs are able to achieve relatively quick service gains in the primary care and community services setting, with clinical governance being a key lever in this process.
- The commissioning of secondary care services by PCOs is more challenging, and the jury is still out as to whether significant progress in this area can ever be made by PCOs.
- The relationship between a PCO and its supervisory tier is important in terms of the degree of devolution and freedom of operation that the organization is allowed.
- PCOs have the potential to combine sensitivity to the needs of individual patients with a population-based public health perspective when planning and managing the delivery of health care services.

The Policy and Management Agenda

Primary care trusts have been in place in all areas of England since 2002. Following a period of extensive policy change and organizational turmoil over the period 1997-2002, it appears that PCTs are now being given the space to develop as organizations and demonstrate their capacity to deliver improved health and services for local populations. Further organizational change in the form of mergers of PCTs may be back on the political and policy agenda after the next General Election, this being a symptom of the apparent failure by policy makers to heed the research evidence concerning the limited benefits to be gained from organizational mergers (Fulop et al, 2002) and an ongoing desire to try and find ways in which PCOs, as funders of care, can have 'clout' in relation to reshaping secondary care.

Wider system change is however evident in a number of important policy initiatives. Firstly, the establishment of a first wave of foundation trusts for hospital services in 2004 signals the creation of a new tranche of local health organizations operating within a degree of devolution and management freedom previously unseen in the NHS (Walshe, 2003). This presents PCTs with an additional challenge regarding their attempts to achieve service change through the commissioning process, given the relative independence of foundation trusts from local and national performance management processes. Secondly, the introduction of a new financial regime of 'payment by results' into the NHS in 2004 marked a return to the use of market forces in the NHS as a means of seeking to improve quality and develop contestability between providers (LeGrand, 2003). The use of a standard national tariff for pricing hospital services also underpins a new policy of 'patient choice' whereby NHS resource follows a patient or GP's choice of care provider. This calls into question the nature and future purpose of commissioning by PCTs, seemingly suggesting that PCTs will have to follow patient/GP decisions about the location of care rather than setting a strategic context for service provision by means of the process of negotiating contracts with NHS trusts and other providers (Smith et al, 2004).

A third key policy development has been the encouragement of integration in the roles and functions of primary care trusts with local authorities. While the NHS Plan (Department of Health, 2000) reinforced the central role to be played by PCTs as both the commissioners and providers of health care, it also called for 'fundamental reform' to make the NHS and social services work more effectively together to create 'seamless' services tailored to patient needs. As a result of this policy, the government removed key barriers to integration by legalising the transfer and pooling of resources between local authorities and PCTs (Department of Health, 1999) creating the foundations for the creation of 'care trusts' envisaged in the NHS Plan as single multi-purpose organizations designed to be responsible for the commissioning and provision of all local health and social care. It was suggested that they would be created from the extension of PCTs, thus providing a new 'end point' in the direction of travel for both integrated care development and the progression of different forms of primary care organization.

However, unlike the development of PCTs, the care trust model appears to have been sidelined as a political priority with the result that only seven examples had emerged by April 2004 (Glasby and Peck, 2004) with all but one case restricting its focus to a single client group rather than a local health economy. Though not formally evaluated, reviews of developments suggest that this slow uptake represents well-founded scepticism of the costs and benefits of organizational restructuring (Hudson, 2002), the absence of an evidence base that care trusts improve services (Henwood, 2001) and difficulties in securing ownership and long-term commitment between partners with different cultural values and financial obligations (Glasby and Peck, 2004). Only one further care trust had been launched by April 2005, though several more were in the process of development (Sinha, 2005). PCTs, therefore, will continue to have a lead role in developing partnership working with local authorities, but how coherent such strategies can be developed within an emerging policy context prioritizing choice, contracting and provider pluralism remains to be seen.

Conclusions: Lessons for Research and Practice

The introduction of GP fundholding into the NHS in 1991 set in train a course of events that few could have foreseen at the time. The idea of having a 'primary care-led NHS' with GPs and other primary care professionals at the forefront of organizations that seek to shape and commission population health and health services has its roots in this single policy initiative introduced by Kenneth Clarke. The subsequent emergence of a range of different models of primary care organization, culminating in the establishment of PCTs, has made the English NHS a fascinating case study of the development of such approaches within health policy and management internationally.

Perhaps the most striking feature of the examination of research into primary care organizations set out in this chapter is the frequency with which certain messages and lessons recur over time (Smith et al, 2004). This suggests that there is a pressing need for managers and policy makers to develop a more attuned corporate memory. There is a tendency in the fast-moving world of the 21st century to dismiss policies and practices developed just a few years ago, often in the name of a need for 'modernization'. What an examination of the research into the development of primary care organizations shows is that the experience of GP commissioning pilots, total purchasing pilots, and primary care groups is as relevant today as it was at the time of the original research. The labels applied to the latest incarnation of primary care organization may change, but the challenges of enabling GPs, nurses, managers and others to work together to achieve truly primary care-led commissioning and service development remain constant.

Chapter 4

Evaluating the Development of Primary Care Organizations

Since the mid-1990s, PCOs in the NHS have been subject to a series of policy evaluations. TPPs, introduced in 1995, became the first major policy innovation of its kind in the NHS to be formally evaluated from the outset (Mays et al, 2001). The genesis of this evaluation stemmed from political pressure on the Conservative Government to undertake independent evaluation of their ongoing quasi-market reforms, a specific reference to the lack of any independent analysis of the controversial fundholding initiative (Goodwin, 1996). Seemingly, this created a precedent whereby all future major re-organizations within primary care would be subject to evaluation (Clarence and Painter, 1998). This included the national evaluations of GP commissioning groups and PCG/Ts (Regen et al, 1999, 2001; Smith et al, 2000; Wilkin et al, 2000, 2001, 2002) and many other primary care-based initiatives such as Personal Medical and Dental Service Pilots (Walsh et al, 2001; Hill et al, 2003).

This chapter reflects on the experience of designing and implementing evaluations of primary care organizations and the difficulties involved in such research due to their high-profile nature politically and to the extremely dynamic policy environment in which they operate. The following sections examine how research teams have formulated and adapted their evaluation frameworks, methodologies and analytical concepts. It presents the key challenges facing researchers in this field and the ways in which they have endeavoured to evaluate progress. The chapter then considers the appropriateness of the research methods that have been employed before examining two important issues in the evaluation process – understanding and interpreting the evidence presented; and the politics of working independently within a Government-sponsored evaluation. The chapter concludes with the implications for policy and practice that have resulted from the experience of evaluation together with the lessons that can be drawn for future studies of primary care organizations.

Developing an Evaluation Framework

The Evaluation Challenge

The evaluation of complex policy initiatives such as PCG/Ts represents a challenge since it is essential to understand both their *impact* in achieving set goals and the *process* by which any observed benefits were accomplished. One review of the evidence concerning primary care-led commissioning highlights the relative lack of evidence concerning the *impact* of such approaches, compared with the wealth of material exploring issues of *process and organization* (Smith et al, 2004). However, understanding cause and effect is problematic: the definition and scope of the issues change over time; the criteria for success are not necessarily specific or measurable; and primary care organizations are usually at different stages of development or working in very different local environments. In the case of PCG/Ts, fundamental challenges were presented because there were no opportunities for making comparisons with alternative models or control cases. Moreover, the implementation of PCG/Ts was not an experiment but a given policy direction with a strong political dimension. As a consequence, evaluations have dropped the unrealistic burden of excessive 'scientific' expectation in favour of a more pragmatic approach (Judge and Bauld, 2004). Indeed, evaluations have never been designed to fundamentally challenge the basis upon which emerging PCOs were founded. Instead, the principal feature of evaluations into PCOs has been to identify lessons emerging from their operation in order to inform their future development and implementation.

Another fundamental challenge to evaluators arising from the pragmatic nature of investigations has been the absence of theory through which to 'test' innovations. In part, this reflects the 'manipulated emergence' of PCOs from a broad ideology that promoted a 'primary care-led NHS' (Harrison and Wood, 1999). Evaluations have necessarily developed a more pragmatic analysis because mainstream theories lack the sensitivity to explain the complex interactions between the context, content and process of change that result in observable outcomes. Instead, evaluators have consistently adopted a 'contextual approach' to their analyses following empirical observations that local contexts (such as cultures, geographies, politics and key agencies) had played an important role in influencing the progress of PCOs in meeting their objectives (Mays et al, 2001; Regen et al, 2001). Whilst pragmatism in research design might be considered a virtue, the lack of a theoretically-based approach remains an underlying criticism of the evaluation experience (Evans et al, 2001).

The Design of the HSMC National Evaluation of PCG/Ts

The national evaluation of PCG/Ts carried out by the Health Services Management Centre at the University of Birmingham was designed to explore the implementation and impact of these organizations, but with a specific brief to inform lessons for their future development (Regen et al, 2001). From the outset, the research recognized that examining new primary care organizations required an approach flexible enough to tackle the dynamic nature of change during their ongoing transition period to PCT status. The approach taken, therefore, was designed to ensure that the key messages and themes emerging from the operation of PCG/Ts could be fed back to the Department of Health at regular intervals to help shape policy and practice (Smith et al, 2000).

The study of PCG/Ts had originally been intended to examine 40 GP commissioning groups established in 1998 to pilot a more collaborative and alternative form of commissioning to that of fundholding (Department of Health, 1997b). Following the emergence of the PCG agenda in 1999, the evaluation was significantly adapted to examine 12 case studies focusing on lessons to inform the establishment of PCG/Ts (Regen et al, 1999). The potential for such national policy changes to influence the subject material of the evaluation was recognized from the outset. Consequently, the evaluation adopted a research framework robust enough to withstand such contextual changes. The framework employed analyzed primary care organizations in terms of their structures, processes and outcomes following an approach to quality assessment first postulated by Donabedian (1980). The approach was flexible enough to follow the continual development of new organizations and be sensitive to the management development and relationship-building issues within them. This evaluation framework is shown in Table 4.1, an approach now commonly referred to as a 'process evaluation'.

Table 4.1 The evaluation framework for the national evaluation of PCG/Ts

---

The Investigation of **Structure** focuses upon issues such as:
- The size and configuration of the PCG/Ts
- Organizational arrangements
- Management, budgetary and IT arrangements

Issues of **Process** include an examination of:
- PCG/T core functions
- The functioning of the PCG/T board and/or professional executive committee
- Relationships between board/executive committee members
- The involvement of PCG/T constituents and stakeholders
- The transition from PCG to PCT status

Analysis of **Outcomes** assesses:
- The impact of the PCG/Ts in terms of their out-turn against budget
- Prescribing, activity and waiting times
- Achievements against stated objectives and core functions
- The impact of PCG/Ts upon patients

Source: Smith et al (2000).

In addition to the research within its case study sites, three parallel studies were undertaken in order to collect more detailed information on research questions of particular policy relevance: prescribing, user involvement and GP engagement.

Prescribing in PCG/Ts This element to the evaluation used the expertise of health economists to assess the impact of PCG/Ts in relation to the management of the prescribing budget. The study involved the analysis of PACT (Prescribing Analysis

Cost) data combined with questionnaire data gathered during the course of the evaluation (McLeod et al, 2000; McLeod, 2001).

Studying user involvement in PCG/Ts This study was undertaken in the context of Government policies emphasizing the prominent role to be played by service users and members of the public in the decision-making processes (NHSE, 1998; Department of Health, 2001b). A combination of research methods was used including documentary analysis of public/user involvement strategies; semi-structured telephone interviews with lay board members and other local community representatives; a postal questionnaire examining the nature and level of resources invested in public and user involvement; and additional fieldwork at four sites to explore in-depth examples of participative approaches (Elbers and Regen, 2001).

Studying GPs' views and involvement in PCG/Ts This study sought to examine the experiences and involvement of grass-roots GPs (Regen, 2002). A postal questionnaire was sent out to all non-board GPs in PCGs and/or non-PCT executives in the case study sites over two years and sixteen follow-up telephone interviews were undertaken to explore in greater depth levels of GP involvement and their perceptions of PCG/T impact.

Such add-on, or complementary, research had also been a key feature of the TPP evaluation where in addition to the main 'process evaluation' which examined the set-up and operation of TPPs, analysis was also undertaken of transaction costs, prescribing, routine activity, and specific service areas including maternity services, services for the the seriously mentally ill, complex community care, and emergency admissions (Mays and Wyke, 2001).

Selecting Appropriate Research Methods

The examination of complex policy initiatives, such as the development of PCG/Ts, requires qualitative in-depth analysis because outcomes are dependent on a highly context-specific and complex range of inter-related factors. As Murphy (2001) points out, qualitative research is well suited to studying the processual and dynamic nature of phenomena such as PCG/Ts. Rigorous analysis of data related to the context in which an innovation took place helps facilitate the application of findings beyond study settings. The approach provides a credible alternative to 'traditional' evaluations that emphasize the primacy of experimental methods since these are often inappropriate in complex, community-based, situations (Green and Tones, 1999).

Due to the complexity of qualitative investigations, it is practically impossible to undertake in-depth examinations in all cases. By implication, in-depth investigations require a *selective* case study-based approach concentrating on a retrospective analysis, and potentially some formative observation, of the complex processes involved. This has the advantage for researchers in their ability to infer meanings by observing action in context. In the evaluation of PCG/Ts, such close scrutiny enabled, for example, the factors that sustained professional engagement, or inhibited patient participation, to be more readily identified (Regen et al, 2001).

Whilst qualitative research is well suited to answering some questions about the delivery and organization of health care, the approach is frequently accused of anecdotalism and of little practical use to policy makers and practitioners (Stake, 1995). Qualitative research, therefore, must seek to inform our understanding beyond the subject of study since the justification for funding is to discover which findings can be extrapolated to other cases. Whilst some writers reject generalizability as a goal of qualitative research, thoughtful and targeted sampling frameworks across several case studies may enable observations to be upheld elsewhere (Seale, 1999; Murphy, 2001).

A Case Study Approach

Case studies are used to explore a contemporary phenomenon where complex inter-relational issues are involved and can be exploratory, explanatory, descriptive or a combination (Mays and Pope, 1996). Case study evaluations have been commonly used in PCO-based research in order to investigate important practical and policy questions of implementation and effectiveness. As Keen and Packwood (1996) suggest, case studies are most valuable where broad, complex questions have to be addressed and where the detail of whether an intervention succeeds or fails depends on how the general context influences the outcome.

Case studies are often thought to be 'less scientific' than alternative experiential approaches but their use is entirely appropriate in settings that are inaccessible by any other research method. The examination of primary care organizations requires micro-level qualitative investigation because the outcome is dependent on many parallel and complex changes over time and because suitable control groups are usually unavailable. Moreover, given the extent to which primary care-based initiatives have changed through policy interventions (see Chapter 3) it is often not clear at the outset whether an initiative will be fully implemented. Case studies also enable a rigorous descriptive base to be developed that provides policy makers and practitioners with sound knowledge upon which to make informed judgments about success or failure.

Much of the value of case study investigations is the discovery of previously unknown factors and issues that influence change. Hence, a legitimate strategy in case study research is an iterative design in which the key themes and questions emerge during the research process. This type of research design is termed ethnography and has often been advocated in studies of government policies in health systems (Mays and Pope, 1995; Keen and Packwood, 1996; Harrison et al, 2004).

In the HSMC national evaluation of PCG/Ts case study investigations were used to assess their dynamic nature of development through a formative and iterative design. The approach taken enabled data to be captured on those essential features that helped (or hindered) certain aspects of PCG/T activity. Such factors could later be used to help interpret the evaluation of progress between PCG/Ts by focusing on the key aspects related to success and/or failure. Such an approach ensured that the evaluation team could feed back key messages to the Department of Health at regular intervals to inform future policy decisions in taking the PCG/T agenda forward.

Selecting Case Studies

The selection of case studies sites within an evaluation such as that for PCG/Ts is very important since selection must promote generalizability. Choice of sites, therefore, needs as far as possible to focus on 'typical' cases or, where a number of different categories of site emerge, attempt to examine across the spectrum. Replication of results across sites also helps to increase external validity (Patton, 1990). Within the HSMC national evaluation of PCG/Ts, twelve case studies were selected that were all former GP commissioning pilots. The groups in the study were selected on the basis that their configuration remained the same or similar following transition to PCG status and that they were broadly representative in terms of size, background, former fundholding coverage, nature of area, level of commissioning responsibility and PCT intentions. The generic lessons to be learned from their experiences could thus be maximized.

Case Study Research

One of the key design features of case study-based research is the ability to use a range of different data collection methods including semi-structured interviews, questionnaire surveys, focus groups, observational and documentary analysis, as well as the examination of local statistical data on costs or activity. The combination of approaches enables the essential process of 'triangulation' to be performed that enables the validity of results to be increased when all the evidence from the different methodological elements are combined. Furthermore, 'triangulation' of results across a range of selected cases using clear (potentially iteratively derived) research questions enables evaluators to put forward highly coherent and rigorous accounts about how events have and can take a particular course (Yin, 1994). This 'triangulation' process was facilitated in the PCG/T evaluation through the combination of several data collection methods including: the content analysis of documents; postal questionnaires; surveys; telephone and face-to-face semi-structured interviews; focus groups; and observational analysis of meetings.

Content Analysis of Key Documents Content analysis systematically examines relevant documentary sources, or parts of them, to categorize or summarize the information therein through the use of a set of pre-defined themes, codes or questions. The purpose is to help offer an account of what is embedded in written material in a form that helps to answer, or contribute knowledge to, the research questions posed. In the national evaluation of PCG/Ts, sites were asked to provide copies of their most recent primary care investment plans, annual accountability agreements, health improvement programmes, and other supporting documents such as strategies for engaging with the public. These documents served to provide essential baseline information on the PCG/Ts and helped formulate questions to be explored in subsequent fieldwork (Regen et al, 2001).

Postal questionnaires, surveys and telephone interviews Postal questionnaires and surveys are often used in qualitative research studies to gather factual information about processes (such as staffing and management arrangements) but are also commonly employed to gather the opinions and perspectives of a larger number of individuals than would otherwise be impossible through direct face-to-face contact. In the PCG/T evaluation, postal questionnaires were used to compile a detailed factual profile of each case site including data on demography and background characteristics; PCG/T objectives and organizational arrangements; management costs and support; budgetary information and commissioning responsibilities; service level agreements; and main providers and local authority boundaries (Regen et al, 2001). In this way, the evaluation sought to uncover much of the underlying contextual terrain within which PCG/Ts were operating and which might influence their ability to make progress against objectives. Postal questionnaires and telephone interviews were also employed to gather the views of a wider constituency of stakeholders from GPs to patients and user representatives (Elbers and Regen, 2001; Regen, 2002). Additional phone interviews were undertaken with lead managers and GPs at six-monthly intervals to update on project objectives, achievements, problems and plans for the next phase. Information collected from these helped revise fieldwork tools and enable rapid feedback to the Department of Health within policy briefing papers. The design of these surveys necessarily used a set of 'closed' questions within pre-defined thematic categories.

Face-to-face semi-structured interviews Qualitative interviews with individuals are perhaps the most widely used methodology in case studies. Such interviews enable the perspectives of different consitituencies to be recorded, such as patients, professionals and managers. The adoption of 'semi-structured' interviews also attempts to reduce the potential distortion that can result from the use of more standardized categories used in postal and telephone surveys. In the national evaluation of PCG/Ts, each of the twelve case study sites was visited on an annual basis by two lead academics over a two-day period. During these visits, one-to-one interviews were conducted with PCG board and/or PCT executive board members and with a local health authority contact, usually the director of primary care (Regen et al, 2001). The rationale for the selection of interviewees was based upon the need to gain a variety of perspectives in order to obtain as accurate and as valid a picture as possible of the implementation and operation of PCG/Ts.

The semi-structured questions posed were formulated in the context of the evaluation framework, the baseline data compiled through postal questionnaires, and background documents. Whilst many of the questions followed a standardized format, with researchers working from an interview guide that specified the key topics, the interview schedules varied slightly depending upon the particular interviewee. This enabled the evaluation to gather data that reflected individuals' particular experiences and areas of expertise, thus making the interview process more meaningful. In addition, researchers were encouraged to use their interview guides flexibly, allowing informants to discuss topics in any order and to propose new areas of relevance. In this way, informants could express their own definitions of their experiences and to define what was important or significant helping to extract a more accurate version of events.

Focus groups Focus groups are designed to obtain perceptions of individuals in a defined area of interest in a permissive, non-threatening environment. Group members interact to ideas and comments in a discussion usually based around pre-set themes and under the facilitation of the researcher (Krueger, 1994; Greenbaum, 1998). In order to discuss progress made regarding PCG/T core functions, four separate focus group discussions were held in each of the twelve sites on the following topics: health improvement, commissioning, clinical governance, and primary care development. Participants varied significantly but tended to include board/executive committee members with lead responsibilities for such areas or work. In addition, co-opted members from local trusts or the local authority were often involved. In year two, focus groups were disciplinary (for example, GPs and nurses) in order to gather additional data relevant to the progress or otherwise being made against core PCG/T functions.

Observational analysis This form of research involves an individual researcher engaging with the daily life of the group under study and listening and recording what happens in everyday interactions. Such research can involve a long-term observational period over several months to assess how a system works (see Guillemin and Holmstrom, 1986) but can also be an intensive study of a particular setting or interaction at several sites in order to extend the generalizability of findings. Data analysis is usually based on the taking of detailed field notes, often with the use of a focused guide on which to explore interactions between individuals (Mays and Pope, 1995).

Fieldwork visits in the PCG/T evaluation in its third year were organized to coincide with board meetings in order that researchers could observe their conduct and process and add richness to the data on the functioning of PCG/T boards. A standard observational framework for interpreting small group decision-making was used (Fisher and Ellis, 1990) with attention focused on the contributions and interactions between board members and the range and type of behaviours exhibited – for example, the extent of 'information giving', 'supporting', 'disagreeing' and so on. Such observational research served to illustrate the dynamics of group behaviour amongst the key players in a PCG/T leading to the support of significant conclusions such as the level of GP dominance of the agenda and the lack of interaction and inclusion of certain representative groups (Regen et al, 2001; see Chapter 5).

The range of qualitative methods employed to investigate the processes involved in the development of PCG/Ts across twelve case study sites and over a three-year period of activity was a conscious effort on behalf of the research designers to increase the validity of their research findings. The ability to 'triangulate' across a wide range of different source material provided greater confidence in their ability to make robust conclusions and policy recommendations.

A result of the 'process' evaluation methodology used in the PCG/T research has been the ability of researchers to show policy makers those key aspects of organizational working that has enabled organizations within different contexts to function effectively. However, a key drawback is the limited ability of the approach to address whether or not new initiatives had any impact on patient care. An influential 2004 review of the evidence related to primary care-led commissioning, for example, found that there was little research evidence to demonstrate that *any* commissioning approach had made any significant impact on the cost, quality and delivery of hospital care services except in relation to waiting times (Smith et al, 2004). This review concluded that more systematic efforts were needed in the future to assess impact of initiatives such as PCG/Ts in terms of their ability to achieve specific service and patient quality objectives.

Understanding Change in Primary Care Organizations

A common component to UK-based evaluations of primary care organizations has been the use of a contextually-based analysis. The approach has helped evaluators to uncover the impact of different issues locally which, across a range of sites, enabled the creation of important generic observations on those key factors that enabled PCOs to succeed or fail. The approach of researchers, therefore, has followed the school of 'realistic evaluation' encapsulated by Pawson and Tilley (1997) who identified a model of 'scientific realism' in which organizational outcomes are triggered by the interplay between mechanisms operating in a particular context. The model gives great importance to contextual factors in understanding causality, a conceptual approach which they termed 'generative causation' (see Figure 4.1). More simply put, the theory can be summarized by the basic equation: Context + Mechanism = Outcome.

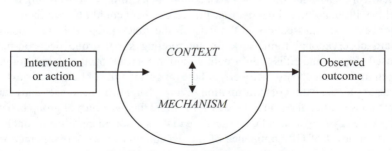

Figure 4.1 The 'scientific realistic' model of generative causation developed by Pawson and Tilley

Source: Adapted from Pawson and Tilley (1997).

The 'contextual approach' to understanding change was first adapted as an analytical framework in the national evaluation of TPPs which drew on the concept of 'receptive' and 'non-receptive' contexts for change outlined by Pettigrew et al (1992, 2004) and the contextual theories for change developed by Goodwin and Pinch (1995). By adapting such concepts, the TPP evaluation was able to show how the dynamic and multi-faceted nature of context meant that it was not possible to identify causality based on any static variable. Consequently, the research concentrated its analysis on the interplay between the mechanisms used to implement change and the range of contextual variables that influenced their ability to do so effectively (Goodwin et al, 2000; Evans et al, 2001).

The contextually-based evaluations of primary care organizations have since combined with the 'realistic evaluation' concept put forward by Pawson and Tilley (1997) to create an analytical paradigm that has gained prominence in the field of policy studies in health services research. The approach does not escape from the atheoretical nature of such investigations, which remain predominantly 'process' driven, yet it underpins the point that 'context matters' to enable distinctions to be made between generic factors of causality and those that are more context-specific.

The Impact of Contexts

According to Pawson and Tilley (1997), context refers to those contingent factors which influence the relationship between causal mechanisms and probable outcomes. They illustrate this in a physical science example: that gunpowder has within it the potential to explode, but whether it does so depends on it being in the right conditions. By extrapolating the concept to the development of primary care organizations, the TPP evaluation was able to uncover a number of contextual variables which were influencing the ability of TPPs to 'take off'. In the PCG/T evaluation, analysis of contexts enabled similar factors in progress to be uncovered including whether boundaries were coterminous with local authorities, whether PCGs were undergoing a process of mergers, and whether there was a history of good relationships and trust between local stakeholders (Regen et al, 2001). Crucial to both analyses was the changing national political context. For example, larger TPPs were placed at a contextual advantage once the direction of national policy was set towards locality-based PCGs (Goodwin et al, 2000).

The Impact of Mechanisms

A key conceptual task for evaluators is to tease out those key mechanisms, or causal factors, that both enable and prevent primary care organizations in achieving their objectives. Hence, the evaluator is looking to determine those key elements of process that enable change to occur across contexts. The findings from the TPP evaluation suggested three central mechanisms were crucial to making progress – budget holding and contracting; inter-agency co-operation; and key leaders with willing followers (Mays et al, 1998). Policy recommendations, therefore, emphasized that holding a 'real' budget was a prerequisite for change to be combined with a collaborative (rather than combative) style of negotiation with providers (Goodwin et al, 2000). In the PCG/T evaluation, where progress was observed primarily in terms of organizational development, success mechanisms included the articulation of a clear and sound vision, and developing an inclusive and collaborative (rather than imposed) decision-making process (Regen et al, 2001). Such findings show how achieving change in the larger and multi-professional world of PCG/Ts required far greater investment in relational and consensus-building initiatives before progress could be made.

The Interplay Between Context and Mechanism

The key conceptual issue in understanding change in individual PCOs is that of the *interplay* between context and mechanism over time. The likelihood of a particular PCO to reach a desired outcome is thus dependent on the abilities of those in the process of change to overcome contextual barriers or optimize contextual advantages. This process is represented diagrammatically in Figure 4.2 in which the vertical axis represents the context in which PCOs operate and the horizontal axis the mechanisms, or way in which PCOs have gone about their business. Each cell represents the likely consequences for a PCO. Thus, where context is 'receptive' and mechanism 'appropriate' the more likely it is for achievements or progress to be made.

Receptive		**'UNDER-ACHIEVEMENT'**	**'OPTIMAL ACHIEVEMENT'**
CONTEXT			
Non-receptive		**'LOW/NO ACHIEVEMENT'**	**'STIFLED ACHIEVEMENT'**
		Inappropriate	*Appropriate*

MECHANISM

Figure 4.2 Achieving objectives in primary care organizations: the interplay between context and mechanism

Source: Adapted from Goodwin et al (2000), p. 61.

The value to this model of interpretation is that most PCOs have struggled to reach the 'optimal' scenario since a mix of contextual and processual problems have restricted progress. The identification of these factors through qualitative case-study research enables a judgment to be made as to whether the PCO policy itself is being 'stifled' by non-receptive contexts (such as entrenched cultural values, policy shifts, or lack of management resources) or whether sites are 'underachieving' due to inappropriate mechanisms (such as top-down imposition of governance rules, or the unsophisticated use of contracting methods with providers). By studying these dynamics, evaluations have identified generalizable mechanisms that are more likely to lead to successful outcomes whilst being aware of the contextual blockages. For example, the structure-process-outcome analysis in the PCG/T evaluation was able to identify the inhibiting and facilitating factors in the transition from PCG to PCT status (Table 4.2).

Table 4.2 Transition to PCT status – key facilitating and inhibiting factors

	Facilitating Factors	**Inhibiting Factors**
ELEMENTS OF CONTEXT	Coterminosity of boundaries with local authority	Lack of coterminosity of boundaries with local authority
	Avoidance of merger	PCG merger and splits
	Local ownership of PCT plans	Loss of local ownership
ELEMENTS OF PROCESS	Inclusive planning process to promote joint ownership and acceptance of PCT	Imposed changes – not inclusive planning to promote joint ownership and acceptance
	A clear vision and well articulated PCT business case	Lack of vision and lack of agreement on case for PCT
	Fast pace of change with a willingness to move forward	Political interference, bureaucracy and unwillingness to change
	Hard work and commitment	Burn-out and excessive workloads
	Planning based on the benefits to patients via move to PCT status	Structure-driven and non patient-focused
	Clinical engagement	Professional disenfranchisement
	Adequate management and IT support arrangements	Lack of management capacity

Source: Adapted from Regen et al (2001), pp. 125-126.

The crucial point to make in understanding change in PCOs is that the mechanisms required to achieve similar objectives may need to vary depending on the context within which they are operating. Hence, success in securing appropriate hospital services might be best served through a contestable strategy where competition exists between providers for PCT contracts, but such an approach lacks feasibility in a monopsony provider environment where more relational commissioning may be required. It follows that national initiatives need to be sympathetic to the role of contexts and avoid a 'one size fits all' policy that is overly centralist. Furthermore, policy-makers should be encouraged to facilitate an enabling contextual climate for PCOs by, for example, investing in management training or by allowing new initiatives the freedom to 'bed down'.

The Politics of Evaluations

Evaluation of health services in the UK is intimately bound within a highly-charged political environment over the performance of the NHS. As Dash et al (2003) report, policy-makers are often concerned about the timeliness of evaluation studies since, to be useful to them, findings need to be made available when political decisions are being made. Indeed, NHS managers in a changing political environment have often criticized evaluation studies for lacking relevance and being poor value for money. Researchers, on the other hand, are often reported as frustrated because their work is not more widely used by managers and policy-makers and often feel that their work is undervalued or poorly applied (Dash et al, 2003). This section, therefore, examines these key issues in the relationship between policy-makers, practitioners and researchers.

Responding to the Changing Policy Context

A key characteristic of evaluations is their concern with policies that are on the current agenda of policy makers (Berk and Rossi, 1990). However, changing policy contexts in England have been an occupational hazard when researching PCOs due to their emergent and developmental nature. During the course of the TPP evaluation, a General Election led to major changes in health policy which abolished fundholding in favour of locality-based PCGs. As a result, the purpose of the TPP evaluation was forced to change from 'identifying best models in which to further the development of fundholder-based purchasing in primary care' (Department of Health Research and Development Directorate, 1995, pp. 1-2) to a question based on what could be learned from TPPs that would help PCGs perform best. The evaluation had to be significantly altered since single-practice sites were no longer useful cases. New data were collected concentrating on case studies of the larger multi-practice TPPs where the lessons for emergent PCGs would be most relevant (Goodwin et al, 2000).

The national evaluation of PCG/Ts similarly had to respond to two major policy upheavals during its lifetime. Originally, the research had been established to examine GP commissioning groups that were piloting a more collaborative and alternative form of commissioning to that of fundholding (NHSE, 1997b). However, the emerging PCG agenda meant that policy developments had overtaken the pilots and it became clear that the evaluation should become focused on providing early lessons to inform the establishment of PCGs (Regen et al, 1999). Accordingly, the evaluation adopted a formative and iterative design, seeking to identify key lessons to help shape the development of PCG policy and practice. A further stage of organizational reforms following 'Shifting the Balance of Power' (Department of Health, 2001a) meant that the evaluation team had to further amend its design to examine issues related to the transition from PCG to PCT status. Fortunately, the formative design enabled the evaluators to adapt to these changing policy contexts relatively easily.

Influencing Policy and Practice

Since politicians are central to the policy making process, evaluations have been intrinsically enmeshed in a complex political process. During the marketization policies of the early 1990s, evaluations were avoided to 'stop academics crawling all over the reforms' and to avoid opponents using them as a way of delaying change (Evans et al, 2001). That evaluations of emerging primary care organizations were embraced in the mid 1990s reflects a more collaborative, evidence-based approach to the development of policy (Martin and Sanderson, 1999). However, as Klein (2000) observed, what was far less clear is whether politicians could accept the logic that, having commissioned major pieces of work, they should then base policy decisions on the findings.

The history of evaluation studies in health care as a whole suggests evidence to support only a limited direct impact on policy making (Walt, 1994, Övretveit, 1998). For example, in the national evaluation of TPPs, a key finding was that small and single practice organizations had achieved more in their first 'live' year (Killoran et al, 1999). However, this finding did not fit with the political opposition to single-practice budget holding that was regarded as having contributed to both 'two-tierism' and to high transaction costs. Conversely, following a return to the concept of practice-based commissioning in 2004 (Department of Health, 2004b), the benefits of the approach as perceived by the Department of Health appear to be highly selective of the known evidence (Smith et al, 2004). 'Technical guidance' provided to PCTs in 2005 (Department of Health, 2005b), for example, explain the potential of the approach to make providers more responsive and to reinvest resources in primary and community care, but seemingly overlook issues to do with transaction costs and potential service inequities. This provides evidence for the selective way in which research findings can be used to suit political objectives.

In the national evaluation of PCG/Ts, the evaluation team was able to inform the Department of Health of certain key findings and policy implications, but this did not necessarily have any influence on policy in the short term. In particular, their research concluded that 'many PCG/Ts are operating on the edge of what is sustainable and sometimes well beyond it. Individuals are at times close to "burning out", and the additional pressure of moving to PCT status is placing an almost intolerable burden on organizations and those leading them' (Regen et al, 2001, p. 143). Concerns over workload combined with the need to establish organizational and management infrastructure led to the policy recommendation that PCGs needed to be allowed the time to develop as organizations and deliver tangible service changes before moving to trust status. Indeed, consensus had emerged across the case study sites that a greater number of more senior and experienced managers were required for the leadership and management of PCTs (Smith et al, 2000). However, in the following year, the pace of the transition was accelerated dramatically following the publication of 'Shifting the Balance of Power' (Department of Health, 2001a) which made it clear that no such time would be available.

The experience of the evaluation of primary care organizations suggests that it is probably naïve to believe that evidence from research and policy analysis can influence policy-making. As Mays, Wyke and Evans (2001) argue:

> The limits of evaluation are clear. Evaluation is only likely directly to influence policy where it addresses questions on which policy makers have yet to make up their minds, it offers them insights which enable them to develop emerging policy options and is unopposed by conflicting political pressures (p. 419).

Apart from the political dimension, there are clearly sound empirical reasons, such as changing political and local contexts, which limit the generalizability of findings that might be applied more widely (Raine, 1998). However, at a local and more practical level, the dissemination of findings through reports, conferences and workshops has helped address some of the developmental needs of PCG/Ts. As with the TPP evaluation, the national evaluation of PCG/Ts was never established as a piece of 'action research' in which findings from, and recommendations to, individual organizations could be fed back as part of a developmental process. Nonetheless, the process of case study evaluation highlighted a significant need for the development of workshops or training programmes. Whilst there was no shortage of independent and Government agencies developing initiatives to support such needs, the evaluations themselves were left on the cusp between traditional evaluation and policy development. The balance between maintaining a distance and providing feedback to those PCG/Ts was often difficult, but it was clear that the evaluators' role did not include developmental work with sites.

In 2004, the Labour Government announced a return to the policy of delegating budgets to GP practices in order to address a number of concerns including the ability to provide patients with a choice of provider at the point of referral for elective care; the need to address flagging GP involvement in the commissioning of services; and the ability to introduce market pressures on providers and incentivize primary-care based alternatives (Department of Health, 2004a). A number of review studies were subsequently undertaken to analyze the potential for this new policy and to provide lessons from the past (NERA, 2005; Lewis, 2004; NHS Alliance; 2004a; Smith et al, 2004). It will be interesting to observe the extent to which policy-makers will heed the messages from this body of evidence and, in particular, fund research to examine whether practice-led commissioning makes any impact on the costs and outcome of care provision – a key missing element in past evaluation studies.

Working with Research Funders

When undertaking Government-funded research, evaluators must accept that their client works in a political context. Not only does this mean that reports need to be delivered on time but that evaluators need to be ready to brief officials at short notice on emerging findings or key issues, especially if they may be responding to a question raised in Parliament. Furthermore, research needs to retain its 'usefulness' and be able to address new questions following policy changes. This means that researchers are often required to adapt protocols to address new demands, a process that evaluators might be wise to anticipate.

One of the key issues in working with a Government sponsor is managing the potential conflicts involved in being 'useful' whilst retaining an independent focus. This becomes particularly important if and when research discovers findings that are potentially controversial or challenging to the client. In order to avoid any potential conflict, it has been important for evaluation teams to 'manage upwards' through the provision of regular written updates, face-to-face consultations and involvement of the client on project steering groups. Given close working relationships, and aided by the developmental nature of the research questions posed, evaluation teams have generally managed to maintain their ability to be objective, challenging and yet supportive.

A major problem with process evaluations in the highly politicized environment of the NHS is the ability of researchers to retain their independence. Where research uncovers unpalatable messages, the relationship between researchers and policy makers has sometimes become fraught. As Bate and Robert (2003) reported, the potential impact of some process evaluations examining NHS modernization processes became compromised due to the need of Government-based funders for the evaluations to provide more positive policy messages to suit current political objectives. A key future issue for process evaluations, therefore, is to redefine the relationship between policy-makers, practitioners and researchers to ensure such tensions are minimized. As Dash et al (2003) conclude, independent organizations may be more suited in bridging the tensions in the way each stakeholder works together.

Assessing the Evaluation Process: Lessons for Research and Practice

The evaluation of primary care organizations in England has involved the assessment of highly complex initiatives using a wide variety of primarily qualitative research methods. The evaluation process has highlighted the importance of developing contextually-aware frameworks for data collection and analysis within a changing political context requiring a reflexive and responsive attitude to the needs of policy-makers. Undertaking such evaluation is of itself a necessarily more complex methodological task than experiential approaches such as the randomized control trial within clinical settings. To improve the quality and relevance of such work for policy development in the future, a series of key lessons for research and practice present themselves:

Lessons for Research

- Learning about complex initiatives should be encouraged to make a virtue of pragmatism, but clear evaluation frameworks based on an agreed set of research questions should be employed.
- Contextual analysis provides an important basis for investigation, but there is a need to develop greater theory-based approaches to the design and implementation of evaluations.
- Evaluations need to be multi-disciplinary since there is added value in having a mix of social scientists, health economists, and other disciplines in research teams.
- Evaluations should be formative and iterative to ensure flexibility, but as a result methodologies should employ a range of data collection methods to improve the validity of the results observed.
- Collecting baseline information is crucial as PCOs develop quickly over time. Having documented information also helps clarify objectives, research questions and success criteria.
- Evaluators should be aware of the changing policy context and employ a robust research design adaptable to change. Without losing focus on the longer-term issues, evaluations must meet the demands of policy makers.
- Evaluators have to accept that funders work in a political context. They should manage upwards to ensure good relationships through regular forms of feedback but retain their sense of independence.
- The relationship between researchers, practitioners and policy-makers needs to be redefined to ensure that findings are not compromised. Independent research funding help might help in this regard.
- Research should examine in more detail the costs and impact of innovations rather than simply the processes which make them function.
- The organization of evaluation teams will involve many individuals, so a dedicated project manager, clear roles and responsibilities amongst members, and regular team meetings with actionable outcomes are required.
- Evaluations have maintained a clear separation between the participants in the implementation process and the researchers. Given the developmental needs of newly emerging primary care organizations, more interactive activities such as workshops or training programmes within an 'action research' model should be considered.

Lessons for Practice

- Evaluation plays an important role in informing policy options and guiding new policy initiatives. Policy-makers should re-invest in research, evaluation and developmental activities since there is a lack of knowledge on how PCTs can best adjust to new arrangements such as nGMS contracts, practice-based budget holding, out-of-hours arrangements, and new models of commissioning based on 'payments by results'.
- PCOs would benefit from engaging in research and evaluation studies as apart of a continuous process of learning and should be prepared to change working practices in the light of what is observed.
- There is scope for developing models of evaluation where PCOs become 'partners' in the research process through developmental networks in which feedback and learning from evaluation studies can be discussed and shared.

Chapter 5

Exploring the Organizational and Governance Arrangements of PCG/Ts

This chapter examines the organizational and governance arrangements put in place by primary care groups and trusts in England over the period 1999-2004, using this as the basis for distilling lessons for researchers and practitioners about the design, implementation and evaluation of effective governance arrangements for primary care organizations. Consideration is given of the growing sophistication of organizational forms adopted by primary care organizations, and the associated increase in bureaucracy and management costs associated with running PCG/Ts. This development of PCG/Ts as larger and more complex organizations is seen to be a consequence of their expanding remit, and the fact that they have evolved from local GP-run and – developed organizations into statutory NHS bodies largely operating in accordance with national agendas and priorities.

Typology and Characteristics of PCG Organizational Arrangements

Primary care groups (in place in England from April 1999-2002) operated within a nationally defined framework of organizational form and function. This contrasted sharply with those primary care organizations in place prior to 1999 (such as GP commissioning groups, GP multifunds, and total purchasing projects) that had been free to determine their own organizational arrangements. PCGs were sub-committees of health authorities, and as such were not free-standing statutory bodies. The membership of PCG boards was also prescribed through Department of Health guidance in 1998 (NHS Executive, 1998), and required the following:

- 4-7 general practitioners;
- 1-2 community nurses;
- 1 social services representative;
- 1 lay member;
- 1 health authority non-executive director; and
- a PCG chief executive.

However, PCGs were free to develop their own management arrangements in support of the board, using a specific government financial allocation for this purpose, plus other resources made available from their local health authority, NHS trusts, or other sources. The discretion over the level of management arrangements available to PCGs was reflected in the range of organizational forms adopted by PCGs for the provision of management support, the characteristics of which were often influenced by past experience. For example, PCGs in the HSMC evaluation study had evolved from previous GP commissioning pilots, and their management arrangements and sources of funding for support as PCGs to some extent reflected the particular history and ways of working of the pilots as well as the new organizations (Smith et al, 2000).

HSMC's national evaluation of PCG/Ts identified four broad categories of management support. These four models reflected the level and nature of dedicated management support within the PCG and the degree of integration between PCG support and that provided by health authorities (Regen *et al*, 2001). The four categories are summarized in Table 5.1 below and reveal a gradation in the extent of management support arrangements.

Table 5.1 Categorization of PCG management structures, 1999-2001

- Type A: *Basic PCG infrastructure*, relying almost completely on health authority links and teams for many functions
- Type A2: *Enhanced PCG infrastructure,* relying on health authority links and teams for main functions
- Type B: *Extended PCG infrastructure,* with minimal reliance on health authority support
- Type C: *Integrated PCG/health authority management support arrangements*, with clarity of roles, responsibilities and job design

Source: Regen et al (1999).

Type A: Basic PCG infrastructure The type A 'basic' PCG infrastructure had very limited management arrangements usually comprising a chief executive, a secretary, and in some cases a primary care development or commissioning manager. This being the case, the groups relied heavily on their host health authorities for the provision of management support including commissioning, public health advice, financial management, information technology support and contractor services.

Type A2: Enhanced PCG infrastructure Similar to the basic PCG infrastructures, these groups had secured two to four additional staff (working on clinical governance, health improvement or commissioning) over and above the chief executive's immediate team. These groups continued to rely heavily upon their host health authorities for management support such as public health advice, finance and information functions, commissioning, prescribing advice and core functions such as human resources and pay-roll.

Type B: Extended PCG infrastructure Type B PCGs had a more extended management infrastructure with some ten to twenty people working as part of a dedicated PCG support team, usually located in separate PCG management offices. Posts in these structures included the chief executive, a business support manager, finance manager(s), health improvement/needs analysis staff, primary care development managers, clinical governance managers, prescribing advisors, and secretarial and administrative support. These groups had used their management allowance to set up relatively freestanding organizations but still relied upon their host health authority for support in the areas of public health, commissioning and finance. Extended structures were facilitated by a significant degree of devolution of resource and personnel from the local health authority to the PCG.

Type C: Integrated PCG infrastructure The type C model with integrated PCG/health authority management arrangements represented something of a middle way between types A2 and B described above. Here, PCGs and health authorities had negotiated management support for the PCG in a way that treated many of the health authority functions as being part of the PCG's management resource. Typically, this meant that the PCG had a number of core staff, for example, chief executive, administrator, primary care development manager, and information officer, supplemented by specified health authority support formally attached to the PCG. Some of these posts were line-managed by the PCG chief executive exclusively or on a joint basis with the health authority. PCGs had direct access to health authority support such as public health, commissioning management, clinical audit input, and financial and management accounting.

Funding the Management of PCGs

In 1999/00, the average management cost allowance made available to the twelve case study PCGs was £2.92 per head (Smith et al, 2000). This figure was slightly below the indicative sum of £3.00 per head stated in central guidance (NHS Executive, 1998). In 2000/01, the average management cost allowance made available to the PCGs in the study had increased to £3.50 per head. As Figure 5.1 shows, PCGs with basic infrastructures were associated with smaller PCGs, while those with extended infrastructures had the largest average population size, demonstrating a clear and unsurprising link between size of PCG and complexity of management arrangements (Regen et al, 2001).

PCGs with basic infrastructures were associated with smaller PCGs, while those with extended infrastructures had the largest average population size, demonstrating a clear and unsurprising link between size of PCG and complexity of management arrangements (Regen et al, 2001). Table 5.2 shows the size/complexity relationship of PCG management arrangements as found in the HSMC study.

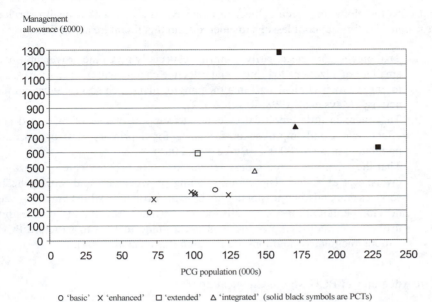

Figure 5.1 PCG management allowance by structure type in 2000/2001

Source: Regen et al (2001), p. 65.

Table 5.2 Management structure and population size of PCGs in HSMC's National Evaluation of PCG/Ts

Type of PCG Structure	Number of PCGs	Mean PCG Population	Population Range
A – Basic	2	93,000	70,000 to 116,000
A2 – Enhanced	4	100,000	73,000 to 125,000
B – Extended	3	165,000	104,000 to 230,000
C – Integrated	3	139,000	102,000 to 172,000

Source: Regen et al (2001), p. 63.

Caution is required when considering the size and infrastructure of a primary care organization, particularly if one is tempted to assume that big is generally better. The relationship between the size of a primary care organization and its ability to carry out core functions, has been subject to extensive analysis within health services research. The three overall lessons to emerge from this literature are as follows:

1. That bigger is not necessarily beautiful, especially given the proven ability of smaller organizations to bring about effective change within primary care and to engage their clinical staff in a meaningful manner in service development activity (Mays et al, 1998; Regen, 2002).
2. That there is little empirical evidence to support claims of increased cost effectiveness and improved performance for a primary care organization population of over 100,000 (Bjoke et al, 2001).
3. That the key issue is the fitness for purpose of a primary care organization (Walshe et al, 2004). The commissioning of secondary and tertiary health services demands a larger population base than 100,000, whilst practice-based development of primary care calls for smaller management units, thus leading to the conclusion that size alone is not a guide to how to structure PCOs – more imaginative solutions are required (Smith et al, 2004).

The Adequacy of PCG Management Support

A very common finding of evaluations of primary care organizations in the UK has been that they struggle to access adequate levels of management support in relation to the scale of tasks they are required to fulfill (Regen et al, 2001; Wilkin et al, 2001; Dowling and Glendinning, 2003). Regen et al (2001, p. 143) noted:

> There is an inevitable relationship between the degree of management resource made available to organizations and their ability to perform the functions required of them. Our research suggests that many PCG/Ts are operating on the edge of what is sustainable and sometimes well beyond it.

Dowling and Glendinning (2003), in drawing together the conclusions of the three-year National Tracker Survey of 71 PCG/Ts, pointed out that PCG/T chief executives viewed the lack of organizational capacity, particularly shortages of staff, as being the primary barrier to progress in each of the three years. The percentage of chief executives reporting organizational, and in particular management, capacity as the key barrier to progress increased from 40 per cent of PCGs in 1999/2000 to 61 per cent in 2001/2002 (Dowling and Glendinning, 2003).

When set in the international context, there is strong evidence to suggest that UK PCOs are indeed relatively starved of administrative and organizational support. For example, there is a striking difference between the management resources typically available between US and UK primary care organizations. In a comparative study of US managed care organizations and PCTs, Weiner et al (2001) pointed to a hundredfold disparity between the management resources available to PCGs in the UK and health maintenance organizations serving a similar population base in the US. This disparity may in part be due to what some commentators see as the wasteful and over-administered nature of the American medical management system (Himmelstein and Woolhandler, 1998). Nevertheless, concerns remained that PCG/Ts were being expected to deliver a much more managed approach to primary care with some features akin to those of US primary care organizations but with grossly inadequate management resources and capacity (Smith and Walshe, 2004; Weiner et al, 2001).

The Evolution of Primary Care Group Boards

As noted earlier in his chapter, all PCGs operated within a nationally specified board structure. In almost all cases, GPs represented the largest professional group within a PCG board, a fact that reflected both the board composition suggested by central government guidance and the influence of the medical profession as a lobby group during the process of developing policy related to PCGs.

In studies of the first year of operation of PCGs, researchers found that organizations had spent much time and effort in developing their board members and establishing the PCG board as a corporate entity (Smith et al, 2000; Wilkin et al, 2000). A key area of concern related to board development at this stage was the apparent dominance of GPs on boards (Smith et al, 2000). Evidence in 1999/2000 suggested that GPs had a tendency to dominate discussion within board meetings, and more generally in shaping the PCG agenda around clinical and medical issues. One reason for this was felt to be that the non-medical members of the board were still in the process of establishing themselves, but a note of particular concern was sounded in relation to nurse members who appeared to be very enthusiastic and competent board members whilst lacking real influence within PCG decision-making processes (Smith et al, 2000 and see Chapter 7). A year later, in 2000/2001, the issue of GP domination remained a concern for half of the PCGs within the HSMC study. For example, one social services representative noted:

> The core group of GPs see it [the board] as inclusive but other board members feel excluded. I'm never really sure why I'm there – except to fly the flag (Regen et al, 2001, p. 76).

In groups such as this, many board members highlighted a continued emphasis on practice-based primary care development activities and the commissioning of hospital services, to the detriment of partnership working, health improvement and public involvement work (Regen et al, 2001). This was witnessed by the fact that PCG board agendas were often found to be very primary care and medically dominated.

Other groups, however, reported that the balance of involvement and influence within their PCG board was improving, with a shift in emphasis away from GPs towards lay, social services and nurse members. This shift was largely attributed to the growing confidence of these board members and their increasing understanding of PCG issues and ways of working.

Intra-Board Relationships and Relative Levels of Influence

GP board members The relative contributions of different members of PCG boards inevitably affected the overall effectiveness of the organization, and the sense that board members had of relationships within the board. In HSMC's report of PCG research carried out in 1999, one of the most frequently reported issues regarding the contributions of particular board members concerned the role of GP board members and the perception that some were not giving appropriate time and attention to PCG work (Smith et al, 2000). A year later, this problem appeared to have eased, with the resignation of 'ineffective' GP board members having been sparked in some cases by discussions about their performance within the board. In 2000, there was still concern about the differential contribution of board members (usually GPs), this being a key source of tension for some boards. One chief executive summed up this issue as follows:

> We're more divided between those who do and those who don't – some are taking on a far bigger burden than others and it's causing tension between the GPs (Regen et al, 2001, p. 77).

Nurse board members In earlier studies of GP commissioning groups and PCGs, a key concern was that the nursing contribution to board working, especially at a strategic level of decision-making, was less than ideal, despite obvious enthusiasm for PCG work on the part of nurses (Regen et al, 1999; Smith et al, 2000; Wilkin et al, 2001). In research carried out in 2000, the picture remained mixed. A majority of PCG nurse board members felt that they were valued by their GP and managerial colleagues and were able to 'have their say', although some pointed out that it had taken time and effort to reach this position, and it had required constant reinforcement of the nursing contribution. The difficulty of nurses wielding true influence at PCG/T board level was underlined by the National Tracker Study findings in 2002 (Wilkin et al, 2002), where only 11 per cent of PCG/T chairs rated nurses as having considerable influence on the policies and priorities of the organization, compared with 28 per cent seeing GPs as influential and 98 per cent seeing the principal officers (lay chair, PEC chair and chief executive) in this light. In the HSMC study, researchers observing PCG board meetings reported that only a minority of nurses participated in an active manner in discussions, or challenged their colleagues at board meetings. There was a tendency for nurses to focus on providing information related to their areas of work rather than contributing actively to more general discussions (Regen et al, 2001 and see Chapter 7).

The fact that the issue of nurse influence at a strategic level within primary care organizations has emerged in both of the major UK studies and at each stage of research, suggests that this is a key organizational issue facing those who seek to develop truly inclusive and diverse PCT boards. It shows that it is not sufficient to have structures in place that enable nurses to sit at the top table alongside doctors and senior managers. There are clearly factors that mitigate against their effective engagement and influence at a strategic level, and evidence from other research suggests that these include issues of gender, the traditionally subservient nature of nursing relative to medicine, and the lack of effective political mechanisms to fight nursing's corner at senior levels (Wicks, 1998; Hennessy and Spurgeon, 2000). For nurses working at a senior level within primary care organizations, gaining significant strategic influence is a major challenge and one that requires skilled and sustained organizational and personal development support. This issue is explored further in Chapter 7.

Lay and social services board members When the lay member and health authority non-executive roles on the PCG board were announced in government guidance in 1998, they were viewed as a significant departure, drawing a lay perspective into the previously GP-dominated preserve of fundholding and commissioning groups. Despite the GP majority on almost all PCG boards (a feature that was negotiated by the British Medical Association as a right for general practice in 1998), the government was clearly intent on broadening the composition of PCG boards and linking primary care organizations more clearly with their local communities.

In HSMC's study of PCG/Ts, board members reported their appreciation of the lay members' role in developing user involvement on behalf of the PCG, but others commented on what they felt was a rather token role in terms of its impact on PCG decision-making (Regen et al, 2001). The health authority non-executive director's role was viewed as being somewhat ambiguous, with some colleagues being unsure as to their true allegiance (health authority or PCG?). Others noted the value of the non-executive's contribution, particularly with regard to enacting principles of corporate governance.

Issues relating to the contribution of social services representatives on PCG boards centred upon their level of appointment and their attendance and input at meetings (Regen et al, 2001). Some chief executives and chairs felt that a social services appointment at director or assistant director level would have facilitated the development of joint working at a strategic, rather than operational level. Indeed, some of the social services representatives interviewed in the HSMC research recognised and shared this view (Regen et al, 2001). In addition, several acknowledged that they could not be as active in the PCG as they wished to be because of time pressures and lack of support.

What is evident is that the development of a corporate board within a primary care organization is a lengthy and challenging process. The PCG board (and now the PEC) is a microcosm of many of the professional and tribal tensions inherent in NHS primary care and health care management more generally. Long-standing cultural factors such as a tendency on the part of nurses to defer to doctors in meetings (for example, HSMC's research noted that in some boards, doctors referred to nurses by their first names, whereas nurses always addressed their medical colleagues as 'doctor') are not easily transcended. The fact that primary care organizations in the 1990s were almost exclusively developed, led and governed by GPs is important context to the emergence of PCG/Ts. Whilst on the one hand PCGs and PCTs can be rightly criticized for failing to be adequately inclusive in elements of their operation and governance, the same organizations are simultaneously challenged about the need to reclaim the grassroots GP support and engagement that appears to have been lost in the move to more mainstream primary care organizations (Regen, 2002; NHS Alliance, 2003).

The dynamics of PCG boards as described above was examined in each case study in the HSMC evaluation in 2000 through an analysis of the behaviours of board members during meetings using a standard observational framework for interpreting small group decision-making (Fisher and Ellis, 1990). Attention focused on the contributions and interactions between board members and the range and type of behaviours exhibited. Approximately sixty-five per cent of the content of board meetings in all PCGs was concerned with the giving and receiving of information with far less time spent 'proposing', 'supporting' or 'disagreeing' through discussion and debate. Such interactions are vividly portrayed in Figure 5.2 which show the relative contributions (by width of line) and direction of interactions between board members at meetings observed during fieldwork in two typical PCGs (Regen et al, p. 83). The observational data gathered gave support to the view that PCG board meetings were essentially a forum for the ratification and approval of decisions rather than the creation or discussion of PCG policies.

The Importance of the Chair/Chief Executive Relationship

In HSMC's research in 1999, all PCG board members in the twelve case studies were asked to identify where they thought that key decisions about the development of the PCG took place. An overwhelming majority of respondents cited the chair/chief executive pairing as being the locus of PCG decision-making. It was also noted that the chair/chief executive pair was typically the leading influence on strategic as well as operational decisions, presenting suggestions and proposals to the board for discussion and ratification. The degree to which chief executives and chairs were themselves comfortable with this apparently significant organizational influence clearly varied. One PCG chair noted:

> Decisions should happen at sub-board level. The chief executive and I differ in our view about this – he thinks it is all about papers going to the board to ratify, but I think it is more about involving the wider PCG, for we have a member organization elected by constituents (Smith et al, 2000, p. 73).

In 2000, when PCGs had been fully operational for over a year, researchers once again posed the question about decision-making to members of PCG boards. As was the case in 1999, the vast majority of board members said the chair/chief executive pairing was the key influence on PCG decisions, although many pointed out that for operational issues this was largely appropriate.

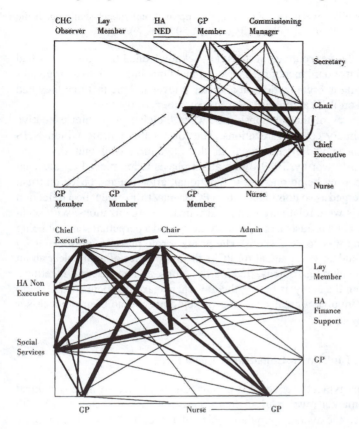

Figure 5.2 The contribution and interaction between PCG board members in two typical PCG board meetings in 2000

Source: Regen et al (2001), p. 63.

On matters of PCG strategy, research in 2000 again suggested a picture of the chair and chief executive formulating proposals and then taking these to the PCG board for comment and approval. Observations by researchers of board meetings confirmed this implied role of the board as a ratifying and checking body rather than a decision making body. Relatively few decisions were required at board meetings, with most items being presented for information, and when decisions were taken, these were usually preceded by a short discussion serving to clarify points of information rather than to debate issues. Some interviewees were however at pains to point out what they felt to be the important role played by the board in considering and taking final decisions:

The chair and the chief executive come to us for approval, not rubber-stamping. If the board doesn't like it, the board will say (Regen et al, 2001, p. 79).

Several chairs and chief executives in the study acknowledged the power they had within the PCG and its board meetings. They attributed this influence to their greater experience of working in organizations at a strategic level and the fact that they had more time to spend on PCG activities than other members of the board.

Clearly, the primacy of the relationship between the chair and chief executive is not unique to primary care organizations. The role of this pairing within NHS organizations has been widely discussed in the literature (Wall and Baddeley, 1998; Robinson and Exworthy, 1999), with an emphasis being placed on the vital importance of the pairing being one that is functional, effective and based on trust. That the pairing emerged as so dominant within PCGs may to an extent be a reflection of the fact that PCGs were relatively small and immature organizations, with scant management support and infrastructure in many cases, and a perpetual sense of being a staging post on the way to PCT status. The primary role played within PCGs by this 'two at the top' did however signal for PCTs the importance of being clear about arrangements for developing strategy, making decisions, and conducting meetings, for as is evident from the analysis below, the governance arrangements of PCTs are more complex and involve a greater number of key players than their predecessor PCGs.

Ensuring Effective Links with Constituent Localities

Primary care groups typically covered a population that reflected a geographical locality such as a market town, parliamentary constituency, or sector of a health authority area. Given the average population size of 100,000, PCGs could in many cases be regarded as locality-based organizations. With the advent of PCTs, however, and the increase in average organizational size to 180,000 population, maintaining a locality focus for PCT activity has proved to be more of a challenge. In many PCTs, a common element has been the retention of a locality or divisional structure (Regen et al, 2001; Wilkin et al, 2002). These divisions, primarily made up of groups of GPs, were retained for two key reasons: first, to provide like-minded or geographically different groups of GPs, thus enabling a sense of representation and ownership within the PCT (as they had within the PCG); and second, to allow for the potential of devolving tasks, such as prescribing or elements of commissioning, to a more local level. The use of localities as a method for facilitating local professional and public involvement and for organizing devolution of budgets and other responsibilities is not of course new. Many primary care organizations in the 1990s operated in this manner (Mays and Dixon, 1996; LeGrand et al, 1998; Smith et al, 1998).

The Use of Sub-Groups

As well as seeking to engage localities within the work of the PCG/T, local managers and health care professionals have worked hard to find ways of ensuring that their constituent primary care colleagues are properly involved in the work of the primary care organization. One of the most frequently reported ways of doing this is by means of the use of multidisciplinary sub-groups of the board or PEC.

HSMC's interim PCG evaluation report noted that all PCGs had established sub-groups to which PCG boards delegated operational areas of work on topics such as prescribing, clinical governance, commissioning and health improvement (Smith et al, 2000). Subsequent research in 2001 suggested that sub-groups (or task groups) had become increasingly important within PCGs, with such groups taking responsibility for whole areas of work, reporting on these to the board and making recommendations about proposed courses of action. Many PCGs comprised a mixture of topic-based sub-groups such as prescribing, clinical governance and commissioning, combined with client-based or service-specific sub-groups such as mental health, coronary heart disease and older people.

Structures for Involving Local Stakeholders in PCG/T Work

PCG/Ts are much more than just their boards. Their constituency includes local general practices, primary health care teams, voluntary organizations, and local authority staff and managers working in health and social care in the locality. HSMC's interim PCG evaluation report found that groups were in the process of developing a range of structures for ensuring effective communication and involvement with different stakeholder groups (Smith et al, 2000). Subsequent research suggested that most PCG/Ts had consolidated work in this area, with the majority now having nursing forums for primary care and community nursing staff in the PCG/T and GP forums/open meetings. In addition, during the period September 1999-August 2000, several groups had established practice managers' groups and practice nurse forums. In some cases, these groups were open to all stakeholders in the particular category, and in others the PCG/T had sought representatives from each practice, clinic or sub-locality area.

Developing Robust Corporate Governance Arrangements

One of the most frequent criticisms levelled at the GP-led primary care organizations in the NHS in the 1990s was the relative lack of corporate governance in comparison with that expected of NHS trusts and health authorities (although many GP groups were of course sub-committees of health authorities and hence subject to their overall governance arrangements). HSMC's interim PCG research found that corporate governance was being taken seriously by PCGs. (Smith et al, 2000). Fieldwork carried out in 2000 suggested that this remained the case as groups continued to operate within either health authority or PCG adapted standing orders and standing financial instructions, and registers of members' interests. Observations of PCG board meetings generally served to illustrate the good progress made by PCGs with regard to issues of probity and corporate governance. Declarations of interest were usually sought at the beginning of meetings and main motions and decisions were formally expressed and moved by PCG chairs.

While generally pleased with progress regarding corporate governance during the period September 1999-August 2000, a few chief executives highlighted examples of poor practice, particularly in relation to the conduct of GPs. Some GPs failed to declare their interests while others had raised inappropriate issues at board meetings. Chief executives felt that in the main GPs accepted the need for probity but sometimes 'forgot' about it in practice. In this context, several chief executives underlined the need to continually reinforce the importance of corporate governance to board members, possibly through regular training sessions.

Public Accountability

Perhaps the most significant area of weakness regarding governance concerned the issue of public accountability in relation to PCG board meetings. While groups recognized accountability as an important aspect of their public sector role, few were successful in actually using board meetings as a mechanism for strengthening public accountability. Of the eight public board meetings observed, only three had managed to attract 'genuine' members of the public, as opposed to NHS employees. Overall, PCG boards appeared to be divided on the extent to which they regarded their board meetings as 'board meetings in public' (and therefore not concerned with engaging the public) or as 'public board meetings' (concerned with encouraging public attendance and participation).

The Organizational and Governance Arrangements of PCTs

Primary care trusts are free-standing NHS organizations that operate at what was outlined as 'level 4' in the evolution of PCG/Ts envisaged in the NHS White Paper of 1997 (Department of Health, 1997). PCTs are at once commissioners of health care for their local population *and* providers of primary and community health services. This inevitably blurs the purchaser-provider divide and raises the potential for conflicts of interests that need to be accommodated in what ever governance arrangements are put in place. Commentators pointed to the risk of such conflicts of interest at the time of establishing PCTs (Mays and Goodwin, 1998), and this continues to be a challenge to the development of effective commissioning arrangements that assure appropriate accountability and governance (Smith et al, 2004).

The governance arrangements of PCTs in some senses draw from both their predecessor bodies PCGs, and from NHS trusts. The professional executive committee (PEC) of the PCT is similar to the board of a PCG and is intended to be the main forum where policy is shaped and decisions taken about PCT activity, described in government guidance as the 'engine room of the PCT' (NHS Executive, 1999). The PEC is made up of GPs, other primary care professionals, and the senior managers of the PCT, with GPs continuing to be the single largest professional group – once again sounding warning bells about possible GP dominance of the agenda and proceedings of primary care organizations.

The PEC reports to a PCT board that is constituted in the same manner as an NHS trust board, with a lay chair, and equal numbers of executive and non-executive directors (there has to be a lay majority overall). The board is responsible for overseeing the PEC and the organization as a whole, and for ensuring that the core public service values of accountability, probity and openness are properly applied to the strategy and operations of the PCT.

There is an important third dimension to the governance and leadership of PCTs, namely the executive management team. It is common practice for the PCT chief executive to meet with his or her executives and service heads on a weekly or fortnightly basis, as would be expected in any major organization. What this means is that there are three key groups involved in leading and governing PCTs: the board, the PEC and the management team (see Figure 5.3). The different groups inevitably lead to the possibility of overlap, tensions and confusion for those involved in these processes and for the staff and stakeholders they relate to.

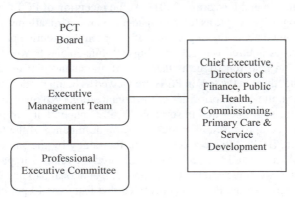

Figure 5.3 Typical organizational structure of a Primary Care Trust

Source: Adapted from Regen (2001), p. 135.

If the potential tensions between PCT Board, PCT Executive Committee and internal executive management teams are not adequately resolved within a PCT, there is a real risk that professionals may feel that their influence and leadership has been compromised (especially in comparison with that which they had in PCGs and other predecessor primary care organizations). Indeed, there is some evidence of professionals feeling that 'their' organization has been 'taken over' by NHS managers (Regen, 2002; NHS Alliance, 2003; and see Chapter 12). Similarly, lay members of

PCT boards may feel disempowered if they end up 'rubber-stamping' policy made in the PEC and management team, and hence viewing themselves as token local people rather than a key part of the overall accountability and governance of the PCT.

The tensions described above are emblematic of the paradox at the heart of PCTs – are they the latest stage of development of primary care-led commissioning and provider organizations representing real devolution of responsibility to 'frontline professionals' and users, or are they a bureaucratic device to draw primary care professionals (and GPs in particular) into the mainstream of NHS organization and management? Evidence from the experience of developing primary care-led organizations in the international context warns of the danger of developing models of primary care governance that are overly 'corporate' in nature, in particular because of the threat maintaining effective professional engagement (Smith and Walshe, 2004; and see Chapter 12).

The 'Three at the Top' in PCTs

The three core elements of PCT governance – the board, PEC and management team – are in turn reflected in the triumvirate that leads the organization. The 'three at the top' who share the leadership of the PCT are the lay chair, the PEC chair and the chief executive (Robinson and Exworthy, 2001). At the inception of PCTs, commentators noted that having three people as the core leaders of an organization was a challenge, given what is known about the importance of chair/chief executive pairings, and the inherent difficulties in three-way relationships (Robinson and Exworthy, 2001).

Evidence from research suggests that as with the chair/chief executive pairing within PCGs, the 'three at the top' in PCTs are viewed as being particularly influential in relation to the policies and priorities of the organization (Wilkin et al, 2002). Early research evidence suggested that in some PCTs, PEC chairs felt that their influence might have been compromised in favour of the predominance of the lay chair/chief executive pairing (NHS Alliance, 2002). A further study by the same organization in 2004 (NHS Alliance and NCGST, 2004) explored the relative impact of the PCT board, PEC, chief executive and management team, and local patients/community in shaping the priorities of the PCT. This revealed that just over 40 per cent of overall influence was attributable to the chief executive and management team, compared with just under 30 per cent to the PEC, 20 per cent to the board and 10 per cent for patients and the community. The NHS Alliance noted: 'What is clear is that few PCTs currently have a 'balanced score card of influence' and that the PEC is significantly marginalized in a number of others' (NHS Alliance and NCGST, 2004, p. 60). Thus it would appear that the trend towards greater managerial and reduced clinical influence within PCTs has continued. Renewed policy interest in practice-based commissioning (Lewis, 2004; Department of Health, 2004) is testament to the growing recognition of the emerging imbalance in relation to the three dimensions of PCT leadership, and the need to redress this by re-energizing clinical engagement at all levels of PCTs.

Governance and Accountability in PCTs

In PCTs, the governance arrangements are more formally defined, given the statutory nature of PCTs as freestanding NHS bodies, constituted in a manner very similar to that of NHS trusts. As such, a PCT's board is publicly accountable for the overall performance of the organization, with the chief executive being the formal accountable officer in terms of financial and clinical governance activity. The duties of the board are set out in guidance from the NHS Appointments Commission as follows:

- to be responsible for making sure that the organization carries out its duties and responsibilities properly and in line with Department of Health policy, and legislation; and
- to be expected to make decisions about local policy and strategic direction of the organization (NHS Appointments Commission, 2002).

PCT board meetings have to be held in public, and many PCTs have learnt from the experience of PCGs, using a range of local venues to try and facilitate public attendance at meetings, varying the time of meetings, and having specific agenda items where members of the public are invited to ask questions and make comments on PCT policy and services. For others, PCT board meetings continue to be relatively formal and traditional public sector gatherings, with attendance by the public being a relatively rare occurrence. What is clear is that great strides have been made in terms of opening up the governance of primary care organizations in the NHS to public involvement and scrutiny – compare the GP multifunds of the 1990s that operated as private organizations with no opportunity for the public to attend meetings or comment formally on policy. What is less clear is the extent to which the development of more formal processes of governance and accountability for primary care organizations has stifled GP and other professional engagement in PCTs, as national and local processes of health care management have increasingly drawn PCTs unto themselves. These issues are considered in more detail in the next two chapters examining the role and engagement of GPs and nurses in PCG/Ts.

Conclusions: Lessons for Research and Practice

The organizational arrangements of PCTs are almost unrecognizable from those of 'simple' PCGs that started out in 1999 in the English NHS, and are even further from some of the structures used by predecessor primary care organizations in the UK in the 1990s. PCTs operate as formal statutory NHS bodies and have a board and executive structure that have more in common with the governance arrangements of NHS provider trusts than with those traditionally associated with primary care led organizations. As will be seen in the following two chapters, the development of such arrangements, whilst largely appropriate to the scope of activity now falling to

PCTs, there is a price to be paid in terms of clinical engagement in PCTs, and this raises the question, is that price worth paying?

Lessons for Research

- Comparative analysis of management arrangements enables PCOs to explore the degree to which their organizational structure is appropriate to its overall size, and allows them to consider the likely implications in terms of 'corporatization' of any merger or increase in size of the PCO.
- Carrying out non-participant observation of the public meetings of PCOs offers valuable additional insights into the intra-board dynamics of the PCO team.
- Questioning PCO members about their perceptions of their own and others' influence on decision-making offers important learning in terms of the relative power of different professional and lay groups within PCOs, and points to those actions required to address evident imbalances in influence.
- It is important to return to PCOs on a regular basis to assess the degree to which deficiencies in terms of governance (for example the relative influence of nurses as opposed to doctors) have been addressed.
- The lessons gained from research into organization and governance have been strikingly similar in PCOs throughout the 1990s and into the 21st century, demonstrating the importance for PCOs and policy makers in terms of heeding messages from research and not dismissing findings as being related to 'out of date' organizations and contexts that are perceived to have subsequently changed.

Lessons for Practice

- The optimum size for a PCO is an ongoing subject of debate, but should nevertheless be revisited on a regular basis by PCOs to check that the organization is not becoming unduly complex, bureaucratic and distant from its original stakeholders.
- There is a need to beware the risk of the chair/chief executive pairing overly influencing the strategy and operations of the PCO.
- Where a triumvirate leads a PCO, it is crucial that steps are taken to ensure that the clinician lead does not get squeezed out by the more traditional chair/chief executive pairing.
- Careful, well-targeted and sustained processes of organizational development are required, particularly in relation to defining and reviewing the respective roles of boards, professional executive committees, management teams and other constituencies.
- Enabling nurses to play a truly influential role in the strategic decision-making and direction of PCOs is a major challenge that requires attention to deep-seated cultural barriers to involvement.

- Developing effective input by lay people to the boards of PCOs requires skilled management and careful facilitation, given the varying professional backgrounds of board members, and the risk of tokenism regarding public involvement.
- Keeping a proper locality focus to the work of PCOs is a key challenge, especially in larger organizations that risk becoming distant from general practices, health centres, and local communities.
- Engaging professionals in the work of PCOs is time-consuming and requires multiple approaches, but to neglect this is to abandon the original spirit and strength of PCOs.
- As a PCO becomes more mainstream within health care management and thus takes on a greater degree of formal public accountability, there is a real risk of disenfranchising those professionals who developed and shaped PCOs in the first place.
- There is a need for greater dissemination of examples of good practice related to developing new forms of public accountability for PCOs, including those related to the purpose and conduct of public meetings.

Chapter 6

The Role and Engagement of GPs within Primary Care Groups and Trusts

The creation of PCG/Ts has been a conscious attempt to engage local stakeholders, particularly GPs, in the management and governance of the NHS. That GPs should be the lead stakeholder in the development of PCG/Ts was enshrined in successive Government directives that trumpeted the need to devolve power and resources to frontline professionals such that the development of local health services would reflect local patients' needs (Department of Health, 1997, 2001a; NHS Executive, 1998b). The rationale for GP leadership was also a condition of GP co-operation within PCG/Ts in order to retain the power and influence over decision-making that they had begun to enjoy through previous primary care-led purchasing schemes. Hence, the leadership and business conducted in PCG Boards and PCT professional executive committees have been GP dominated (Regen et al, 2001; Dowling et al, 2003 and see Chapter 5). Nevertheless, this lead role has been tempered by new collective responsibilities to work with quality guidelines, cash-limited budgets and in 'equal' partnership with other primary care professionals in multi-agency teams.

The aim of this chapter is to examine the role, function and effectiveness of GP involvement within Primary Care Groups and Trusts in order to draw out lessons and recommendations for future managers of primary care organizations. The discussions in this chapter draw directly from a range of evaluations of GP involvement but in particular on the in-depth research on GP participation undertaken by the National Evaluation of PCG/Ts between April 1999 and April 2001 (Smith et al, 2000; Regen et al, 2001; Regen, 2002).

The Challenge of GP Engagement in PCG/Ts

A key challenge for Primary Care Groups and Trusts has been to develop their corporate governance responsibilities in order to effectively undertake the growing powers they have in the planning, provision and commissioning of care. However, the history of GP involvement in the NHS has not embraced the issues of public involvement, accountability and corporate strategy that PCG/Ts needed to establish (Peckham and Exworthy, 2003). Moreover, there was no guidance that dealt with how PCG/Ts could engage with general practitioners effectively. As Starey (2003) points out, helping GP board members to understand the needs of corporate governance was underestimated.

Research on emerging primary care organizations has tended to focus on the processes of developing new primary care organizations, and their progress against objectives (Audit Commission, 2000; Mays et al, 2001; Smith, Regen, Griffiths et al, 2000; Wilkin et al, 2001; and see Chapter 4). Examining the micro-process of appointing GPs onto board positions, assessing their roles and influences, and providing guidance as to how GP engagement can best be maintained has largely been neglected (Regen and Smith, 2000; Smith et al, 2000). However, consideration of the process of GP engagement within PCG/Ts is important since the process is likely to have a major impact on their ability to meet core functions effectively (Dixon and Sweeney, 2000; NHS Alliance, 2003). Throughout many of the forthcoming chapters in this book, the need for active clinical involvement and support within PCG/T activities is a recurring theme in their ability to make progress. This is true at all levels, for example, in managing performance (Chapter 8), developing and improving primary care services (Chapter 10), and in making a reality of the commissioning function (Chapter 11).

The Role of General Practitioners within PCG Boards and Professional Executive Committees

The prescribed composition of PCG Boards saw GPs dominate in terms of representation by allowing up to seven GP board members as well as a GP chair (NHSE, 1998b). Moreover, unlike nurse and lay representatives, newly appointed GP board members were rarely provided with any role specifications or competency frameworks leading to concerns about the consistency of the appointment process and the ability to develop corporate accountability in PCGs themselves (Regen and Smith, 2000). In the early days of PCGs, research revealed concerns regarding the overwhelming dominance at board meetings of the GP view and of discussions that were primarily clinical and medical in nature (Smith, Regen, Griffiths et al, 2000). Whilst the level of GP dominance has become less acute over time, particularly following the move to PCT status where GPs no longer have an effective monopoly of representation, agendas have tended to remain primary care/medically oriented with the contribution of nurses, social services representatives and lay representatives growing, but smaller in comparison (Regen et al, 2001). Given the Government's vision of a multi-disciplinary approach to service development (Department of Health, 1997) the fact that the majority of PCG/Ts reported high levels of GP dominance suggests a continued need to redress the imbalance.

The role of the GP within PCG/Ts differs radically from the clinical professional role of the general practitioner. In particular, the function of GPs within PCG Boards and PCT professional executive committees encompasses more the roles of strategy developer, clinical manager, and leader of peers as the mindset has shifted to focus on the need of a whole PCT population rather than just their own practices and patients. This section examines the roles GPs play *within* PCG/Ts, and the level of power and influence they have exerted.

The PCG and PEC Chair

The chairs of PCG boards and PCT professional executive committees have predominantly been GPs. The contribution of the GP chair has consistently been rated as more significant, and more enthusiastic, than any other Board member (Table 6.1) other than the chief executive in every evaluation undertaken (for example, Dowswell et al, 2002; Regen et al, 2001; and Wilkin et al, 2002). While individual styles of chairs have varied, each has performed a leadership role in introducing agenda items, responding to stakeholders' questions, summarizing views, and formulating strategies. Indeed, it became increasingly common for chairs to undertake personal development activities such as leadership training or participation in learning sets as this element to their role has grown (Regen et al, 2001). As Smith, Regen and Griffith et al (2000) found, board members themselves tended to be happier when chairs operated in a facilitative manner, thus enabling all members the opportunity to discuss and air their comments. However, in over half of the cases studied, chairs tended to dominate discussions rather than be inclusive or interactive (Smith et al, 2000).

During and following the transition to PCT status, it was reported that chairs were playing a less active role in service-development issues whilst the strategic aspect to their jobs had increased (Regen et al, 2001). The main components of the role were seen as providing leadership and vision, developing relationships with constituents and stakeholders (especially other GPs, local authorities and hospital trusts) whilst facilitating the functioning of the board or executive committee. Hence, when asked to describe personal achievements at the end of 2000, most highlighted the development of corporacy and team-working within and between board members as a crucial success factor (Regen et al, 2001). PEC chairs reported how this strengthened the sense of power and control both as an individual but also to the PCT as an organization. Research by the NHS Alliance into the role of the PEC chairs similarly found that helping other clinicians to realize their full potential in PCTs was a key task and one requiring considerable skills such as appraisal, mentoring and motivation as well as talent spotting for future clinical champions (NHS Alliance and Clinical Governance Support Team, 2004). In all studies, however, workloads have been a challenge and it would appear that as PCG/Ts have grown so chairs have devolved many of their responsibilities to the chief executive and to an ever increasing range of directorates. Moreover, in 2004, it was reported how many PEC chairs were planning to withdraw from their roles with few other family doctors keen to take their place (NHS Alliance and Clinical Governance Support Team, 2004). In the future, the provision of high quality operational support to chairs will be vital if they are to properly fill the strategic role required of them and clinical champions will need to be sought since succession planning appears an urgent imperative.

Board GPs

Board GPs generally take on 'lead' roles on various aspects of PCG/T work such as prescribing, clinical governance, commissioning, coronary heart disease and mental health. This role has involved chairing sub-groups, attending meetings with external stakeholders, formulating policy papers and, in the case of prescribing and clinical governance, making visits to individual practices. However, the *active* involvement of GP board members has been variable. In over half the case studies within this research, tensions were reported between 'active' and 'passive' GP board members due to the unequal distribution of tasks taken between them. During the transition to PCT status, many PCGs found difficulties recruiting their full complement of GP board members (Regen et al, 2001).

Table 6.1 Overall ratings of influence and enthusiasm of board members within PCG/Ts, 1999-2000

	Influence Overall rating*		Enthusiasm Overall rating*	
Board Member	1999 (n=69)	2000 (n=56)	1999 (n=69)	2000 (n=56)
PCG/PEC Chair	4.62	4.51	4.84	4.56
Chief Executive	4.45	4.42	4.81	4.70
Board GPs	3.48	3.75	3.68	3.49
Nurses	3.07	3.13	4.39	4.27
Social Services Rep	3.16	2.76	3.67	3.26
Lay Representative	2.87	2.74	4.10	3.89

* Members of eleven PCGs (except GP board members) were asked to provide a rating of influence (decision-making power) and enthusiasm of each board members on a 0-5 scale where 0 = no influence/enthusiasm and 5 = great influence/enthusiasm. The table gives the overall average rating.

Source: Adapted from Smith et al (2000) and Regen et al (2001).

One of the most influential GP roles within PCG/Ts has been that of the clinical governance lead. As Campbell and Roland (1999, 2000) reported, almost all clinical governance leads were GPs (though some shared the role with lead nurses) and many were regarded as more senior, influential and committed than other board members (Dixon and Sweeney, 2000). An effective clinical governance lead was particularly important in providing legitimacy and peer leadership to enable support and compliance from constituent practices to new accountability arrangements for monitoring and appraising the quality of primary care provision (NHS Executive, 1998). Since primary care had previously lacked any explicit objectives relating to the quality of care, and there had been no previous notion of corporate responsibility for monitoring standards, a strong and committed clinical governance lead played a crucial part in engaging participation amongst practices and health professionals. In this process, clinical governance leads have needed to play a key role in helping to avoid a negative performance management culture in which professionals blamed each other when things went wrong (Shekelle, 2002). Moreover, as Campbell and Roland (2003) reported, clinical governance leads also needed to be careful not to let nationally-set priorities 'squash out' local innovations.

Despite signs of growing apathy from rank and file GPs, the emphasis placed by GP board members to their own role appears to have shifted over time from that of 'representing the views of the GP population' (Smith et al, 2000) to becoming more active in task groups and service delivery issues on behalf of the PCG/T (Regen et al, 2001). Hence, there has been a subtle change in attitude from a 'them and us' representative role, to a more supportive developmental role. Indeed, GP-led task groups have been one of the underlying driving forces for participation. However, as Regen et al (2001) report, PCG stakeholders expressed concern that GP-led subgroups were recommending decisions, subsequently approved, without proper consultation.

The main source of difficulty for active GPs on the boards has been workload pressures compounded by a lack of management support. The evaluations showed growing concern that the time taken on PCG/T activities was adversely affecting their own practices, sometimes risking tensions with GP partners over the reduction in time spent in surgeries (Regen et al, 2001). This was also related to the cost and difficulties of finding suitable locum cover. Indeed, the lack of grass-roots support to their own role within PCG/Ts was reported by some GP board members as a source of pressure. Later investigations by the NHS Alliance into the roles of GP PEC members reconfirmed these pressures concluding that practices needed proper support to allow GPs to carry out their PCT work. It also pointed to the need for clear job descriptions, competency frameworks, training and peer support to enable GPs to feel like clinical leaders with an ability to influence PCT strategy (NHS Alliance and Clinical Governance Support Team, 2004).

As Table 6.1 shows, GP board members were rated the third most influential stakeholder group on PCG boards, behind chief executives and chairs, though within the figures was a discrepancy between highly active and influential GPs (such as clinical governance leads) and those far less interested and active. As Chapter 12 considers in more detail, PCG/Ts have found it difficult to develop and sustain GP engagement as many have been 'switched off' by the dilution of professional leadership across other professional groups and the growth of managerial control (Locock et al, 2004). Such issues, combined with workload pressures, have meant that GP board members have been less enthusiastic than other colleagues.

The Influence of GPs within PCG/Ts on Board and PEC Decision-Making

Research into decision-making at board-level in PCGs (Wilkin et al, 2001; Regen et al, 2001) concluded that many PCG/Ts have had acute difficulties achieving a common view since different interests pursue minority or sectoral aims. As Bond and LeGrand (2003) suggest, the lack of corporacy should not come as a surprise because GPs in particular have never been used to participating in collective decision-making structures. In reality, the evidence suggests that PCG/Ts lacked any formal decision-making process and that key actors, particularly the chief executives and GP chairs, have dictated strategy. The chair-chief executive pairing has commonly been regarded as the main locus of power and source of policy generation (Smith et al, 2000; Regen et al, 2001; Wilkin et al, 2001).

Over time, however, the structure of PCTs has created several new power dynamics including a degree of leadership sharing between PCT board chair, chief executive and PCT executive chair. This dynamic has been termed 'three at the top' in recognition of this triumvirate of key decision-makers (Robinson and Exworthy, 2000; see Chapter 5). In the 2001 National Tracker Survey, 98 per cent of PCT chairs felt that strategic influence was exerted primarily by these three principal officers (Wilkin et al, 2002). Indeed, the survey suggested that the transition to PCT status had led to a greater concentration of power and influence amongst the officers of the organization and a corresponding reduction in the influence of broader professional constituencies.

The emerging relationship within this triumvirate structure has not always been easy as the roles and functions of each individual have taken time to mature. Compromises have had to be made across both clinical and managerial interests. Despite these changing power dynamics, no significant tensions were observed between the different professional stakeholders. Seemingly, the multiple interests of other representatives have tended to fall more into a consultancy and scrutiny role than as leaders of strategy and service development. Indeed, due to time and work pressures, there is evidence to suggest that other board members found this model both acceptable and appropriate. The chief caveat to the model being given the time to consider and comment on proposals so presented so as to avoid a potential 'fait accompli' (Regen et al, 2001).

The implications of these findings for the working of PCT professional executive committees is that more GPs need to be found to work actively within the system as overall enthusiasm and participation has been sub-optimal. In order to facilitate this, GPs need adequate resources in terms of funded time, provision of locums/assistants, and management support, if they are to contribute more fully without compromising their practice commitments. They also need to feel the support of the wider GP constituency behind them, but as the next section shows, this has not necessarily been the case.

The Level and Nature of General Practitioner Involvement within PCG/Ts

The support of general practitioners outside of central PCG/T decision-making structures is regarded as fundamental to the success of these organizations. For example, the National Tracker Survey of PCG/Ts found that 97 per cent of chairs rated the support of local GPs as important to the success of the PCG/T (Wilkin et al, 2001). However, a 2001 survey of NHS chief executives raised concerns about the waning level of local GP support, particularly as a result of the rapid transition period to PCT status (Walshe and Smith, 2001). Further research on the involvement of 'grass-roots' GPs similarly found a deteriorating level of active interest and participation in PCT work (Regen, 2002; NHS Alliance, 2003). As Peckham and Exworthy (2003) suggest, rank and file GPs remained 'largely oblivious' to the managerial decisions of PCG/Ts with GP chairs acting as the 'buffer' between them and external management pressures.

Given that a key task of PCTs has been to engender clinical leadership, the level and nature of 'grass-roots' GP involvement is an important cause for concern. In the National Tracker Survey, PCG/T chairs were asked to estimate the total support among local GPs for their organization. In the first year of the survey, 1999/2000, only 40 per cent felt that at least half of their local GPs were supportive (Wilkin et al, 1999). By 2000/2001, this figure had risen to 61 per cent (Wilkin et al, 2000). However, at least one in five GPs were regarded as 'negative or antagonistic' in a quarter of the PCG/Ts surveyed. These figures, however, hide a 'reality gap' between the observations of managers and GP leaders with other 'frontline' GPs. In answer to the question 'are clinicians more likely to be engaged with their PCT today than they were a year ago?' a national survey of clinician engagement in 2003 discovered that only 5 per cent of frontline GPs agreed compared to 25 per cent of GP leaders and 57 per cent of managers. Seventy-nine per cent of frontline GPs felt clinicians would be less likely to be engaged with their PCT (NHS Alliance and Primary Care Report, 2003).

Involvement in PCG/T Activities

The findings presented in this section are based upon detailed case-study research undertaken by the National Evaluation of PCG/Ts (Regen et al, 2001; Regen, 2002). As part of a longitudinal study, postal surveys to collect the views and experiences of grass-roots GPs were undertaken across twelve PCG/Ts in October 1999 and again a year later. By the second year, three of the twelve case studies had become PCTs and five were actively planning to 'go live' in April 2001. Pressure of work in the transition phase led to a reduced response rate to the GP postal surveys in 2000 (44 per cent (n=306/700)) compared to 1999 (60 per cent (n=414/712)) though these rates can be regarded as typical for surveys of this type (Kaner et al, 1998). In addition to the postal surveys, sixteen in-depth telephone interviews were undertaken during April and May 2001 to explore in greater depth reasons for levels of involvement in PCG/T activities (Regen, 2002).

These surveys found that GPs were involved in both an *indirect* and *direct* way. *Indirect* methods primarily meant the work of a GP representative, usually a PCG/T board/executive committee member. Their role has primarily been to represent constituents, informing GPs about PCG/T proposals and activities, eliciting GP views, and feeding these thoughts back to the PCG/T committees. The role of the representative as the 'voice' of the rank and file GP was regarded as important as a mechanism for developing corporacy and legitimacy across the PCG/T as a whole, though in practice there was significant variation in terms of the formality, frequency and contact these representatives had with their GP colleagues (Regen, 2002). Indeed, Regen's (2002) survey showed that 25-35 per cent of GPs did not know the functions performed by their GP representative. The responses reveal either an underlying ambivalence from GPs to their PCG/T or a failure on behalf of these primary care organizations in communicating effectively and/or regularly with their local GPs. The degree of *direct* involvement of grass-roots GPs with their PCG/T appears to have been undertaken in six main ways:

1. Attendance at board meetings;
2. Participation in sub-groups;
3. Involvement in GP forums and locality meetings;
4. Attendance at away-days;
5. Comments on discussion documents; and
6. Participation in education events

Attendance at board meetings As Table 6.2 reveals, most grass-roots GPs 'rarely' or 'never' attended PCG/T board meetings. This was regarded as a cause for concern since one role of the GP board/executive committee was to provide a channel of communication to GP constituents. Since most meetings were held mid-week and during the day, finding and paying for locum cover may have been a constraint. However, as other research has found, PCG/T executive members had little expectation that other GPs would attend board meetings (Regen et al, 2001; Wilkin et al, 2001).

Participation in sub-groups The nature and level of participation in sub-groups varied considerably by PCG/T. Whilst overall figures (Table 6.2) suggest that about one-third of GPs 'always' or 'sometimes' attended PCG/T sub-groups, a much lower percentage was observed in large rural areas, where travelling distances inhibited participation, and in large urban PCTs comprising a high percentage of single-handed practitioners. In those PCG/Ts where participation was highest, these were either small enough to engage at least one GP from each practice within a task group, or were larger PCG/Ts that had developed sub-locality structures in order to provide a local focus for GP participation. Moreover, participation varied by sub-group type, with the most well attended being generally in the areas of clinical governance and prescribing with far less interest in areas such as commissioning.

The lack of direct involvement in task groups was a significant concern to PCG/T chairs and chief executives (Regen et al, 2001) as they were the main mechanism through which GPs and other health care professionals could work together to influence service development. Members of the PCG/T management team reported that the absence of significant GP input meant they were taking on a greater variety of roles than had been originally anticipated. Greater support from grass-roots GPs was seen as essential in sharing out workloads and providing support to GP boards and/or professional executive committee members. However, it was reported that workload and remuneration were key barriers to direct GP involvement in sub-groups leading to a 'missed opportunity' to shape services (Regen, 2002). As one chief executive in the research put it:

> GPs are happy to come to the forum meetings to discuss things but when it comes to actually getting them to take things on it is very difficult. Very few come to PCG sub-groups or would agree to represent the PCG in its various forms (Regen, 2002, p. 11).

Involvement in GP forums and locality meetings Higher levels of GP involvement in long-established GP forums and locality meetings were uncovered in the surveys (Table 6.2). The forums were often used by chairs and chief executives to canvass GP opinion (Regen et al, 2001). Indeed, where work in sub-groups was low, attendance within GP forums was strong suggesting that, in some PCG/Ts, GPs preferred to discuss matters within their own professional community.

Attendance at away days Many PCG/Ts organized multi-professional events and away days to help generate priorities and contribute to the strategic development of their organizations. The events were also seen as an opportunity to promote GP involvement and ownership. However, over 60 per cent of GPs in the survey reported that they 'never' or 'rarely' attended such events (Table 6.2). Again, the level of participation varied by PCG/T and the research suggested that such events were most useful where GPs worked in relative isolation both socially and geographically and did not, on the whole, have high levels of participation through sub-groups (Regen, 2002). This suggests that GPs in different locations have chosen to engage with their PCG/Ts in very different ways – some 'hands-off' and strategically, other more directly.

Table 6.2 Grass-roots GP participation in PCG/T activities, 1999-2000

October, 1999 (n=414)

Question	Always	Sometimes	Rarely	Never	Blank
Attend PCG/T board meetings	6%	6%	7%	69%	12%
Attend PCG/T sub-group	16%	20%	8%	48%	8%
Attend locality meetings/GP forums	15%	41%	14%	25%	5%
Attend PCG/T events and away days	7%	16%	10%	54%	13%
Comment on discussion documents	9%	36%	18%	25%	12%

October, 2000 (n=306)

Question	Always	Sometimes	Rarely	Never	Blank
Attend PCG/T board meetings	4%	6%	5%	75%	10%
Attend PCG/T sub-group	11%	22%	8%	52%	7%
Attend locality meetings/GP forums	17%	34%	11%	31%	7%
Attend PCG/T events and away days	8%	20%	7%	55%	10%
Comment on discussion documents	8%	34%	19%	27%	12%
Attend PCG/T education sessions*	16%	45%	12%	22%	5%

*Asked in 2000 only

Source: Regen (2002).

Commenting on discussion documents The opportunity to comment on discussion documents was a strategy used by PCG/Ts to engender a significant form of involvement and was regarded as crucial in providing ownership and credibility to PCG/T policies. This process was particularly apposite when producing papers on issues that impacted directly on GP roles, such as clinical governance procedures, prescribing incentive schemes, criteria for allocating General Medical Services bids, and the transition to PCT status. Since this form of involvement was less time consuming, it appears to have been a more popular mode of involvement.

Participation in education events In contrast to strategic away days, many PCG/Ts have organized educational events for GPs, such as topics related to clinical governance objectives or primary care development issues. The comparatively high level of GP participation in such events (Table 6.2) compared to other forms of involvement suggests that GPs craved both practical information and peer support.

Explaining the Level and Nature of GP Involvement in PCG/Ts

The research into the level and nature of GP involvement in PCG/Ts suggests strongly that GPs tend to engage in less active and time-consuming methods of involvement (Wilkin et al, 2001; Regen et al, 2001; Dowswell et al, 2002; Regen, 2002). The vast majority of GP respondents in the survey by Regen (2002) found that almost 70 per cent spent either 'no time' or 'up to one hour' only upon PCG/T activities in a typical week. Moreover, 73 per cent of GPs in her 1999 survey, and 60 per cent in the 2000 survey, felt that this limited contribution was already 'about right' or 'too much'. These figures support overall concerns over the low level of GP involvement and suggest that seeking to increase direct involvement in PCG/T activities is difficult. Indeed, whilst 40 per cent of GPs suggested they contributed 'too little' to their PCG/T in 2000, the level of input had not increased.

The nature and level of involvement has varied considerably between PCG/Ts with some areas experiencing fundamental, deeply rooted challenges to all forms of direct GP involvement (Regen, 2002). Size, location, management capacity and previous history of fundholding/commissioning were contributory contextual factors. In the larger PCG/Ts, sub-locality structures tended to have had a positive impact. In explaining the overall lack of GP involvement in PCG/T decision-making, there is a breadth of evidence from a wide range of studies (Audit Commission, 2000; North et al, 1998; Regen et al, 2001; Locock et al, 2004; North et al, 1998; Smith et al, 2000; and Wilkin et al, 1999, 2000, 2001). From these studies, four key explanatory factors are recurrent:

1. Workload, time and remuneration;
2. Perceived lack of influence upon PCG/T decision-making;
3. Perceived ineffectiveness and impotence of PCG/Ts; and
4. Resistance to the development of PCG/Ts due to the wider policy context.

Workload, time and remuneration The main explanation put forward to account for a GP's lack of active involvement in PCG/Ts has revolved around a series of practical constraints relating to increased workloads, time and money. Regen (2002), for example, reported how GPs felt that the introduction of PCG/Ts had increased their day to day workload such that they could not spare the time to become involved. Moreover, the cost of finding adequate locum cover and the perceived over-bureaucratic regime of meetings and paperwork were not seen as conducive to support. Two comments from GPs in Regen's (2002) telephone survey illustrate this view:

> I have no interest in being involved with the PCG actively – though I do read mail and newsletters. I have actually chosen to avoid the PCG due to lack of time and the fact like most GPs – I am over-committed!

> As a single-handed dispensing GP I find little time to engage in management and health planning activities – hence my low level of involvement. I find that the time I need to spend with patients being increasingly squeezed by organizational tasks and general morale is low. I find the pace of change taking place in primary care both depressing and frustrating.

Perceived lack of influence upon PCG/T decision-making In contrast to the influence of GPs *within* PCG/Ts, the evidence suggests that the engagement and influence of grass-roots GPs has remained low. For example, the National Tracker Survey showed that only 28 per cent of PCG/T chairs rated local GPs as having any considerable influence over decision-making (Wilkin et al, 2001). Amongst the GP community themselves, figures suggest that 76 per cent rated themselves as having 'little or 'no' involvement in PCG/T decision-making in 2000 (Regen, 2002). Many GPs took an active decision to withdraw from the PCG/T environment since they felt 'impotent' in terms of their influence upon decision-making. Key factors for this disengagement included perceived inadequacies in consultation mechanisms and that PCG/T boards, particularly lead officers, were operating in an 'elitist' fashion. This reflects the findings in the previous section that showed how decision-making and strategy has been primarily influenced by those *within* PCG/Ts, an approach that has seemingly disempowered professional constituents. Two GPs in the Regen (2002) telephone survey testify to the issue:

> I think in the end decision-making boils down to the management side despite the fact that local GPs should be making the decisions. Whether clinical or non-clinical people, it is basically the management side that end up making the decisions.

> The PCT are aware of what the grass-roots think, but that is not the same as doing what the grass-roots think!

Perceived ineffectiveness and impotence of the PCG/T One of the key issues for GPs in the early days of PCG/Ts was that these organizations did not appear to be 'delivering the goods' in terms of changes to service delivery or in effectively delivering specific 'outcomes' to key objectives. Whilst it may be argued that achieving change has been difficult due to the developmental needs of these new bodies, the GP perception was that the system had become too bureaucratic and that tangible change was not being delivered quickly enough. For many GPs, this lack of progress led to disengagement as PCGs, in particular, became criticized for spending too much time on 'meetings and paperwork'. As Chapter 5 highlighted, the trend in managers dominating the proceedings of a formerly GP-led system led to significant frustrations amongst GP leaders and 'grass-roots' GPs at the 'corporatization' of PCG/Ts (Smith and Walshe, 2004). The apparent inability of PCG/Ts to address the power of the secondary care sector has been another contributory factor to much of this frustration.

Resistance to the development of PCG/Ts due to the wider policy context As Chapter 12 examines, the wider context of rapid reform in general practice at the time of PCG/T implementation has led to growing workloads and difficulties in recruitment. Kmietowicz's (2001) survey for the British Medical Association found that a quarter of GPs wanted to leave the medical profession with two-thirds describing their morale as low or very low. Moreover, increasing workload demands led to an unprecedented one-day strike as GPs threatened to resign *en masse* due to failings in their contract of employment (Beecham, 2001). Engaging GPs was always going to be problematic given this wider context since PCG/T-related work was not seen as a 'core activity' (North et al, 1999).

A further general resistance towards PCG/Ts was the change that it implied in terms of shifting the GP role from that of medical practitioner to clinical administrator. For many GPs, this shift in emphasis not only threatened the time they could devote to direct patient care but potentially created a conflict of interest between their role as the patient advocate and new responsibilities for priority setting and 'rationing' care (Glendinning, 1999). Moreover, many GPs remained critical of the abolition of practice-level fundholding. As Chapter 2 discussed, in Northern Ireland the primary care system has yet to recover from this process as GPs have refused to take any active part in Local Health and Social Care Groups resulting in a stand-off between the medical profession and government. The perceived erosion of GP autonomy and independence has thus led to an underlying resistance to PCG/T activities.

Conclusion: Lessons for Research and Practice

One of the main attractions of the PCG/T policy to innovative GPs was the ability to exert greater local independence than had been possible under the aegis of health authorities. Indeed, Wilkin and Coleman (1999) showed how greater autonomy in decision making was regarded as a more important factor than the ability to focus on local needs and services. However, the devolution of roles and responsibilities to PCG/Ts has been accompanied by top-down policy prescription and centrally-driven targets that have constrained autonomous decision-making. In the third round of the National Tracker Study (Smith et al, 2002) over two-thirds of PCG/T chairs rated national priorities, policies and targets as having the strongest influence over decision-making, with only five per cent rating local priorities as more influential. As Dowling et al (2003) point out, it is questionable whether the GP support for PCG/Ts observed in the study can be sustained in the longer term, a prediction seemingly coming to fruition in the greater alienation between doctors and PCTs and tumbling GP morale observed in a number of subsequent surveys (NHS Alliance, 2003; NHS Alliance and Clinical Governance Support Team, 2004).

According to Regen (2002), most GPs utilize a range of methods to inform and comment on PCG/T activities and priorities. However, given the evidence, it is difficult to argue with her observation that 'whilst GPs are generally on board, they are occupying the back seat rather than the driving seat in primary care organizations' (Regen, 2002, p. 31). Since most commentators point to the work of frontline GPs as essential to the overall success of PCTs (Dixon, 2002; NHS Alliance, 2003), the fact that so many grass-roots GPs remain uninvolved in decision-making is alarming. In particular, the lack of GP engagement appears to be a major contributor to the lack of progress in core functions such as commissioning (Smith and Goodwin, 2002), addressing health needs (Harrison et al, 2001) and delivering integrated services (Moon and North, 2001).

This growing disengagement between GPs and PCTs reflects an agenda that is perhaps neither relevant nor important at a practice-level. As Dowling et al (2003) surmise, the problem appears to reflect wider features of the current 'modernization' agenda in which a fundamental tension exists between shifting power to frontline staff and the expectation that they will then prioritize national targets over local priorities. It appears that the GP's sense of professionalism has been fundamentally undermined by 'hard nosed management' that appears to put more emphasis on numbers than on quality (Ham and Alberti, 2002). Some commentators, however, believe that GPs owe it to themselves to end their isolationism and foster a kind of stakeholder relationship with PCTs that may help end the unhappiness and demoralization that many apparently feel (Smith, 2001; Starey, 2003). However, as Locock et al (2004) conclude, unless PCTs can establish an identity that champions some commonly held cause and/or provides necessary incentives then the majority of GPs will continue to contest the managerial control of PCTs. In this regard, much may be learned from the experience of IPAs in New Zealand where clinical leadership and the minimization of bureaucracy has helped to manage potential professional-manager tensions (Jacobs, 1997). The lessons from the IPA experience are examined in Chapter 12.

Lessons for Research

- Evaluations of primary care organizations have tended to view the level of GP engagement as a key contextual variable affecting their ability to achieve objectives. To help PCTs understand better how GP engagement can be improved, research should focus on the micro-processes and dynamics of manager-professional relationships and the incentives psyche of GPs.
- Understanding the clinical and professional competencies of GPs working in PCTs remains underdeveloped, particularly in important key functions such as commissioning, needs assessment, and clinical governance. Research

can contribute to the development of a set of core competencies for various aspects of GP work and identify the necessary training needs and personal development plans to help GPs fulfill these roles effectively.

- Effective clinical leadership is an important contributor to the level of local GP engagement. Research that identifies the core characteristics of effective clinical leaders and clinician-managers may prove to be helpful in identifying future leaders and generating a positive organizational culture in PCTs.

- Monitoring levels of engagement and research that provides regular feedback on the motivation and reaction of GPs over time should help enable PCTs to understand the issues in sustaining and developing engagement.

Lessons for Practice

- PCTs need to promote their activities to GPs as an opportunity to deliver improvements to patients and engage them via their clinical interests. GPs should be encouraged to take leadership of the agenda within PECs and help define PCT objectives.

- PCTs should strengthen channels of communication though GP representation and forums. The more GPs are informed about PCT activities, the more likely it is for them to become directly involved. Such consultation and decision-making processes must include meaningful GP participation and debate.

- Sub-locality structures in large or rural PCTs may be an effective way of retaining a locality-focus and increasing GP involvement.

- PCTs need to identify future clinical leaders from the grass-roots to build necessary capacity and to plan for succession to managerial positions.

- PCTs must ensure access to training and education to help GPs fulfill their roles and responsibilities and core competencies.

- PCTs need to reduce bureaucracy to ensure that workloads are manageable and rewards are maximized.

- PCTs need to demonstrate tangible improvements to services.

- Funding practices for locum cover and/or reimbursement to those participating in PCT activities appears to be crucial. GPs should be fairly rewarded for meeting the expectations of their PCT.

Chapter 7

The Role and Engagement of Nurses within Primary Care Groups and Trusts

Nurses working in primary care have, until recently, been largely concerned with the personal care of individuals rather than the strategic functions of health improvement, or the organizational process of care management. As Klein (2001) reports, the political history of the NHS has for the most part been a history of relations between the government of the day and the medical profession. Though nurses represent the largest group of the NHS workforce, they have not had a major influence on policy-making. The development of nursing services in primary care has tended to be piecemeal and detached from mainstream health policy as a result (Dent and Burtney, 1997; Broadbent, 1998). Nursing also represents a highly varied group of professionals from practice nurses and nurse practitioners to health visitors, district nurses, school nurses, community psychiatric nurses and other practitioners allied to medicine such as physiotherapists (Williams, 2000). Moreover, these different nursing professions have traditionally been organized in a highly heterogeneous fashion such that each retains its own employment and career structure. As a consequence, the primary care nursing workforce has remained fragmented with nurses working separately and often in isolation (Doyal and Cameron, 2000). Thus, even where community and practice nurses work in 'teams', the two groups have often taken different approaches to assessing need, planning treatments, and delivering care (Goodman, 2000).

For primary care groups and trusts tasked with integrating the provision of primary, community and intermediate care services, such fragmentation in nursing services has been increasingly questioned and challenged. This has led to greater opportunities for nurses to work together in teams, develop their professional roles, and to take up roles in strategic planning and service management. These developments appear to coincide with the Labour Government's wider modernization agenda in health care that has advocated extended and specialist roles for nurses. Innovations in nursing practices have proliferated since the White Paper 'The New NHS' (Department of Health, 1997) as policy makers have attempted to address the broader issues of extending access to care in the face of increasing demand for services and GP recruitment difficulties. Nevertheless, a shortage of trained nurses has remained a perennial problem in the NHS with the traditional method of plugging gaps with 'bank' or agency nurses, or through overseas recruitment, not being enough to meet rising demands (Newman and Maylor, 2002). The NHS Plan pledged that nurse numbers would be increased by 20,000 by 2004 through improving their working lives, pay and conditions, and also promoting many nurse-led service initiatives (Department of Health, 2000).

This chapter examines the changing role of nurses in primary care and the engagement of nursing and allied health professionals in the management and functioning of PCG/Ts. Reflecting on the research evidence collected in national evaluations of PCG/Ts, the level of nurse involvement and the ability of nurses to influence decision-making is then assessed. The chapter concludes with an examination of how nurses are likely to play a key part in the management and leadership of PCTs following the introduction of the 2004 general medical services (GMS) contract and assesses the factors that may help ensure the effective engagement of the nursing professions in the future.

The Changing Role of Nurses in Primary and Community Care

The role of nurses has undergone significant and distinctive professionalization in recent years. This has included the introduction of degree-based education and training together with the proliferation of new roles and responsibilities in practice. Whereas much of the traditional work of nurses was complementary to medicine, such as wound care and long-term convalescent care, nurses have increasingly become alternative providers to medical professionals (Wilson, 2000). New forms of nurse-led medical care such as nurse triage, nurse prescribing, diagnostic and treatment centres, walk-in centres, NHS Direct and nurse-led PMS practices have encouraged nurses to become increasingly the main primary care provider and referral agent in the system. Traditional nurse boundaries have become blurred as nurses have begun to adapt their roles and take on new responsibilities such as the treatment of minor illnesses, health promotion and disease prevention. These changes are summarized in Table 7.1.

The growth in nurse specialization has largely been welcomed by patients (Kinnersley et al, 2000; Shum et al, 2000) though the reaction from nurses working to create the new systems has been mixed. For example, some community nurses have perceived the extended role of the practice manager as a threat to their 'own' professional territory whilst others have not necessarily welcomed a movement into the traditional role of the general practitioner (Jenkins-Clarke et al, 1998). This reflects concerns with a policy process that Green and Thorogood (1998) have called the 'double bind' the promotion of nurse specialization without trying to lose the traditional patient-centredness of nursing itself. Such new responsibilities have also led to greater nurse workloads with over two-thirds of all nursing types (community and practice) working longer than contractual hours (Jenkins-Clarke and Carr-Hill, 2001). Moreover, there is little evidence available to make any sound judgment on the policy of substituting nurses for doctors on the grounds of clinical quality (Sibbald, 2000).

Table 7.1 Changing nurse roles in the era of PCGs and PCTs

From	*To*
Personal Care	Health Promotion
Nursing Process	Care Management
Complementary to medicine	Alternative provider of medical care
Reactive	Proactive
Follower	Leader
Performer	Manager
Isolated profession	Team-based nursing

Source: Adapted from Starey (2003), p. 195.

Liberating the Talents

In 2002, a document entitled 'Liberating the Talents' (Department of Health, 2002) was produced as a guide to help PCTs and frontline nurses develop the nursing professions' contribution to the NHS Plan. The document emphasized how extending the role of nurses, midwives and health visitors was an essential part of the strategy. In particular, it was envisioned that enhanced nursing services could be developed to lead the process of first contact care, enable the provision of a 24 hour care service, promote chronic disease management, and address both health promotion and ill-health prevention. In order to achieve this, the document developed the idea of a 'skills escalator' for nurses to develop incrementally the competencies needed to take on more clinical tasks. Ten key roles for nurses were outlined showing both the development of nurse roles in clinical care but also their role as leaders in primary care organizations (Table 7.2).

Table 7.2 Ten key roles for nurses

1. To order diagnostic investigations such as pathology tests and x-rays
2. To make and receive referrals direct, say, to a therapist or pain consultant
3. To admit and discharge patients for specified conditions and within agreed protocols
4. To manage patient caseloads, say for diabetes or rheumatology
5. To run clinics, say, for ophthalmology or dermatology
6. To prescribe medicines and treatments
7. To carry out a wide range of resuscitation procedures including defibrillation
8. To perform minor surgery and outpatient procedures
9. To triage patients using the latest IT to the most appropriate setting
10. To take the lead in the way local health services are organized and the way they are run

Source: Department of Health (2002), p. 7.

As well as promoting the vision for nurse roles, the document attempted to set out the environment that needed to be created by PCTs for the talents of nurses to be 'liberated'. This included the need for PCTs to provide access to clinical supervision, professional advice and development programmes. A work-based educational scheme was suggested to be facilitated by 'teaching' PCTs tasked with bringing clinical learning into the workplace. By implication, this approach is likely to enhance leadership capabilities in PCTs since lead nurses will have a vital facilitative role in empowering and engaging frontline nurses. Substantial new nurse responsibilities would also have to be developed including strategic leadership, clinical governance, workforce development, professional accountability, and the empowerment of appropriately qualified nurses and allied health professionals to take on a wider range of clinical roles.

PCG/Ts and Nursing Roles

The vision set out in 'Liberating the Talents' (Department of Health, 2002) appears to be somewhat at odds with the original set up of PCG/Ts where boards retained a majority of GPs forming its membership (see Chapter 3). Nonetheless, the establishment of PCG/Ts has encouraged a new management cadre of nursing professionals to develop. The development of PCG/Ts has meant that forward-thinking nurses were given the potential opportunity to do more than simply exhort and encourage health promoting activities, but use a mechanism to develop professional leverage by having more direct strategic and managerial influence.

Initially, each PCG board included two nurse members rising to a maximum of seven members within the professional executive committees of PCTs (see Chapter 5). This has meant that, nationally, over 2000 nurses have been provided with a new role in local health policy formulation, including the ability to influence nurse-led service developments and the integration of community and primary care nursing. Due to the nature of nursing, nurse board members do not represent a single professional group but a range of nursing staff working in primary and community care settings, including the allied health professionals. For most nurses, their involvement in policy development in the initial stages of PCGs was an unfamiliar and challenging task, particularly in the face of a system that was GP-led at the time (Antrobus and Bailey, 1998; Smith et al, 2000).

The guarantee of a role in decision-making has been offset by working within primary care organizations that have been dominated by GPs. For example, just two nurses were appointed as chairs across 481 PCGs in April 1999 (Richards et al, 2000). The development of PCTs from 2000 onwards allowed nurses to gain an equal number of seats on professional executive committees yet only one nurse PEC chair was elected in the first two waves of PCTs suggesting that nurse roles at a strategic level have continued to struggle to gain parity with the power of doctors (Robinson and Exworthy, 2000). Nevertheless, the nurse role within new primary care organizations in England has developed rapidly to the point where there has never been a better time for nurses to contribute to the decisions that affect patient care (NHS Confederation, 2003d). Drawing from the key national evaluations of PCG/Ts, the next sections examine how the roles and experiences of nurses have developed together with what is known of their influence on decision-making.

The Role and Experiences of Nurses within PCG/Ts

The Role and Experience of Nurses in the Transition to Primary Care Groups, 1998-1999

In the lead up to the launch of PCGs, nurses often reported a sense of confusion in what their role as a board member should entail. Many nurses considered that their main responsibilities were to represent their community nursing colleagues and to use their knowledge and experience to advise PCG boards on nursing issues (Titheridge, 2000). This understanding had been carried forward from the roles nurses had been playing in GP commissioning group pilots, the immediate forerunners to PCGs. Evaluation of nurse involvement in these GP commissioning groups by Regen et al (1999) showed that just over two-thirds of the commissioning pilots had nurse representation at board/steering group level, usually comprising a combination of community (district nurses and health visitors) and practice nurses. Nurses in a number of sites had established multi-disciplinary nurse forums that helped promote communication by providing a mechanism for exchange of information and ideas about the work and direction of the pilot with other nurses. Significant nurse involvement was reported in sub-groups, for example in producing formularies and guidelines for disease management based on clinical effectiveness (Regen et al, 1999).

In GP commissioning groups, nurses questioned their real influence and recognized their limitations at board level. Whilst most nurses felt that GPs valued nursing input, the agenda was regarded as GP dominated with an emphasis on prescribing and other general practice priorities. Indeed, some nurses found board meetings 'intimidating', 'overly-formal', and 'threatening' though most were confident that this would improve as nurse representatives 'found their feet' (Regen et al, 1999). However, the research concluded that if future PCGs were to sustain nurse involvement this would not be achieved without them having some real influence:

> Nurses are enthusiastic about involvement in PCGs, but the crucial issue for groups is to determine ways of ensuring that they are able to participate in decision-making on an equal basis with GPs (Regen et al, 1999, p. 89).

The research into GP commissioning group pilots also showed how many nurses were struggling to cope with the workload required in terms of attending meetings, reading papers, conducting research, and networking with colleagues. The problem was felt most acutely by 'grassroots' nurses who had to juggle work for the emerging PCGs yet continue with a full clinical workload (Regen et al, 1999).

The Role and Experience of Nurses in Primary Care Groups, 1999-2000

In the first year of the National Tracker Survey of PCG/Ts that was carried out towards the end of 1999, a self-completion postal questionnaire of nurse board members asked them to describe their views about their role within PCGs and their experiences of board membership (Wilkin et al, 1999). Of the 106 nurse board members who completed questionnaires, the sample comprised a mix of practice nurses, health visitors, district nurses, and nurse managers, with over 90 per cent being female. The survey found that only 26 per cent of respondents felt they had been 'prepared' to take on their PCG role and that whilst most had attended some training only 6 per cent of these found such training helpful (Dowswell et al, 2002). The majority also considered their role as representing nurse views and feeding back PCG policies to their constituencies through local meetings rather than taking a strategic lead within the PCG itself (Wilkin et al, 1999). Indeed, there appears to have been a lack of understanding by the wider nursing community to the nurse role on PCG boards. For example, many local nurses viewed their community nurse representative like a trade union representative rather than an executive board nurse (Benson and Wright, 2002). Moreover, nurse board members perceived that nursing issues were given limited attention in relation to other issues such as commissioning hospital services.

The roles of PCG nurses at this time were given greater attention in the case study research of the National Evaluation of PCG/Ts reported in Smith et al (2000). This research confirmed that the majority of nurse board members came from a community nursing background, typically district nursing or health visiting, with no practice nurses represented on any boards in the study. Approximately a quarter of nurses interviewed had previous involvement in GP commissioning group pilots and saw their role as a natural progression from this previous work. For those with no prior involvement, PCGs were seen more as a chance for nurses to participate in decision-making and influence change on an 'equal footing' with GPs. Thus, in contrast to the National Tracker Survey findings, the research revealed a subtle shift in ambition from nurse representatives from that of a representative role to making a more formal contribution to PCG policies (Smith et al, 2000). This change in role emphasis had been encouraged in government guidance at the time (NHS Executive, 1998).

In order to reflect a perspective based upon the views of their constituents, nurse board members in over two-thirds of the PCGs established regular nursing forums. These provided nurse board members with a mechanism for meeting with nurses directly as a conduit between the PCG and nurse constituents. This was regarded as a crucial role for the nurse board member at the time, though they were also reported as taking a lead role in prescribing, clinical governance, community nursing and the development of health improvement programmes (Smith et al, 2000). Indeed, 25 per cent of nurses had taken a joint-lead role for developing clinical governance strategies whilst over half reported being actively engaged in specific roles such as leaders of sub-groups where they might make a 'worthwhile contribution' to the PCG decision-making process (Wilkin et al, 1999).

Like nurses in GP commissioning groups, nurses cited workload as the least satisfactory aspect of their role. Time commitment to PCG activities varied from half a day to two days a week and it was commonly reported how difficult it had been to combine the time required to undertake PCG activities with their other work commitments (Wilkin et al, 1999). In particular, it was reported how fieldworker nurses were not always able to organize their professional work/caseload around the demands of their role on the PCG or arrange necessary cover. Although PCG business was meant to be covered by their local employer NHS trust, cover for nurses was not always available meaning that PCG duties often encroached into the personal time of nurses (Smith et al, 2000). As a consequence, many PCGs had to rely solely on goodwill, dedication, commitment and enthusiasm (Titheridge, 2000).

The influence and involvement of PCG nurses, 1999-2000 The research undertaken by both national evaluations reported that PCG boards remained medically-oriented and GP-led (Wilkin et al, 1999; Smith et al, 2000). Whilst most nurses reported that GP colleagues listened to and valued their opinions, there remained a sense of subservience to the leadership of GP colleagues. The research by Smith et al (2000) rated the board nurses as the fourth most influential stakeholder group within PCG boards, though it appears that their influence had grown from the year before (Table 7.3).

Table 7.3 Percentage of stakeholders considered as well-represented by PCG/T chairs, 1999-2000*

PCG/T Stakeholder	1999	2000
GPs	76%	91%
Social service representatives	56%	65%
Nurses	49%	64%
The public	9%	30%
Voluntary agencies	13%	19%

* PCG/T chairs' rating of the degree of participation based on a five point scale from 1 (no representation) to 5 (very well represented). The percentages in the table relate to chairs rating representation as a 4 or 5 on the scale.

Source: Wilkin et al (2001), p. 8.

In the first National Tracker Survey, 106 nurse board members in the first-year of PCGs were asked to rate the influence of different board members on PCG decision-making (Wilkin et al, 1999; Dowswell et al, 2002). The influence of nurses was generally perceived as highly limited with only one quarter of respondents rating their influence as 'great'. However, the overall view was one of the growing potential of nurses to contribute and lead activities in an otherwise GP dominated agenda. As one board nurse in the 1999 National Tracker Survey reported (Dowswell et al, 2002, p. 39):

> As a nurse board member I am aware that we have an uphill struggle to gain influence on the board. However, I feel we are now beginning to be accepted as equal members by the majority of board members.

Nurses attempting to demonstrate the significance and value of good nursing practices to their PCG, such as disease prevention techniques or the promotion of independence in the elderly, faced considerable difficulties in voicing their ideas because agendas at board level tended to prioritize budgetary management, prescribing and organizational development issues (Titheridge, 2000). Nurses within the evaluations pointed to the need to be more assertive and to 'prove themselves capable' by taking on specific areas of work in order to reach a more influential position (Smith et al, 2000). More importantly, action within PCGs was needed to maximize the nurse contribution to PCG board work in order to sustain a meaningful level of input.

The enthusiasm of PCG nurses, 1999-2000 The nurses surveyed in the 1999 National Tracker Survey generally held an enthusiastic view of their participation in PCGs (Wilkin et al, 1999). Indeed, ratings for enthusiasm at this time were reported as significantly higher amongst nurses than board GPs due to their observable positive attitude and hard work within PCG boards (Smith et al, 2000; see Table 6.1). Nonetheless, whilst nurses commented on how much they were enjoying the challenge of their new role, many still considered themselves to be representing the various branches of nursing rather than working together to provide some strategic view of nursing services as a whole. Partnership between nurse board members, therefore, was limited.

The Role and Experience of Nurses in PCG/Ts, 2001-2002

The nursing contribution within PCG/Ts was expected to become incrementally more equal to that of GPs as PCGs entered their second year of operation and began to make plans for the transfer to trust status. However, according to the final report of the HSMC National Evaluation of PCG/Ts, board nurses interviewed felt that it was taking time for their contribution to be valued and that their influence upon decision-making was relatively low (Regen et al, 2001). This was despite continued high levels of enthusiasm and growing involvement in specific aspects of PCG/T work, notably as leads for clinical governance and health improvement. As a result of this involvement and a growing understanding of their role, half of those nurses interviewed felt they had become more confident and as a result were 'more questioning and challenging'. However, observational analysis of board meeting suggested the limited contribution nurses were making at this level with only a minority participating in an active manner in discussions or in challenging their colleagues. Nurses tended to provide information on specific areas of PCG/T work rather than contribute to more general strategic debates. According to Regen et al (2001) the main reason for this was the continuance of a medically-dominated agenda, though they also argued that more senior nurse appointments at board level were needed to achieve any real influence with the primary care organizations.

The second report of the National Tracker Survey, which elicited views from PCG board chairs and PEC chairs, suggested that nurses were being increasingly consulted about clinical governance, health improvement and primary care development than the year before, though still less frequently than GPs (Wilkin et al, 2001). Moreover, as Table 7.3 shows, though numbers had increased, significant numbers of chairs did not feel active support and engagement from nurse board members in comparison to GPs.

A particular focus for PCG/Ts during this period was the development of structures and opportunities to enable the inclusion of practice nurses and professions allied to medicine within PCG/T activities. The lack of representation from these nurse groups was considered a key weakness in 1999-2000 (Smith et al, 2000). From 2000 onwards, however, the establishment and consolidation of nurse forums, together with increased involvement from practice nurses in sub-group working, were reported as key achievements (Regen et al, 2001). Moreover, all nurses (as opposed to one-third in 1999-2000) had undertaken some type of formal personal or leadership development programme which was regarded as important to acquire knowledge and skills, as well as opportunities for networking and boosting individual confidence (Regen et al, 2001). Nonetheless, there remained a perceived need to make further progress in involving nurse constituents as proactive participants. As in earlier years, difficulties in managing PCG workloads with their clinical or managerial responsibilities was a major barrier to progress.

The transition to PCTs has had important implications for nurses and a greater emphasis has been placed on them to lead on service development issues within new directorate structures under the PCT professional executive committees. As PCTs have developed, the roles of different nurses have become more clearly defined with some taking a more strategic and managerial role. For example, it has been reported how new nurse executive committee members began to see their role in a more corporate sense – working and representing the PCT as much as the nurse community (Regen et al, 2001). Other nurses were also reported as being more proactive within the different directorates in service development and design issues leading to a 'measured growth' in confidence amongst nurses occupying such roles within PCTs, potentially resulting in increased influence and opportunities for nurses to shape local health policies (Regen et al, 2001).

Engaging Non-Board Nurses

The involvement of non-board nurses in the activities of PCG/Ts was explored in a series of interviews with chief executives, nurse board members and focus groups in the National Evaluation of PCG/Ts (Smith et al, 2000; Regen et al, 2001). The findings from the research revealed a significant amount of engagement through nurse forums and in sub-groups, but there was an issue in creating the time and support needed to facilitate the involvement of nurses in a meaningful way. Indeed, engaging certain professions within nursing, such as practice nurses, has been particularly problematic. With few exceptions, practice nurses and parallel professionals such as allied healthcare professionals (AHPs) (that include physiotherapists, occupational therapists, speech and language therapists) have tended not to be involved in professional forums or PCG/T task groups (Smith et al, 2000). The key problem was reported as a lack of structure or means of communication between these staff and those nurses or AHPs leading these groups, resulting in staff feeling somewhat distanced and excluded. As Titheridge (2000, p. 143) observed:

> It is true to say that some of these groups have felt a sense of exclusion, of not truly belonging to the tidal wave of primary health care reform. It is therefore crucial for PCG nurse members to be the strategic voice of nursing and health and not focus on her [sic] specific discipline. It is the knowledge and experience of the community network that makes nurses so valuable to the work of the PCG.

One explanation for this apparent distance between PCG/T nurse members and their nursing colleagues within the community has been a lack of understanding as to the relevance of the primary care organization to them in professional and personal terms. The apparent struggle to get continuing participation from all nurses and AHPs is a key challenge requiring a reduction in apathy and the ability to inspire nurses to bring knowledge, experience and a personal contribution to the work of the PCT.

Developing Structures for Nurse Engagement

Professional nurse forums have served as the key interface between the PCG/T and its nurse constituents. Indeed, by 2001, all twelve case study sites in the HSMC National Evaluation of PCG/Ts had established professional nurse forums compared to just one-half the year before (Smith et al, 2000; Regen et al, 2001). Thus, the innovative multi-disciplinary nurse forums that had developed in some early GP commissioning group pilots, in which nurse board members could meet representatives from the wider nursing constituency, had become the norm. However, several PCG/Ts established more formal structures whereby nurses met regularly, often on a sub-locality basis, offering the opportunity for views from smaller groups to be fed back into larger nurse forum meetings (see Figure 7.1). Their key achievement has been the ability to break down some of the traditional tribalism between nursing disciplines, providing a network within which the different professions could begin to understand the roles of other nurse colleagues.

For many PCGs, nurse forums proved particularly useful during consultations in the transition to PCT status, serving as a crucial channel of communication. As Regen at al (2001) report, both community and practice nurses had become more interested as a result of the transition to PCT status and involvement had thus increased, particularly from practice nurses previously not engaged. To help this process, some PCG/Ts recognized the difficulties and costs in 'freeing up' nurse time to attend meetings so had developed plans to provide backfill and cover to increase levels of involvement.

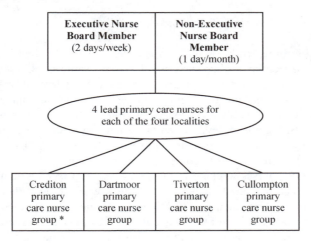

* Each primary care nurses group comprised one representative from ten professional nurse groupings, including the voluntary sector.

Figure 7.1 A structure for nurse involvement: the case of Mid Devon PCG

Source: Smith et al, 2000, p. 100.

Apart from involvement in nurse forums and their associated meetings, the other main way in which non-board nurses were involved was through work in specific sub-groups or projects. Over time, the level of nurse involvement in sub-groups grew significantly. Indeed, many nurses took on lead responsibilities for core PCG/T functions such as health improvement, prescribing and primary care development with some diagnostic visits related to clinical governance (Regen et al, 2001). In terms of reviewing specific areas of service provision, community nurses often led projects on diabetes, sexual health, user involvement and the development of healthy living centres. It was also reported how practice nurses were playing a more active role in the establishment of new PCG/T-wide specialist services, most notably in relation to coronary heart disease, as well as work relating to immunizations and vaccinations, asthma and cytology (Regen et al, 2001). The emerging research into the involvement of the wider nurse constituency up to 2001 suggested growing grass-roots nurse support for their primary care organization. As the National Tracker Survey of PCG/T chairs reported, the level of support from non-board nurses increased from 39 per cent to 66 per cent between 1999 and 2000 (Wilkin et al, 1999, 2001). More recent surveys of PCT nurse members suggest that nurses are continuing to grasp the opportunities presented by strategic involvement in PCTs, but that the pressure exerted centrally on nurses to shift their balance of work has increased workloads reducing the potential for greater engagement in activities (NHS Alliance, 2004b).

Overcoming Barriers to Nurse Involvement and Influence

Issues relating to time, workload and support were frequently cited in evaluations of PCG/Ts as barriers to further nurse involvement (Smith et al, 2000; Regen et al, 2001). In the same way as PCG/T nurse board members have struggled to cope with a dual role so other nurses wishing to attend meetings and undertake PCG/T activities have not been able to engage fully due to the pressures of their own clinical caseloads. Significant levels of participation only tended to occur where the local community trust facilitated their involvement by covering 'backfill' without demanding funding from PCGs to cover nurse involvement.

Thus, like GPs, nurses working in PCG/Ts have been faced with a conflicting set of demands that potentially makes their clinical work suffer as hours spent on PCG/T activities push into their personal time. This issue is cause for concern given the growth in workloads faced by nurses out with PCG/T activities and significant retention and recruitment issues for the profession as a whole. A 2003 survey of members of the Royal College of Nursing highlighted how continued divisions between nursing professions, increasing workloads and new priorities meant there was a need to improve the quality of working life in nurse careers to ensure retention (Ball and Pike, 2003).

Engagement with PCG/Ts has also been influenced by the degree of marginalization that nurses may feel. As Hart (2004) argues, despite having nurse representatives on the PEC, managers within PCTs can seem to 'occupy a parallel universe to nurses' and 'use a different language' that can disempower and exclude nurses from the process. As Titheridge (2000) suggests, nurses and other non-GP members have had to learn a new language to understand such issues as contracting, in-house services, prescribing patterns, and out-of-area referrals. Regen et al (2001) concluded that more effort was needed to avoid inappropriate domination of meetings and agendas by GPs in order to increase the contribution of nurses in PCG/Ts. In particular, it was argued that effective communication between nurse forums to PCG boards and professional executive committees was poor such that ideas generated at a grass-roots level were not reaching higher up the organization leading to perceptions of participation as being tokenistic. As one nurse in their survey responded:

The PCG board is a bit of a black box. It feels very remote. I'm not confident that task groups do feed back to the board and vice versa … sometimes I feel more like an observer in the task group and that I am not actually participating in the process (Regen et al, 2001, p. 101).

For many nurses, therefore, their enthusiasm and commitment feels like an untapped resource. For example, district nurses in the discussion paper 'The Invisible Workforce' felt that their contribution to PCTs was largely unrecognized (Queen's Nursing Institute, 2001) a theme shared in a more recent survey of nurse engagement where a wide range of key barriers were identified (NHS Alliance, 2004b). The key barriers to engagement included:

- the fact that many nurses only want to deal with direct patient care;
- that there was a lack of understanding on issues to do with the PCT agenda;
- that staff shortages and insufficient funding reduced morale;
- that workloads were high and the time for engagement low;
- that there were gender issues and professional barriers to overcome;
- that commissioning activities were seen as an 'entity on its own' and failed to involve nurses and wider multi-disciplinary input;
- that managers often set optimistic yet unrealistic targets and parameters; and
- that community nurses have difficulty challenging GPs (NHS Alliance, 2004b, p. 7).

Disagreements and resistance exist from and within nurse teams on the appropriate direction of nurse roles. Given these considerable barriers to the engagement of nurses, it is not surprising that non-board nurses have been reported as having a very limited impact on decision-making within PCG/Ts. As Table 7.4 shows, though the enthusiasm of the wider constituency of nurses remained higher than most other stakeholders from 1999-2000, nurse influence was regarded as low. This echoes findings reported from the national evaluation of GP commissioning pilots (Regen et al, 1999) suggesting that nurses by 2000 had yet to find an effective voice within their primary care organizations.

Table 7.4 The influence and enthusiasm of non-board nurses compared to other stakeholders, 1999-2000*

Stakeholder	Rating of Influence		Rating of Enthusiasm	
	1999	2000	1999	2000
Non-board nurses	2.32	2.20	3.18	3.00
Health authority	4.48	4.00	2.96	2.79
Non-board GPs	2.96	2.70	2.83	2.85
Other PCG/Ts	3.26	3.05	3.70	3.20
Hospital trusts	3.09	3.05	3.17	2.80
Social services	2.19	2.15	2.55	2.75
Local authority	1.84	1.80	2.28	2.10
Service users	1.77	1.84	1.74	1.78
Public	1.27	1.47	1.26	1.26

* PCG/T chairs and chief executives in 12 case study sites were asked to provide a rating of influence and enthusiasm on a 0-5 scale where 0 = no influence/enthusiasm and 5 = great influence/enthusiasm. The average rating for each stakeholder is presented in the table.

Source: Adapted from Smith et al (2000) and Regen et al (2001).

The Potential Impact of the 2004 General Medical Services Contract

The role of nurses has been undergoing further development as a result of a revised form of contract for the provision of general medical services in primary care. Since 2004, new local contracts for General Medical Services, based on a common national framework, have been developed that are administered by PCTs to primary care practices rather than nationally through the Department of Health to individual GPs. In the new arrangements, primary care practices have the ability to negotiate the level of service they are prepared to provide as well as have the freedom to determine new skill-mixes in which to do so. The contract should help nurses to further sub-specialize in care services such as vaccinations and minor surgeries and supports the trend towards the further medicalization of the nursing profession. The new GMS contract also allows frontline nurses to extend their interests from the clinical to the business aspects involved in running a provider organization. Nurses are able to take a more strategic role within primary care by forming a practice partnership or, indeed, developing a limited company to provide primary care services (as long as at least one GP is a signatory).

For PCTs, administering the 2004 GMS contract will require lead nurses to ensure that all frontline nurses have access to appropriate training, professional advice and continued professional development. As guidelines for the administration of the new GMS contract point out:

All practice-employed nurses are supported [by their PCTs] to participate in clinical supervision and appraisal and have access to professional advice and continued professional development and to information management and technology (Department of Health, 2004c, paragraph 4.20, p. 28).

The new arrangements have considerable implications for nurse engagement with PCTs. For example, nurses must be informed of contract discussions if this means changes to their roles and the guidance encourages nurses to become directly involved in planning the contract specifications and in implementing changes. PCT lead nurses, therefore, will be required to facilitate meetings so that frontline nurses can be involved, give advice and/or voice any anxieties that they may have.

An important element to the new GMS contract is linking payments to the achievement of performance and quality targets. A 'quality and outcomes framework' stipulates a number of organizational and clinical standards to be achieved with remuneration subject to an annual audit by the PCT. PCT lead nurses will be expected to take part in these annual visits to practices/providers providing them with a greater role in undertaking audit. Moreover, since nurses are likely to play a far greater role in providing clinical care, PCT lead nurses will be required to promote access and facilitate work-based learning programmes as well as to assess the attainment of core competencies. As a result, the commissioning, monitoring and educational role of lead nurses will increase and the importance of PCT nurse management is likely to grow considerably. These nurses will also need to have the experience, knowledge and understanding of general practice.

Conclusions: Lessons for Research and Practice

The development of new primary care organizations has combined with a set of other modernization policies to actively encourage nurses to take on more clinical roles and managerial leadership. The evidence reviewed in this chapter suggests that nurses have begun to take a more active part within their primary care organizations in determining local health policies and developing new services. However, a number of key factors inhibiting future engagement in PCTs need to be addressed to ensure that nurses can fulfill their potential new roles effectively.

Lessons for Research

* Nurse roles within PCG/Ts, and of the wider nurse constituency, have primarily been researched using postal and telephone surveys with some observational and focus group work. This has provided knowledge on the issues facing nurses and their perceptions as to their role and influence. However, the nature and depth of the nurse contribution within PCTs has not truly been explored and, in particular, a major gap has been work examining the core competencies required of nurse leaders and managers.
* The research to date has pointed to the importance of professional nurse

forums and other similar methods of engagement as crucial to engendering participation across the profession. However, it remains unknown whether such structures have any real influence on PCT decision-making and further research might be directed at examining the effectiveness of different methods of engagement.

- Nurses working within PCTs are actively being encouraged to take on clinical tasks previously performed by GPs. However, there has been limited research examining the impact of such substitution on the quality of patient care. Given that the development of nurse-led provision and of new types of skill-mix in primary care will be actively encouraged by PCTs through the new GMS contract, research is needed to assess the impact of skill-mix change and to inform PCTs of models of best practice.
- A final lesson for research emerging from this analysis is how the PCT's role in training and continued professional development of nurses will become a core activity alongside a greater role in clinical supervision and monitoring of activity. It is likely such roles in the PCT will be undertaken by lead nurses. Research is needed that can inform PCTs and lead nurses of the most appropriate methods for developing these new tasks.

Lessons for Practice

- Nursing workloads are a significant barrier to engagement, especially where nurses have their own clinical workload as well as dual roles within a PCT. To ensure effective engagement, primary care organizations will need to ensure that workload levels remain sustainable by providing resources for backfill. PCTs may need to consider developing their own 'bank' of salaried nurses for this task, particularly since the new GMS contract allows providers to 'opt-out' of certain elements of service provision.
- To foster service and professional integration, further efforts are needed to bring together the different nursing professions to promote understanding, joint working and the development of generic nurse roles.
- Engaging nurses through professional nurse forums will remain a crucial mechanism for engendering support and participation. However, PCTs will need to ensure better communications between such forums and the PCT professional executive committee so that the views and ideas expressed at a locality level are not seen as 'tokenistic' but as a worthwhile contribution. A sense of real influence is required to sustain nurse involvement with PCTs in the longer-term.
- Providing opportunities for training and the continued professional development of nurses is a core task. Lead nurses need to develop skills in clinical supervision, information technology, advice and mentoring if they are to facilitate educational and training opportunities.
- Lead nurses in PCTs need to be of sufficient seniority to debate and challenge priorities within the PCT itself. At the same time, PCTs would engage the

views of nurses and allied health professionals better if they avoided an overly medical agenda and sustained an active interest in nursing roles.

Chapter 8

Managing the Performance of PCG/Ts

The process of managing and developing performance within primary care organizations in the NHS in the 1990s was, in common with the overall policy environment of the time, relatively diverse, ad hoc and dependent on local systems of management and governance. Over time, however, the advent of PCGs and PCTs, with their formal responsibilities for securing appropriate local health services, necessarily precipitated the development of more robust performance management arrangements. In this chapter, an overview is given of the experience of performance management of PCG/Ts at the individual, practice and organizational level. This assessment of performance management in PCG/Ts is used as the basis for distilling a set of lessons for performance management in primary care organizations.

Performance Management of Primary Care Organizations in the 1990s

The introduction of primary care-led purchasing into the NHS as part of the Thatcher reforms of the early 1990s was aimed at strengthening the accountability of healthcare providers to patients, through their intermediary purchasers, GPs (Ham, 1996). The belief was that GPs would focus on elements of quality of service, as well as price, in making the choice of deliverer of care. In a review of the evidence concerning the performance of GP fundholding, Goodwin (1998) noted that providers were more responsive to the demands of fundholders than non-fundholders, suggesting that in certain respects fundholding did serve to increase accountability within NHS purchasing. This finding is supported by more recent research (Croxson et al, 2001; Propper et al, 2002; Dusheiko et al; 2003).

A system that accorded a new range of powers to GPs clearly required a system of performance management to ensure appropriate governance of public resources. An accountability framework for GP fundholding (Department of Health, 1994) was introduced some three years following the introduction of this new form of NHS purchasing. That it took this long to develop a robust framework for the governance of GP fundholding is testimony to the degree to which the NHS in the early 1990s was characterized by innovation, devolution and a distaste for central control.

Whilst GP fundholding was managed through local accountability agreements with regional health authorities (and subsequently with health authorities at the district level), parallel forms of GP-led purchasing were subject to diverse local performance management approaches. Locality and GP commissioning groups created in partnership with health authorities were typically held to account through the standard performance management processes of the health authority, especially where purchasing budgets had been devolved to localities and/or groups of GPs. Where GP fundholders formed themselves into consortia or multifunds, using their management allowances allocated by government to create new independent management organizations (often constituted as companies limited by guarantee), the process of performance management and accountability was far less clear.

The development of a pilot programme of total purchasing projects (TPPs) in 1996 was underpinned by a much more formal performance management process – budgets were jointly managed by the TPP and the health authority and the TPP itself was made a formal sub-committee of the health authority. In addition, the GP fundholding accountability framework applied to TPPs (Mays et al, 2001). This was at once a reflection of the significantly greater degree of purchasing and financial responsibility held by TPPs and of the wider policy environment that was moving towards stronger accountability processes for local primary care purchasers. Research evidence on TPPs reveals, however, that health authorities tended to take a fairly hands-off approach to the performance management of TPPs, letting them operate with minimal interference from the centre (Strawderman et al, 1996). Commentators suggest that this was a further reflection of the prevailing government view that TPPs, like fundholders, should be 'allowed to get on with it', being able to withdraw from the TPP and fundholding schemes if demands made upon them became too great (Dixon et al, 2001).

Research into the various NHS primary care organizations of the 1990s frequently pointed to the need for stronger systems of performance management and accountability in the next phase of development of NHS purchasing and cautioned against the risk of losing the vital innovation and associate clinical engagement that had typified the emergence of these organizations (LeGrand et al, 1998; Smith et al, 1998; Mays et al, 2001). The announcement of the creation of PCG/Ts in the 1997 NHS White Paper (Department of Health, 1997) revealed that PCG/Ts faced more stringent arrangements for upward accountability to NHS management organizations in comparison with their predecessors, fundholding and total purchasing pilots (Dixon et al, 2001).

Performance Management in Primary Care Groups and Trusts

In contrast to the primary care organizations of the early and mid-1990s, PCGs operated as formal sub-committees of health authorities. As such, they were required to develop strategic objectives located within the health authority's health improvement plan, demonstrating how they were seeking to tackle national and local health priorities such as coronary heart disease, diabetes, and mental health (NHS Executive, 1998). Health authorities varied in their specific approach to the performance management of PCGs, but a frequently used tool was the formal quarterly review meeting between senior health authority managers and the PCG chief executive and chair (Smith et al, 2000; Wilkin et al, 2000; Audit Commission,

2000). Research into PCGs noted that the relationship between a PCG and its host health authority varied greatly. Whilst some PCGs operated in a constructive and yet robust framework of performance management and development, others reported much less positive relationships including the distant/barely interested, and the distinctly controlling and lacking in trust (Regen et al, 2001).

PCGs, as with GP multifunds, total purchasing pilots and GP commissioning groups before them, rapidly realized that they needed performance management tools that would enable them to lever change in key areas of priority, in particular primary care development and clinical governance. As can be seen in the detailed discussion of this topic in Chapter 10, PCGs chose to focus on primary care development as an early and pressing priority, using the process of clinical governance as a lever for developing clear practice-based targets for service provision such as prescribing and the management of chronic disease, incentive schemes to encourage the achievement of such targets, and peer review mechanisms to check progress towards these aims. Researchers noted that this approach to the management of performance in primary care was at once radical (in that it was happening at all and was led by professional peers) and focused on performance development and improvement, yet lacking 'bite' in terms of an ability or willingness to tackle deficiencies in service delivery or practitioner performance (Smith et al, 2000; Wilkin et al, 2000; Roland and Campbell, 2003).

PCTs, in contrast to PCGs, were established in 2000 as statutory NHS bodies independent of the local health authority. Following the abolition of health authorities and the associated extension of PCT powers in 2002 (Department of Health, 2001a), PCTs were placed in a clear formal performance management relationship whereby they were made accountable to the strategic health authority (SHA) for their delivery of corporate objectives and NHS Plan targets. The PCT chief executive became the formal accountable officer for the organization, both in terms of financial and clinical governance targets and performance. In addition, PCTs were now subject to external regulation in the form of Commission for Health Improvement (CHI) visits and reviews – these feeding into the formal 'star ratings' awarded to PCTs (and NHS hospital and mental health trusts) and published on an annual basis.

As noted elsewhere in this book, the move to PCT status has marked the shift for English primary care organizations away from voluntary, relatively informal and clinically-led bodies to being formal, managerially-led and statutory NHS bodies. In place of clinically-led priorities and targets, PCTs were required to deliver on a wide range of nationally determined management and service objectives. This entailed management processes and systems designed to monitor, report on and improve performance in specific areas of health improvement, service commissioning and primary care development. PCTs in turn sought to develop internal performance management processes for the organization that focused on assuring the delivery of both national and local service and health improvement targets. To do this, many PCTs organized themselves into directorates and/or localities, sub-units of the organization that are held to account for their performance of overall PCT objectives. In relation to the performance management relationship between PCTs and their constituent practices, a key tool in this process was the development and use of local contracts for services.

PCG/Ts and the Use of Local Contracts with Primary Care Providers

The NHS White Paper 'Choice and Opportunity' (Department of Health, 1996) proposed the development of flexible local contracts for the development and management of practice-based primary care, initially in a series of Personal Medical Services (PMS) pilot schemes. These pilot schemes were enacted in the NHS (Primary Care) Act of 1997, an Act that had cross-party political support and thus ensured that PMS schemes continued under the Labour administration. The flexibilities offered to PMS pilots by the provisions of the 1997 Act were (Peckham and Exworthy, 2003):

1. Salaried option – GPs able to be employed by the health authority under a separate contract.
2. Personal medical services (PMS) – development of a local contract between the health authority and practices (GPs, nurses and other primary care professionals) to deliver personal medical services within a cash-limited budget.
3. Personal medical services plus (PMS+) – development of a local contract between the health authority and practices that would extend PMS pilots to cover both personal medical services and a range of other healthcare services within a combined primary and hospital/community services budget.

PMS pilots schemes focused on issues relevant to their local situation, and some were radical in their nature, representing new forms of providing primary care services to previously excluded groups such as the homeless, people living on inner city estates without GP practices, and travellers (Walsh et al, 1999; Walsh et al, 2001). In 2002, PCTs took over from health authorities the responsibility for holding and managing both mainstream general medical services (GMS) and PMS contracts. This established the PCT as the commissioner *of* primary care as well as deliverers of these services and commissioners of secondary and tertiary care. In terms of performance management, the PCT now had a powerful tool for specifying what it wanted to be provided within primary care, and to what quality standards (Maynard, 2004).

By 2003, over 40 per cent of GPs in England were working within the PMS scheme, demonstrating an increasing acceptance of locally negotiated contracts and associated quality standards and performance assessment. In many ways, PMS contracts can be viewed as having blazed a trail for the new national GP contract that was implemented in the UK in April 2004, for this new General Medical Services contract (nGMS). The new national GMS contract is held with practices (rather than individual GPs), requires GPs to opt for providing one of three levels of medical services (essential, additional and enhanced) and is underpinned by a comprehensive quality and outcomes framework that links the achievement of key clinical and management quality indicators with additional contract payments. Perhaps the most significant element of the implementation of the new GMS contract is its role as a key tool for PCTs in managing performance within primary care. PCTs in England are now clearly positioned as the commissioners of practice-based primary care, based on a set of national and local performance indicators (see Chapter 12).

That UK primary care has moved into what can be seen to be a much more managed and performance-focused environment over the period of the 1990s and the early 2000s is the result of a number of key environmental factors. The emergence of the primary care organization as a force for drawing together professionals into more managed arrangements, the wider societal push for greater accountability and transparency on the part of professionals, and the impact of well-publicized NHS system failure scandals such as the Bristol Royal Infirmary paediatric heart case and the murders carried out in Manchester by the GP Harold Shipman, all played their part in enabling the introduction of more robust contracts within primary care. In tandem with this, it is possible to detect a 'clipping of the wings' in relation to the traditional autonomy of UK GPs, a drawing into the fold of broader NHS management (Smith and Walshe, 2004).

Determining What Constitutes 'Good Performance' in a PCG/T

This shift within primary care from the focus on the individual practitioner as the manager and co-ordinator of services towards a more corporate model of primary care overseen and developed by a formal NHS organization has brought with it a shift in the definition of what constitutes 'good performance' in a PCT. At practice level, rather than the clinician's perspective being dominant via clinically-led processes of audit and peer assessment (as was the case in the early 1990s), performance standards are increasingly agreed through formal PCT organizational mechanisms, albeit that these bodies include significant clinical input, especially in the form of PECs and clinical governance committees. Similarly, at the level of the organization, what is deemed to constitute good performance has shifted from almost exclusively practitioner-defined factors such as prescribing behaviour, levels of practice-based activity, and development of additional local GP services, towards targets with a clear link to the national NHS Plan, National Service Frameworks and PCT corporate objectives. Such corporate targets include: levels of access to primary care services (reducing waiting times); a focus on seeking to achieve demonstrable health improvement in areas such as mental health, coronary heart disease and diabetes; and reaching national standards in relation to the provision of services for chronic disease management.

The influence of external bodies on the definition of 'good performance' in primary care organizations is not however a new concept. In the 1990s, the local health authority had the responsibility for managing the performance of GP fundholders via their accountability agreements, and, following the introduction of the policy of a 'primary care-led NHS' (NHS Executive, 1994), for overseeing and shaping the contribution of other primary care commissioning groups to local health planning and purchasing. The first official and systematic review of the performance of GP fundholding came in the form of a study by the Audit Commission of the value for money of the scheme (Audit Commission, 1996). This concluded that only a minority of innovative practices actually used the fundholding scheme to transform patient care in a significant manner, and that overall, the transaction costs of the scheme were disproportionately high (Audit Commission, 1996). Perhaps the most significant aspect of this study was the fact that it established the principle that primary care organizations should be subject to external assessment within a framework of public accountability, and that the determination of performance indicators by professionals leading projects was not in itself sufficient.

What can be considered an increasingly centralist approach to managing the performance of the NHS post-1997 has been borne out by the experience of PCTs (NHS Alliance and CGST, 2004). There has been some criticism of the English star rating system leading to an undue focus on national frameworks, targets and assessment, and the fact that these targets are predominantly linked with acute services issues (Roland and Smith, 2003). Similarly, commentators have pointed to the risk of distortion within such a target-based approach to performance assessment, namely that key areas of health care activity might receive less policy and management attention than is appropriate, examples of such 'neglected' areas being maternity services, community nursing, and mental health (Maynard et al, 2004).

National Performance Management Bodies

The Commission for Health Improvement (CHI), known as the Healthcare Commission with effect from April 2004, was established for England and Wales in 1999 as part of the Government's overall policy of developing clinical governance in the NHS (Department of Health, 1997b). CHI was developed as a national inspectorate charged with addressing unacceptable variations in patient care, identifying areas of good practice, and highlighting ways in which care could be improved (Roland and Smith, 2003). Although initially focused mainly on acute sector reviews, CHI commenced pilot reviews of PCTs in 2001/2002, starting a full programme of PCT reviews in October 2002. In 2004, CHI reported on its initial 62 reviews of PCTs in England, concluding with an assessment of what they considered to be a 'good' PCT, this assessment being set out in Table 8.1. In summarizing CHI's view of PCT performance, CHI Chair, Dame Deirdre Hine, commented:

> PCTs have established themselves as new organizations and are responding in particular to national targets for waiting lists and the national service frameworks, which is no small achievement. However, a number of PCTs are struggling to mature as organizations; that is, to learn systematically from experience and monitor progress. Similarly, we have yet to see many PCTs leading improvements in local NHS services or in the health of their population (Commission for Health Improvement, 2004, p. 5).

Table 8.1 The CHI assessment of what makes a 'good' PCT

- PCTs that scored well in CHI reviews tended to have worked hard to develop good engagement with their staff and professionals.
- Many PCTs had difficulty engaging all professional groups and the respective roles of the professional executive committee and the PCT board were often blurred.
- PCTs with strong clinical governance arrangements showed clear evidence of integrated strategic planning and capacity development. This enabled staff to understand PCT priorities and the importance of their own role in achieving these.
- Many PCTs were making use of national levers to improve performance, with high scoring PCTs making imaginative use of initiatives, partnership working, sources of funding and resources to lead change in specific areas.
- The use of information was considered to be central to PCTs' capacity to improve health care, but CHI reviews showed that many PCTS struggle in this respect.

Source: Commission for Health Improvement (2004), p. 34.

This assessment of organizations that were on average two years old at the time of inspection was not surprising. What is, however, of particular note is the conclusion that PCTs had yet to demonstrate any significant achievement in relation to the commissioning and planning of local health services. This concern about PCTs' ability to commission services has been noted in other studies of PCTs (Smith and Goodwin, 2002; Wilkin et al, 2002; Audit Commission, 2004) and is explored in more depth in Chapter 11.

This assessment by CHI of what constitutes 'good' performance by a PCT clearly derives from the three core functions of PCTs, namely health improvement, service commissioning, and primary care development. What CHI's assessment reveals is a clear sense that PCTs should, as statutory local health organizations respond to national targets, but that this should not be at the expense of local planning and service development. Once again, the tension between the national and the local, the collective and the individual focus, is played out in the experience of PCTs.

Setting Targets and Performance Measures in a PCG/T

The tension between the national and the local is mirrored in the dilemma facing PCTs about the level at which targets and performance measures are set and by whom. There are clearly statutory and national imperatives for PCTs that lead to the development of core organizational targets at board/executive team level. These targets typically reflect the star ratings system applied to PCTs and the national aspirations for the NHS as articulated in the NHS Plan (Department of Health, 2000). What is more challenging for PCTs, however, is the determination of performance measures that reflect local issues and priorities, and ensuring that these measures receive appropriate organizational attention when PCT managers are held very clearly to account on the basis of national targets.

Two key ways in which PCTs are intended to remain close to their communities and service users are by means of engaging clinical professionals and staff in their management and commissioning processes, and by having robust and active approaches to involving local people and service users in the setting of priorities and the monitoring of service provision. In relation to the engagement of professional staff, Chapters 6 and 7 revealed the complexity of this task for PCTs and the fact that the increasingly managed and 'corporate' nature of PCTs appears to mitigate against active clinical engagement, thus calling for significant management time and attention to be devoted to the development of real and robust clinical involvement within PCTs. If clinicians are not effectively engaged with the running of their local PCT, it is hard to see how they can play an active role in the development, implementation and monitoring of performance measures. To enable such involvement, the PCT needs to have in place an approach to strategic planning and service development that has clinical involvement as a key component.

This calls into question the role of the professional executive committee (PEC) in determining targets and measures within PCTs. There is evidence to suggest that PECs have struggled to develop a clear role as clinical leaders of PCTs, and that in many cases, the power base in PCTs seems to be located within the executive management team rather than in the PEC, or indeed the non-executive element of the board (NHS Alliance/NCGST, 2004, NHS Alliance, 2003 and see Chapter 5). If this apparent managerial dominance of PCTs and their agendas is indeed widespread, the chances for clinicians to truly influence the nature of PCT activity and in turn its measurement would seem to be doomed to be very limited. The logical consequence of such a situation is that the national, managerial agenda related to performance management will continue to dominate, this in turn serving to further alienate clinicians (see Chapter 12). There are however signs of hope in relation to the possible re-engagement of clinicians within PCTs and the rediscovery of ways of determining local service priorities and measures. NHS guidance issued in the summer of 2004 and implemented from April 2005 onwards, exhorts PCTs to adopt a range of approaches to devolved practice-led commissioning, specifically aimed at enabling practices and localities to develop local priorities and to fund developments in line with these aspirations (Department of Health, 2004b).

The engagement of the public and service users in the strategic management and priority setting of PCTs has to date been universally reported as being something where PCG/Ts employ a range of approaches and techniques, but where evidence about actual impact on strategic or operational decision-making is limited (Regen et al, 2001; Wilkin et al, 2002; Elbers and Regen, 2002; Anderson et al, 2002; Rowe and Shepherd, 2002; Milewa et al, 2003). Further analysis of this is made in Chapter 9. Some commentators suggest that the very use of a diversity of approaches to public involvement may in itself constrain the extent to which users and citizens can fully engage, as partners, in the planning process or challenge professional decisions (Milewa et al, 2003). Milewa et al (2003) point to the centrality of the role of the PCT in determining what constitutes involvement and in demarcating who is a legitimate participant in each aspect of public engagement activity. As with the issue of clinical engagement, this highlights the responsibility incumbent on the PCT in terms of deciding how it wants to operate, what degree of devolution and delegation it wishes to embrace, and to what extent it is prepared to share the responsibility for defining, implementing and monitoring performance measures.

Thus PCTs are faced with a choice in relation to organizational development and overall culture. Do they wish to be participative, inclusive, and devolved, ready to engage clinicians, service users and other stakeholders in the process of setting targets and measures and in responding to progress against such measures? Or will they take a more traditional managed and hierarchical approach, responding primarily to a central Department of Health agenda, making mainly tokenistic gestures in relation to broader engagement and involvement in decision making? This distinction is exaggerated here to make a point, but the underlying message is that it is impossible to separate performance measurement and management from the overall cultural and managerial approach of a PCT. The degree to which a central as opposed to local agenda takes precedence is inevitably intertwined with the organization's readiness or otherwise to devolve responsibility and engage others in the process of shaping plans and priorities. In its review of performance of PCTs, CHI (2004, p. 27) noted that:

> Lack of clinician and public involvement contributes to a commissioning process that is divorced from the needs of patients and users and from evidence based practice.

Performance management is part of the broader process of commissioning and planning, and the lessons concerning effective commissioning (see Chapter 11) and sustaining clinical engagement (see Chapter 12) also apply here.

Managing and Developing the Performance of a PCT

There are two key dimensions to the ways in which the performance of a PCT is managed and developed. Firstly, the means by which the organization itself seeks to manage and develop the performance of individuals, teams, departments, localities and the whole organization. Secondly, the mechanisms applied by external agencies seeking to scrutinize and develop PCT performance, such bodies including strategic health authorities, the Healthcare Commission (formerly the Commission for Health Improvement), local authority overview and scrutiny committees, and numerous agencies such as the National Patient Safety Agency and the Health and Safety Executive.

The Internal Management and Development of Performance in a PCT

At the level of care delivery, the assessment and improvement of clinicians' practice is a key issue for PCTs, this being an essential building block in the overall performance of the organization. Evidence from early evaluations of PCOs in the NHS, in particular PCGs and the early PCTs, pointed to the general reluctance to tackle poor practitioner performance on the part of these organizations (Regen et al, 2001; Wilkin et al, 2001) and a greater readiness, understandably, to focus on developmental and education approaches to improving service quality. It should however be remembered that any moves towards greater consistency and quality in the delivery of primary care services were radical in comparison with the largely laissez-faire to monitoring and developing clinical quality in primary care prior to the mid- to late 1990s.

Work to develop practitioner performance in the NHS has, since 1998, taken place as part of an overall policy of introducing and assuring clinical governance (see Chapter 10). Techniques employed by clinicians and managers leading the development of improved service quality within PCG/Ts have included peer review, the sharing of information about individual and group clinical practice, the setting and monitoring of service standards at practice level, and the application of financial and other incentives as a means of encouraging achievement of such standards (Regen et al, 2001; Campbell and Roland, 2003).

Other external demands have similarly led PCTs to focus on the development of their clinicians' performance, including the introduction of a national system of appraisal for GPs, a requirement for doctors to undergo regular revalidation of their fitness to practice. The development of a stronger commissioning function for primary care has also played its part in introducing a new focus on the management and development of performance within primary care. Initially through local PMS contracts in pilot sites, and now on a national basis through the implementation of the new General Medical Services contract, primary care practitioners are required to sign up to locally defined versions of a national contract that is based on a quality and outcomes framework that seeks to identify targets for primary care practices as a basis for determining appropriate services for local practice populations and associated financial rewards for practices and GPs in particular. This move towards the use of tailored local contracts within primary care and the application of these as a basis for performance development is not now unique to general medical practice. A new local contract for NHS dental practitioners is being introduced with effect from April 2005 and a new national contract for pharmacy is similarly in the process of being developed and negotiated. What this represents is an overall shift towards a more managed form of primary care within a tighter and more locally determined framework of quality standards, the contract being the key tool for managers and PCT clinical leaders seeking to bring about change in practitioner performance within practices (see Chapter 12).

PCTs are not however just made up of practice-based services delivered through NHS contracts. They also directly employ many staff and manage whole services such as community nursing, health visiting and community-based allied health professions. The performance framework for these groups is typically one more closely based on traditional organizational approaches to the setting and monitoring of performance standards as part of the overall management task of appraisal and performance development. PCTs use standard performance management practices in order to set performance objectives for their staff and to monitor progress in relation to these objectives. It should also be noted that PCTs are increasingly seeking to influence their constituent practices to apply the same form of performance assessment and development with staff employed by GPs, dentists, and pharmacists, as part of an overall strategy of developing and assuring clinical governance.

At the level of the locality or broader primary care team, approaches to the management of performance within PCTs would appear to be more diverse, or indeed sporadic, linked with the degree to which budgetary responsibility has been devolved to this level. Although localities have continued to feature as a unit of organizational (and in particular inter-professional) communication within PCTs, they are much less frequently used for budget holding and active service development than was the case in the 1990s (Wilkin et al, 2002; Lewis, 2004). The degree to which responsibility for budgets and service delivery is actually devolved to localities clearly influences the extent of performance management and development being exercised at this level. Once again, we see that performance management is a function of broader decisions taken in an organization about its shape, culture and modus operandi. There has been recognition by the English Department of Health of the need for a return to a greater degree of commissioning and service development activity at the locality level, as set out in its NHS Improvement Plan in relation to practice-led commissioning (Department of Health, 2004b). As PCTs make decisions about how to implement this guidance in the local setting, they will need to ensure that they apply appropriate methods of performance management in place in a manner that is at once sensitive to the professionals engaging in commissioning, and yet robust enough to assure the achievement of PCT commissioning and financial objectives and standards of governance.

Within PCTs, the main governing and performance management bodies are the board (the overall accountable body) and the professional executive committee (PEC) which, as set out in Chapter 5, is the main forum for securing senior levels of clinical engagement within the organization. The need to clarify and capitalize upon the respective roles and talents of the board and the PEC as a prerequisite to effective working and performance management is set out in a report from the NHS Alliance:

> In order to discharge their complex statutory duties efficiently and effectively and to provide the strategic leadership demanded by the quality improvement and public service reform agendas, the Boards and PECs of PCTs need to make the best use of all their aggregated talents and to perform not only as individuals but to function well as 'working social systems' (NHS Alliance/CGST, 2004, p. 76).

For such effective 'working social systems' to be in place, there is a need for an appropriate external environment of regulation, performance assessment and development that nurtures creative and forward-looking organizations.

The External Management and Development of Performance in a PCT

The relationship between a PCO and its supervisory tier or organization is one that research evidence shows to have had a very mixed experience (Shapiro et al, 1996; Smith and Shapiro, 1997; Regen et al, 1999; Regen et al, 2001; Wilkin et al,

2000; Wilkin et al, 2002). The dilemma for strategic health authorities and their predecessor health authorities has been framed as 'holding on while letting go' (Smith and Shapiro, 1997), that is, the classic performance management challenge of how much to trust and delegate and how much to control and closely manage. This dilemma was accentuated by the fact that health authorities were at once the key funders and supporters of emergent PCOs, whilst also having the responsibility of holding them to account for their performance. Research reveals the importance for PCOs of having a constructive and mutually trusting relationship with the host health authority or SHA, both in terms of the development of a positive and supportive approach to performance management, and in order to maximize opportunities for delegation of responsibility and associated management and other support resources (Regen et al, 2001; Wilkin et al, 2002).

Research carried out in twelve case study PCG/Ts in 2001-2002 revealed that a diverse range of approaches to performance management was being used by health authorities, ranging from relatively formal processes to informal processes and cases where little or no performance management was being reported (Regen et al, 2001). This study noted that one-quarter of case study primary care organizations lacked a performance management structure, relying instead on ad hoc meetings between the health authority and PCG/T. What this demonstrates is the inevitable diversity in approaches to performance management that are likely to be adopted by supervisory organizations, in particular when there is no clear national requirement in this regard. Contrast this with the later NHS experience of PCTs, in their capacity as formal statutory NHS organizations, where they are, as noted earlier, subject to formal performance management by strategic health authorities and external inspection and assessment by the Healthcare Commission and a range of other bodies. The approach taken by strategic health authorities (the supervisory tier for PCTs) in managing PCT performance is however likely to vary. Early research evidence on strategic health authorities suggests that they have inevitably different behavioural and cultural preferences in respect of how they choose to relate to PCTs and other NHS bodies, and that the performance management element of their role tends to be predominant, over and above more facilitative and developmental functions (Walshe et al, 2004). The same research warns, however, of concerns in strategic health authorities about the performance of PCTs, suggesting that PCTs are likely to face stringent and focused performance management in the short to medium term.

Conclusions: Lessons for Research and Practice

It is clear that English PCOs have become subject to increasingly stringent and formal methods of external performance assessment and management. This underlines the way in which the Department of Health has drawn PCTs into the mainstream management and scrutiny framework of the NHS, viewing them as formal accountable NHS bodies, a far cry from the relatively informal and unregulated clinician-led PCOs of the 1990s. This said, perhaps the greatest challenge facing PCTs in their next phase of development is to balance the necessary requirement for appropriate external scrutiny and performance management with the need to re-engage GPs and other professional staff in both strategic and operational aspects of PCT work, whilst assuring robust public accountability to local communities. The key lessons to be drawn from this analysis of performance management in PCTs are set out below.

Lessons for Research

- The assessment of PCO performance in the 1990s was largely characterized by a lack of overall national evaluation, with the exception of total purchasing projects and GP commissioning pilots.
- Although there is an increasing body of research evidence concerning the development and implementation of PCOs, it is characterized by a focus on issues of context, structure and process, with little detailed and sustained attention to health outcomes.
- There is a need for research funders and researchers to explore more effective ways of assessing the *impact* of PCOs. Much is already known about process and implementation issues but relatively little about impact.
- The rapidity with which policy makers have changed the form and function of PCOs in the NHS has mitigated against significant longer term monitoring and evaluation of health outcomes that might be attributed to PCOs.
- The new General Medical Services contract and its associated data collection and quality and outcomes framework offer a new opportunity for researching and assessing the performance of PCTs.
- Research evidence on the performance and overall impact of PCOs is generally supported by the findings of external regulatory bodies such as the Healthcare Commission and the Audit Commission. This points to the potential for researchers to work more closely with such bodies, especially in relation to the analysis of routine data.
- Researchers need to find ways of working with practitioners to identify the most appropriate methods of performance management, given the need also to retain clinical engagement within PCOs.

Lessons for Practice

- Where PCOs have developed from a professional, rather than managerial base, performance management is more likely to focus on clinical issues of immediate relevance to clinicians in practices.
- The accountability of PCOs to patients and the public is an area where many approaches and techniques have been applied, but evidence of meaningful outcomes is scant.
- The management of PCO performance by the supervisory tier (e.g. health authorities) has been very variable in the approach used, this finding being consistent across the different phases of PCO development in the NHS.

- PCOs need an effective and mature relationship with the supervisory tier, based on clear and regular arrangements for the review of performance, if the overall experience of performance management is to be productive and constructive.
- Developing PCOs as formal statutory bodies is one possible response to a need for greater accountability and performance management, but such a move comes at a cost, in particular that of clinical engagement.
- The use of locally managed contracts with primary care providers are an increasingly important tool in the management of PCO performance, enabling the development of local standards and targets against which to measure performance.
- In NHS PCOs, the definition of what constitutes 'good performance' has shifted from being largely determined by professionals to a situation where central government, through its overall policy direction and regulatory agencies, sets and monitors key performance targets.
- Whilst central targets are often criticized for skewing the focus of PCTs away from local priorities towards national issues, there is emerging evidence that effective PCTs use such central targets as a way of levering desired local change.
- Given that external assessment of PCT performance, both via research studies and the reports of national regulatory bodies, reveals that whilst good progress has been made in the areas of clinical governance and primary care development, much remains to be done in relation to commissioning and health improvement, it may be that the appropriate scope for a PCO is about developing primary and intermediate care rather than playing a major role in the wider health system.
- PCTs face a constant balancing act in respect of the degree to which national as opposed to local targets and priorities are addressed.
- PCTs have an important choice to make in relation to organizational development and culture, in particular the degree to which they are prepared to be participative, inclusive and devolved in their approach to the management and development of performance.
- PCTs need to develop robust approaches to the management of poor clinical performance, moving beyond purely 'carrots' methods of developing local performance standards.
- PCTs appear to have made effective use of a range of externally driven developments as part of their overall management of performance, examples including the introduction of GP appraisal and revalidation, the implementation of Personal Medical Services and latterly the new General Medical Services contract, and the development of clinical governance.
- The effectiveness of professional executive committees as strategic decision making bodies that have a real influence on the setting and monitoring of performance standards in PCTs remains open to question.

Chapter 9

Creating Partnerships for Improving Health in PCG/Ts

Primary care organizations in England have incrementally taken on the responsibility for improving health and tackling health inequalities locally. This development has occurred within a context in which policies have given, at least in rhetoric, as much emphasis to improving public health as to the creation of better and more accessible NHS services. Following 'The New NHS' (Department of Health, 1997), the programme of NHS reform first required health authorities to develop Health Improvement Programmes to assess local health care needs and inform and guide commissioning. Moreover, a statutory duty was placed on both NHS and local government bodies to work in partnership to reduce health inequalities and tackle the underlying causes of ill-health. By 1999, health authorities in England were responsible for bringing together PCG/Ts and local authorities to develop a joint public health agenda and set mutual objectives. Further restructuring in the wake of 'Shifting the Balance of Power' (Department of Health, 2001a) saw this function devolved to PCTs . As a consequence, primary care organizations in England have been required to diversify from a primarily medically-based model to take a lead role in fostering strategic and operational partnerships with social services and other local authority and community-based agencies. This chapter examines the emerging role of PCG/Ts in health improvement and how managers have addressed the growing requirement to create strategic and operational partnerships with local authorities and the local community. Three themes are explored: the emerging public health role; the developing relationship with local authorities; and relationships with the wider local community. The chapter concludes with a set of lessons for research and practice.

The Public Health Role of PCG/Ts

The culture and practice within primary care in the UK has traditionally reflected the narrow orthodox medical view of health care, suggesting that the potential to realize a public health model of primary care is unlikely in the face of the traditional GP practice based on a small business model of independent contractors (Taylor et al, 1998). As Baggott (2000) observed, the creation of GP-led primary care organizations in the 1990s did not act as a counterbalance to this scenario since attention was placed on interventions and treatments rather than prevention based on wider social action. Research into primary care innovations at this time, such as fundholding and total purchasing, makes it clear that a GP-dominated model of primary care service delivery and commissioning paid virtually no attention to the role of public health (Mays et al, 2001). Furthermore, the health professionals' interpretation of their potential 'public health' role was limited to the identification of disease patterns and standards of treatment (Taylor et al, 1998). As a consequence, many commentators have been pessimistic about the ability of new primary care organizations to address health improvement:

> The persistence of a rather narrow vision of health promotion among those who dominate in primary care [organizations] – the GPs – does not augur well … there is no guarantee that the creation of PCGs and PCTs will automatically lead to a sharper focus on health improvement and, to this end, inter-agency working. Much will depend on their ability to develop a shared perception of health improvement and to build an effective working relationship between stakeholders at local level (Baggott, 2000, pp. 108-109).

The perception that combining primary care and public health approaches is like 'mixing oil and water' is one that pervades (Meads et al, 1999). Indeed, some have felt that the expectation for primary care organizations to fulfill the wider public health agenda flies in the face of evidence suggesting primary care professionals had neither the expertise nor the inclination to do this (Popay, 2001).

The Nature of the Public Health Agenda for PCG/Ts

The emerging role of the primary care organization in England as the leading agent to address health improvement and tackle health inequalities has been growing since the 1997 Labour Government identified and prioritized these issues for grass-roots action (Department of Health, 1997). Before this, responsibilities for public health had been divided between local authority social service agencies undertaking an environmental health agenda, and health authorities examining public health needs and community medicine. From the beginning, the vision for PCG/Ts was not just in disease management but also in the prevention of ill health and the promotion of healthier lifestyles. Moreover, PCG/Ts were seen as the potential vehicle for integrating the organizationally fragmented way public health issues were being managed. This implicated the need for PCG/Ts to lead and work within community-based multi-agency partnerships.

Initially, health authorities rather than PCGs were required to take the lead role in addressing population health needs. To this end, each health authority was tasked with the development of an annual health improvement programme to help guide commissioning strategies, whilst collaboration with local authorities was mandated through a statutory duty of partnership to promote health and wellbeing. Furthermore, a programme of national service frameworks was initiated, each setting national service standards in particular fields such as coronary heart disease or mental health. In addition to these activities, the government initiated two further schemes in 1997 with an explicit community health focus. These were health action zones, an initiative for inter-agency collaboration to address local health needs, develop partnerships and improve services; and healthy living centres, community-based health promotion centres to help tackle the social, economic and environmental factors inhibiting good health. Overall, despite health improvement being a key PCG function, it was the health authorities that retained overall responsibility.

Following the dissolution of health authorities in 2001 (Department of Health, 2001a), the transfer of budgets and key functions to PCTs included a major reorganization of public health responsibilities. PCTs were required to develop a public health directorate to work in partnership with local communities and non-governmental agencies. PCTs were also required to work closely with local authorities and contribute to the creation of local strategic partnerships, a joint health and social care plan.

The Progress and Key Challenges of PCG/Ts in Addressing Health Improvement

The explicit emphasis for PCG/Ts to tackle health inequalities and address health improvement was welcomed by many public health advocates (Baggott, 2000). However, concerns remained as to the extent to which PCG/Ts would take up these issues within a system dominated by health professionals and concerned primarily with care and treatment of individual patients. Early analysis of the progress of PCG/Ts at the end of their first year by two national evaluations suggested very limited progress in forwarding their public health role (Abbott and Gillam, 1999; Smith et al, 2000). At this time, both evaluations excused PCGs in this area since a higher priority was to address fundamental organizational development issues, hence creating time pressures that precluded engagement with the public health agenda. More worrying was the finding that PCGs at this time lacked any understanding of the tasks required to address the public health agenda and suffered from a chronic shortage of public health expertise (Abbott and Gillam, 1999).

A further year into the life of PCG/Ts, the same studies re-evaluated progress in addressing health improvement and concluded that, whilst slow and developmental, some signs of progress had been made (Abbott and Gillam, 2001; Regen et al, 2001). The National Tracker Survey found it encouraging that most PCG/Ts had advanced support systems to develop health needs assessments and influence health improvement plans drawn up by their host health authorities (Abbott and Gillam, 2001). The HSMC National Evaluation of PCG/Ts reported that local health improvement plans linked both to national service frameworks and to specific local priorities. Indeed, some PCG/Ts had begun to work in partnership with local authorities towards more community-focused, rather than clinically-driven, activities (Regen et al, 2001). A number of key management challenges to PCG/Ts were uncovered by these research teams (Abbott and Gillam, 2001; Regen et al, 2001):

- securing staff engagement;
- developing the capacity to address the health improvement agenda;
- finding the time required in the process of partnership building and integration

between different agencies;
- overcoming the bureaucracy involved in bidding for monies for health improvement; and
- the distraction of organizational change and the transition to PCT status.

Other research into the emerging public health function in primary care organizations in the late 1990s by the UK Public Health Alliance (Taylor et al, 1998) suggested that other, more fundamental, barriers existed including:

- the lack of a 'shared language' and common understanding what constitutes public health between primary care and other stakeholders, including the community;
- poor understanding of the key principles of public health amongst primary care professionals;
- medically-dominated organizations and professional values; and
- poor collaborative working between within and between primary health care teams, GPs and other agencies.

These latter observations reveal that one of the key challenges on the agenda of PCG/Ts is how to address their growing responsibilities for delivering health improvement within a historical and cultural context of medically-led and reactive service provision to patients. To improve the health of individuals, communities and populations, primary care professionals now have to do far more than provide accessible or enhanced primary care-based services. At a basic level, primary care professionals need to 'own up' to the public health agenda and engage in what Cornish (2001) describes as 'upstream thinking' to examine the determinants of ill health rather than just treat and care for the sick. This requires primary care professionals to begin an engagement with organizations outside of health care with which they have had little experience, or inclination, to deal with before.

All primary care organizations tackling health improvement will need to develop a range of public health skills and competencies. However, according to Cornish (2001) there is a general lack of understanding of what competencies are required and how primary care organizations might develop them. This is linked to a general need to better understand the concept and definition of health improvement itself. Developing greater support for public health specialists and health promotional staff within primary care organizations is thus a critical issue (Smith et al, 2000). However, whilst the government envisaged the development of a new cadre of non-medical public health directors in PCTs, more than 80 per cent of new posts have been filled by public health doctors from old health authority public health departments (Peckham, 2003).

Partnership Working with Local Authorities

Partnership working between health and social care agencies, particularly for vulnerable groups such as the frail elderly, has been a recurring policy theme in the UK. The rationale for developing an integrated health and social care focus has been underpinned by a central belief that 'joined-up' planning, commissioning and provider functions should help to deliver changes in services that benefit users by providing a more flexible and 'seamless' pattern of care. Moreover, partnership working was also seen to have potential in improving organizational efficiency by reducing duplication of tasks, using resources more appropriately, and redistributing services more equitably across a locality.

Since the 'New NHS', a key aim has been to 'get the NHS to work in partnership by breaking down organizational barriers and forging stronger links with local authorities' (Department of Health, 1997). The White Paper stressed the need to integrate across health and social care in order to deal with those people with multiple needs that had previously been 'passed from pillar to post' between care agents and agencies. These sentiments correlated closely to other key social agendas at this time including combating social exclusion, encouraging welfare to work, and improving health in local communities (Goodwin and Shapiro, 2001).

Developing New Mechanisms for Health and Social Care Partnerships: The Policy Context

The recognition that health and social care services needed to be brought together to serve the best interests of patients has been ever present in policy documents since the functional separation of health and social care activities in 1974 (Woolley et al, 1995; Hudson and Henwood, 2002). The 'New NHS' heralded a sea-change in the nature of health and social care partnerships as agencies became obliged to sign up to new joint investment plans to ensure that services could be co-ordinated and accessible by linking services, for example, in 'one-stop shops' (Department of Health, 1998a). The pace of change quickened following the 1998 publication of 'Partnership in Action' (Department of Health, 1998b) and the subsequent Health Act 1999 (Department of Health, 1999) which provided new mechanisms to encourage health and social care agencies to co-operate more closely.

The role of different agencies in promoting joint strategic plans encompassed three centrally-driven initiatives: health improvement programmes, joint investment plans, and health action zones. A new 'statutory duty of partnership' between PCTs and local authorities followed the Health and Social Care Act 2001. As a consequence, each organization was bound to the creation of local strategic partnerships and the promotion of organizational changes in care provision (Peckham and Exworthy, 2003).

In terms of service commissioning and provision functions, 'flexibilities' contained in the Health Act 1999 allowed NHS and local authorities the opportunity to:

- pool budgets for specific services, with contributions to the 'pool' losing their original identity;
- delegate commissioning to a single lead organization; and
- integrate health and social service staff into a single organization.

The 'flexibilities' became operational in April 2000 and over 130 new partnership plans had been developed with a year, mostly in pooled commissioning budgets for mental health, adult learning disability and older people's services (Hudson et al, 2002).

The change in emphasis of NHS strategy towards a health *and* social care policy became further enshrined in 'The NHS Plan' (Department of Health, 2000). The plan emphasized the need for agencies to take up the mantle of partnership working and set out a vision in which social care staff would work alongside GPs as part of a 'single care network'. Moreover, new intermediate care facilities for older people were promoted, characterized by multi-agency needs assessment, rapid response and the development of alternatives to inpatient hospitalization (Goodwin and Peet, 2004). More radically, the NHS Plan provided a vision of new single multi-purpose legal bodies to commission and be responsible for all local health and social care. These 'care trusts' were intended to be a new level of primary care organization designed to 'remove the outdated institutional barriers between health and social services which have got in the way of people getting the care they need when they need it' (Department of Health, 2000, p. 73).

The development of PCG/Ts emerged in parallel, if not necessarily in synch, to these partnership strategies. As a consequence, the role of the primary care organization as a key player in shaping health and social care partnership arrangements has mostly been inherited from previous relationships developed between former health authorities and local authorities. On the one hand, this has provided many opportunities to develop new and local integrated services, but on the other hand the transition of responsibilities and organizational changes put at risk partnerships that had emerged before the development of PCG/Ts.

The Role of PCG/Ts in Engaging Social Services and Local Authority Agencies

PCG/Ts have always engaged social services due to their allocated representation on boards and professional executive committees respectively. The seniority of social service representation on these bodies has varied. A survey in Northern and Yorkshire and South West Regions, for example, found a near even split between director-level involvement and those where only locality or area managers were represented (Exworthy and Peckham, 1998). It was observed that the seniority of representation was associated with whether PCGs were coterminous with unitary authorities, a finding confirmed by Hudson's (1999) survey of Directors of Social Services. In the latter, more than half of social service representatives were third-tier managers with only 10 per cent having director-level representatives. As Hudson (1999) observed, seniority of representation had implications on the level of partnership between PCGs and social services. Hence, high level representation suggested a more strategic approach, potentially ideal for developing joint commissioning functions, whereas area manager representation was an approach more suited to the development of local services.

The impact of social service representation on PCG boards and PCT professional executive committees appears to have been limited at least in their early years. As the National Evaluation of PCG/Ts uncovered, agendas have remained largely primary care and medically-oriented with the contribution of social service representatives being relatively minor in comparison to GP colleagues (Regen et al, 2001). As one representative in this evaluation reported:

> Despite trying it's almost impossible to get anything social services onto the agenda ... it's very difficult for non-clinicians to be involved. I wanted to be involved in commissioning but the clinicians have taken the lead (Regen et al, 2001, p. 91).

This reflects other research that has observed positive and energetic input from social services representatives on PCG Boards and sub-groups within an overall context of being 'slightly removed' from the PCT's main business (Benaim, 2001). Nevertheless, social services representatives had begun to find it easier to get social care issues onto the agenda as internal organizational issues became resolved. For example, when asked to reflect upon personal achievements over the period September 1999-August 2000, half of those social service representatives interviewed in the National Evaluation of PCG/Ts underlined new developments in joint working but significant difficulties with personal workloads and time pressures (Regen et al, 2001). Within the National Tracker Survey of PCG/Ts in 2000, it was reported that partnership working with local authorities had yet to have any real impact on commissioning and service delivery (Coleman and Glendinning, 2001).

Developing Partnerships Between PCG/Ts and Local Authorities: The Evidence

Before the central drive to partnership working that emerged in 1997, primary care purchasing organizations in the UK such as fundholders and multifunds were primarily interested in securing services for individual patients rather than developing new forms of services that combined with social care (Audit Commission, 1996; LeGrand et al, 1998). Nevertheless, as primary care organizations grew larger in size and remit, their propensity to develop new services in partnership with social service departments increased. Total purchasing pilots, for example, often seconded social care workers onto multi-disciplinary care teams to facilitate services for older people (Myles et al, 1998; Wyke et al, 2001). Locality commissioning groups provided a different mechanism for engaging NHS and local authority organizations, but joint working other than at the strategic level was rare (Exworthy and Peckham, 1999; Hudson et al, 1999).

Since 1997, it has proven difficult for PCG/Ts to translate the political vision of integrated health and social care commissioning and provision into reality. As

Rummery and Glendinning (2000) have argued, significant obstacles to integration work against the objective, including:

- the persistence of differing professional and organizational cultures;
- the lack of alignment between organizational boundaries, and also budgets;
- differing target pressures, such as the clinical governance agenda and waiting list reduction for PCTs against the need for local authorities to demonstrate 'best value' in providing services;
- the continuing policy of charging for social care, but not health services; and
- poorly developed information management strategies and structures through which to share information.

Furthermore, organizational changes to health care institutions have often had a negative impact. For example, the number of organizations developing pooled budgets reduced after the transition to PCTs because they were keen to establish a clear locality focus and identity, leading to fragmentary pressures within existing partnership agreements (Hudson et al, 2002). Analysis of care trust development similarly reported the challenges posed in the transition since PCTs were keen to establish independence and created an unstable environment that did not help partnership developments (Glasby and Peck, 2004).

Research suggests that working in partnership with local authorities remains underdeveloped. Despite evidence of some improved partnership working on the front-line in relation to broader national priorities, such as intermediate care for older people and mental health care services, fundamental barriers to partnership working have persisted. Important issues have included incompatible boundaries, different professional values, and constant organizational change. As a result, there remains a danger that the skills and resources within social services and the wider local authority have not been fully harnessed by primary care organizations. As Hudson et al (2002) conclude, what is necessary for partnerships to flourish are organizational and professional cultures that confront fragmentation and promote holistic approaches to care. Whilst much has been achieved through the central lead on incentivizing partnership working, the process of fine-tuning relationships at a local level need to be better understood and supported.

Developing Relationships with the Local Community

The role of the local community in influencing PCG/T decision-making has become a key focus for development. In policy terms, perceived benefits include the development of a greater understanding and responsiveness to local issues; strengthening public 'ownership', contributing towards accountability, and challenging the historic paternalism of service providers (NHS Executive, 1998). As Lupton et al (1998) suggest, the policy is related to both a *democratic* approach (the need for citizens to have rights and influence) and a *consumerist* approach (the ability of users to have choice and influence).

That user and public involvement should be an integral part of PCG/T activities, engendering a continuous dialogue with local communities rather than mere lip service to them, has been a recurrent policy theme. For example, The NHS Plan (Department of Health, 2000) devoted an entire chapter to the development of community involvement in the NHS, reinforcing the lead role to be taken by PCGs and PCTs. The Plan set out a statutory duty for the NHS to involve and consult the public when planning or changing services, a policy enshrined in the Health and Social Care Act (Department of Health, 2001c). In addition, the NHS Plan set out targets related to increasing the availability of information to help empower patients, develop representation, and strengthen choice.

Developing Methods to Engage the Local Community in PCG/Ts

The literature on public and user involvement suggests a number of levels at which the community may be involved. As Charles and DeMaio (1993) discuss, this may happen at a micro-level, where patient become involved as an active partner in their own care; at a meso-level, where they are involved in the design and delivery of services; and at a macro-level, where citizens are involved in priority setting. However, involving the public directly in PCG/T decision-making was seen as a significant challenge (Smith et al, 2000; Regen et al, 2001) and indeed quite rare (Barnes and McIver, 1999).

As Elbers and Regen (2001) describe, examples of methods used to promote community involvement in PCG/T decision-making can be divided into four categories:

1. Informing or awareness raising, based on a one-way flow of information.
2. Consultation, a one-off exercise where participants give and receive feedback.
3. Participation or partnership, a two-way process expected to be ongoing and integral to the decision-making process.
4. Lay control, in which the community or individuals have decision-making authority.

In practice, most approaches employed by PCG/Ts to involve the public and service users have been conducted at the informing and consulting levels. The former process, for example, has typically included the use of newsletters, posters, the press, websites and so on to provide information and raise awareness of activities and services. Consultation methods have typically included discussions over the transition to PCT status, the development of the health improvement programme, or focus groups and surveys to canvass opinions about certain services or procedures.

Despite government policy being clear that user and public involvement activities in PCG/Ts should be participative and continuous, few examples of genuine public participation had emerged in PCG/Ts in their early years (Regen et al, 2001; Milewa et al, 2003). Indeed, in their review of public and user involvement in PCG/Ts, Elbers and Regen (2001) found but a few good examples of the process. Other research studies on user and public involvement in PCGs and PCTs were undertaken contemporaneously in the late 1990s. These show remarkably similar findings. For example, the HSMC National Evaluation of Primary Care Groups and Trusts (Smith et al, 2000; Regen et al, 2001; Elbers and Regen, 2001) reported that lay members on PCG boards had very low levels of influence on PCG decision-making. Figures from other studies showed that local community groups had been involved in 80 per cent of the PCG/Ts (Shepherd, 2000) and that 63 per cent of PCGs had set up working groups to examine public involvement (Anderson and Florin, 2000). These figures were slightly higher that the HSMC National Evaluation of PCG/Ts with figures of 67 per cent and 42 per cent respectively (Elbers and Regen, 2001). Overall, all surveys reported growing efforts to develop strategies and mechanisms for public involvement even though these efforts appear to have not been related to any attributable outcomes (Anderson and Florin, 2000; Alborz et al, 2002; Anderson et al, 2002; Bond et al, 2001; Elbers and Regen, 2001; Milewa et al, 2003; North and Peckham, 2001; Rowe and Shepherd, 2002).

Assessing Community Involvement: Facilitators and Inhibitors

The limited ability of PCGs and PCTs to engage in community involvement can be shown in the research evidence to be the result of a number of key inhibiting factors. In an analysis of user views, Elbers and Regen (2001) were able to identify several key problems:

- The limited time and resource available for lay input and for developing community participation initiatives;
- Professional attitudes within PCG/Ts leading to a lack of willingness to prioritize public and patient involvement;
- The rapid timescale of PCT implementation and the organizational development agenda;
- The lack of interest on behalf of the general public to become involved in very general issues to do with health care services; and
- Cultural and geographical diversity amongst communities making effective representation of local views to PCG/Ts difficult.

All of these factors are emphasized within other research that examined the development of community involvement in PCG/Ts. For example, Anderson and Florin's (2000) investigation of 27 PCGs found that 88 per cent of lay members were responsible for planning public involvement strategies and yet the time and resources available to them were extremely limited. Perhaps the greatest limiting factor identified was the lack of time and/or willingness of professionals within PCG/Ts to participate in the public engagement agenda. For example, Milewa et al's (2003) case study analysis of 11 PCTs found a degree of institutional unwillingness amongst many professional executive committees to encourage community involvement.

Scepticism on behalf of GPs as to the merits of community involvement in decision making is a well known and common theme (Dixon et al, 2001). Indeed, where attitudes of board members were more supportive of user views then more progress in developing community involvement systems was present (Elbers and Regen, 2001). Indeed, the presence of health action zones, healthy living centres and other local authority-based partnerships were positively associated with community involvement (Shepherd, 2000; Wilkin et al, 2001). An active community health council was also a facilitating factor in promoting participative practice (Elbers and Regen, 2001), but these have subsequently been abolished in the NHS in England. Other key factors to have facilitated user involvement included the development of dedicated public involvement officers with a specific remit (and resource) to develop community and public involvement as well as pro-active and vocal lay representation within PCG/Ts.

The Future Influence of the Local Community on PCG/T Decision Making

The Government's emerging strategy for involving the community in the work of the NHS was set out in 'Involving Patients and the Public in Health Care' (Department of Health, 2001b). The result was the controversial phased abolition of community health councils, the local health community watchdog and advisory service, to be replaced by a series of new bodies including a Patient Advice and Liaison Service (PALS) for each NHS provider organization, a Commission for Patient and Public Involvement in Health (CPPIH), and patient forums to be established in NHS trusts and PCTs as independent statutory bodies responsible for monitoring the quality and delivery of local health services.

Since April 2002, every PCT has been required to set up a patient forum drawn from patients and local residents through which consultation about services and commissioning decisions should be discussed. These forums are passive in that they inform, rather than steer, PCT decision-making. However, patient forums have also been tasked with promoting local people in consultations with PCTs and each forum makes use of representation on PCT boards through a non-executive director. The research evidence suggests that there remains a lack of public awareness to the existence of patient forums and problems with gaining membership due to the inability to directly resource participants (Taylor et al, 2004). Issues of resources, space, time and support are reflected in the history of patient participation initiatives in primary care over many years (Anderson et al, 2002). Questions have been raised as to the breadth of these new mechanisms and their ability to engage willing local people and hence whether they are truly representative to local communities (Milewa et al, 2003).

PCTs have also been tasked with establishing PALS that act as a conduit of information to individuals. A key role of PALS is to monitor trends and highlight any deficiencies in local health services which they then report to the PCT for action. PCTs are now also obliged to produce an annual prospectus for patients. At a more national level, the CPPIH was established in January 2003 to monitor the performance of patient forums and conduct reviews into how to improve the role of patients and the public in decision-making. The Commission was to report to the Secretary of State for Health on the overall performance of these arrangements but was abandoned following a review of 'arm's lengths bodies' by the Department of Health in July 2004, part of a strategy to reduce the size of the Department itself by one-third (Department of Health, 2004d).

The lack of a central body pushing for the development of patient forums, combined with research suggesting practical difficulties in their creation, casts doubts on whether such mandated attempts at improving the accountability of PCTs to local communities will result in greater influence over decision-making. Nonetheless, they provide a stronger element of compulsion for PCTs to include the public and patients as legitimate stakeholders. If community involvement strategies are to flourish, PCT managers will need to undertake assertive steps to develop links between professionals and user groups and show how the process can have a demonstrable and positive impact. Without this, centrally imposed structures for patient consultation may quickly become a bureaucratic chore that primary care organizations must address within their ever increasing range of responsibilities.

The future of local community engagement with the NHS will also be heavily influenced by two further emerging policies – patient choice and foundation hospitals (see Chapter 3 for more on these policies). The patient choice initiative has been promoted since 'Delivering the NHS Plan' (Department of Health, 2003) with the aim of allowing patients to choose any NHS or private provider by the end of 2005 (Appleby and Dixon, 2004). In theory, individuals become an active partner in their own care and play an important role in influencing how care is provided through exercising their right to choose. Foundation hospitals, enjoying independence from government control, will be held locally accountable to a Board of Governors where directly elected representatives from the local community will reside (Department of Health, 2002b). Local residents can become members of the foundation hospital securing them the right to be directly consulted as well as to vote on membership of the Board of Governors itself. In theory, such direct democratic accountability should ensure that the interests of the local community are served. Many commentators, however, have cast doubts on whether either initiative would substantially improve community participation or patient-centred care (for example, Pollock et al, 2003; Wall, 2003; Walshe, 2003). Indeed, Klein (2003, 2004) reports on how predictable apathy to foundation trusts led to 'appallingly low' turnouts in the elections of board members within the ten first wave trusts, even amongst staff. Whether either policy has a significant impact on the future influence of local communities in their local NHS remains to be seen, but it is clear that PCG/Ts will not be the only forum through which patient participation policies will be sought.

Conclusions: Lessons for Research and Practice

This chapter has shown how partnership working for health improvement has been a problematic and developmental process for PCG/Ts. In developing public health roles, new primary care organizations have struggled to find the capacity, time and skills to develop effective public health teams and have only recently developed public health directorates. Partnership working with social services and the wider local authority has not been a key priority in most PCG/Ts and has been hampered by a triumvirate of organizational, financial and cultural barriers. Similarly, the development of community participation has generally been slow to materialize.

Within each of these fields of activity a number of common problems have been encountered. First, the impact of constant organizational upheaval (and the prospect of further radical change) has been a source of turbulence making the cementing of new partnerships, or the retention of existing ones, highly problematic. Second, the enormous challenge for PCTs in taking over the functions previously performed by health authorities at the speed and pace required has led to severe capacity issues in performing key functions. As a result, most PCTs have needed to prioritize other 'core' activities to the detriment of partnership activities. Third, the evidence suggests that health care professionals leading PCG/Ts, influenced heavily by a range of government-imposed targets, remain primarily engrossed with the efficient development of a treatment-oriented service rather than one based on the wider promotion of health and wellbeing to local populations. Professional and cultural barriers need to be broken down if the functions of public health, partnerships with social care agencies, and community participation are to be advanced.

Despite these issues, it is clear that new primary care organizations in England have made steady progress in developing new approaches to health and social care provision and in promoting community involvement. The key management task within PCTs will be to break down remaining barriers to partnership working which is likely to be helped through the establishment of protected time to facilitate these activities and, more importantly, by the creation of legitimacy for these new partnerships by showing how they may make a positive difference. The role of central government may be a catalyst to the process through the creation and imposition of new mechanisms aimed at facilitating partnerships.

Lessons for Research

- To help PCTs better understand how to engage with professional and develop new partnerships, research needs to focus on the dynamics of professional relationships.
- The outcomes for patients and staff of public health focused and partnership-based PCT activities need to be addressed to establish the costs and benefits of such approaches on staff and patients.
- Research should also attempt to contribute to the development of the competencies for public health staff, and to professionals working in posts

across institutions.
- Assessment should be made of the impact and effectiveness of patient forums and other forms of community engagement to establish progress and derive lessons for PCTs and policy makers on how best to take forward this agenda.

Lessons for Practice

- PCTs need to make a priority of the public health agenda and work with partner agencies and social care professionals to avoid an over-medicalized approach to care.
- PCTs need to work to break down cultural barriers that exist to fulfilling the public health agenda. This might best be achieved through the marketing of best practice and highlighting examples that have 'made a difference' to the lives of patients. Primary care professionals would be wise to 'own up' and engage with this agenda.
- Investment in support and training is required to develop public health skills, roles and competencies.
- For partnerships with local authority and other agencies to develop, PCTs need to identify and address professional and organizational fragmentations and promote holistic approaches to care.
- Senior representation on PCT professional executive committees would facilitate better strategic alliances on such issues as joint commissioning.
- Government targets for PCTs have tended to make priorities of other agendas leading to under-investment in the skills and time required for the public health and partnership agendas to flourish. Central expectations and targets for PCTs need to be revisited to help PCTs focus and prioritize on these core functions of their activity.
- For community involvement strategies to flourish, PCTs need to develop active links between professionals and patient groups and support the establishment and development of patient forums.

Chapter 10

Developing and Improving Primary Care

Primary care development was specified as a core function of PCG/Ts (NHS Executive, 1998a) and research evidence from the UK (Wilkin et al, 2000; Smith et al, 2000; Mays et al, 2001; Wilkin et al, 2002) and internationally (Malcolm et al, 1999) highlights the strong tendency of PCOs to focus on practice-based primary care development. Attention is typically focused on investment in primary care infrastructure, the development of local core standards for services provided by practices, the financial and quality management of prescribing, and the development of new and extended services within primary and intermediate care.

This chapter sets out an exploration of the progress made by PCG/Ts in developing and improving the range and quality of primary care services, with a focus on distilling the management and research lessons about the factors that facilitate or inhibit such progress. Topics explored include primary care development in practices, the management of prescribing by PCG/Ts, and the implementation of clinical governance in primary care.

Primary Care Development in Practices

In their first year of operation (1999-2000) PCGs focused primarily on gathering basic data from practices in order to inform primary care investment and clinical governance plans (Smith et al, 2000). This process was in itself relatively radical, for much practice level data had previously been considered almost 'commercial in confidence'. Reducing inequity in service provision across practices via the 'levelling-up' of services was a prime objective, and several of the groups were in the process of reviewing former GP fundholder services as part of this activity. The main areas for investment identified by PCGs included: information management and technology; prescribing support to practices; primary care staffing; practice premises and surgery developments; and training and development of staff (Smith et al, 2000).

By 2000, research undertaken by HSMC's national evaluation identified that progress had been made by PCGs in a number of key areas:

- primary care infrastructure;
- information management and technology;
- primary care staffing;
- practice premises and surgery developments;

- training and development;
- the development of practice-based services;
- chronic disease management;
- initiatives to promote alternative primary care provision; and
- the use of incentives.

Primary Care Infrastructure

Approximately half of the PCG/Ts within the study had established sub-groups to oversee primary care development activities. In addition, five of the twelve PCG/Ts in the evaluation had established separate panels to make decisions about the allocation of general medical services (GMS) monies for primary care investment. What this demonstrated was the determination of PCG/Ts to focus on the development of primary care at a practice level, seeking to address variation in the level and quality of services provided to patients, and to find new forms of service provision within and across local practices. Despite significant constraints in terms of resources for management support, PCG/Ts made sure that they could sustain all-important yet basic work in improving local primary care.

Following the implementation of 'Shifting the Balance of Power' in 2002 (Department of Health, 2001a), and the associated expansion in the responsibilities of PCTs, many PCTs established primary care directorates incorporating primary care development for practices, prescribing support, primary care nursing advice, premises development, and the management of contracts with GPs, dentists, pharmacists and optometrists. In this way, primary care infrastructure continued to be a core focus of PCTs, albeit as one function amongst a growing portfolio of tasks.

Information Management and Technology (IM&T)

Research shows that IM&T development was an important and yet challenging priority for PCG/Ts (Audit Commission, 2000, Wilkin et al, 2000). Mapping exercises carried out by PCG/Ts revealed a great deal of variation in terms of the level of computerization in practices, the clinical systems in use and the actual use of IM&T within general practice. As a result, and with the aim of producing greater standardization, most of the groups within the study invested significantly in practice information technology development during the period September 1999-August 2000. Having invested in upgrading practice IT systems, most of the groups within the study highlighted the importance of providing IT training to GPs and practice staff in order to ensure the effective use of systems.

The area of information management within primary care had, in 2001, generally received less attention than issues relating to IT infrastructure and communication. However, several groups had made some progress and this is discussed later in this chapter in the context of clinical governance. Over the period 2002-2004, PCTs were required to develop and implement local information management strategies as part of the Department of Health's wider 'Information for Health' initiative aimed at ensuring local health care professionals would be at the centre of the decision-making process (NHS Executive, 1998c). In practice, this work has built on the earlier IM&T infrastructure work carried out by PCG/Ts, but became much more focused on issues deemed to be of national strategic importance, including the development of electronic patient records and systems that can be integrated across practices and hospitals.

Primary Care Staffing

In most of the groups within the HSMC study, mapping exercises conducted in 1999 to inform initial primary care investment plans revealed inequities in the distribution of staff within practices, including practice nurses, administrative and clerical staff. In this context, in 2000, just over one-third of the groups had strategies to increase levels of resources available for practice staffing through the distribution of growth monies allocated to health authorities. Practices below the PCG average were given priority in bids for additional staffing and several groups had produced criteria to assist this decision making process (Regen et al, 2001).

Box 10.1 Practice staffing initiative in Harrow East and Kingsbury PCG

Within Harrow East and Kingsbury PCG, the levelling up of practices was addressed following agreement from practices regarding a new system for the allocation of funds. Additional funds were targeted at practices with low levels of resources and practices were assisted in devising and implementing development plans that were intended to result in the employment of additional staff. They were also supported in ensuring an appropriate skill mix, which was planned to enhance service provision in line with local health improvement objectives. The PCG developed a scoring system for investment in practice staffing based upon the following criteria:

- existing staff budget per head of practice population
- practice opening hours
- existing skill mix in nursing and management/administration

In order to qualify for consideration for additional resources, practices were required to do the following:

- submit a practice business plan that identified development areas relating to the Health Improvement Plan and clinical governance
- plan an appropriate skill mix of clinical and administrative staff
- give a commitment to fund 25% of staff costs
- demonstrate financial accountability
- agree to appropriate staff training and development

Source: Regen et al (2001), p. 33.

In addition to addressing inequities in the provision of practice staff, most groups within the study had gathered information to underpin future workforce planning. Age profiles of GPs, practice nurses, practice managers and community nurses were being compiled on databases in order that potential recruitment issues could be addressed in a proactive manner. In terms of the medical workforce, almost half of the groups had identified potential problems stemming from forthcoming GP retirements. In order to address these areas of need, some PCG/Ts were considering the use of flexible local contracts for new forms of primary care services using the personal medical services (PMS) pilot scheme (Regen et al, 2001) – see Chapter 8 for more details. In terms of nursing services, several groups had undertaken reviews of practice nursing across the PCG/T. In some cases, these had revealed significant variation in the distribution, roles and skills of practice nurses. What this shows is that PCG/Ts adopted workforce planning and analysis techniques as an early priority, collecting what might be seen as very basic demographic data from practices and using these data as the basis for PCT action plans. An example of one PCG's approach to practice staffing is set out in Box 10.1 above.

Practice Premises and Surgery Developments

An early priority for many PCG/Ts was to undertake an audit of access to, and within, GP practices as the basis for investment and development programmes within them (Smith et al, 2000; Wilkin et al, 2000). Such audits were typically being carried out as part of the PCG/T's work to meet the requirements of the Disability Discrimination Act 1995 (Secretary of State for Health, 1995). In addition to issues of access, most PCG/Ts had attempted to identify practices failing to meet the national Department of Health minimum standards with regard to premises and, where appropriate, had worked with them in developing improvement plans. Research revealed an emphasis upon bringing practices up to minimum standards with investment targeted upon 'sub-standard' provision (Smith et al, 2000). With effect from 2003, many PCTs have been using the provisions of the NHS Local Improvement Finance Trust (LIFT) programme as the primary vehicle for pushing forward capital plans and developments involving primary care and community health premises. LIFT is a form of public-private partnership whereby the NHS enters into a formal partnership with a private company to develop specific local primary care premises developments such as the rebuilding of practices, and the development of new polyclinics, health parks, and community health centres (Department of Health, 2000).

Training and Development of Staff

HSMC's interim PCG/T evaluation report (Smith et al, 2000) found that an analysis of the training and development needs of primary care staff had formed an important part of the process of devising primary care investment plans for all practices. One year on in 2001, research revealed that the majority of groups had produced training and development plans for primary care staff and in some cases, these were beginning to be implemented. It is important to note that such plans were being developed in the context of PCG/T clinical governance activity. With regard to GP training, most groups within the study initially focused on arranging a series of seminars or education events for GPs. These were typically linked to local health improvement programmes and clinical governance priorities such as coronary heart disease, diabetes, or asthma management and took place on a monthly or bi-monthly basis. Evidence from a survey of all GPs in the twelve HSMC case study PCG/Ts in 2000 revealed that over 60 per cent of GPs 'always' or 'sometimes' attended such events (Regen et al, 2001). Such high levels of attendance illustrate a clear commitment to the primary care development/clinical governance agenda on the part of GPs.

Box 10.2 Practice staff development programme in Carlisle and District PCG

> PCGs in the North Cumbria area had access to a dedicated PCG training manager as a result of a new post funded via regional Non Medical Education and Training resources. The training manager set up a management competency-based programme for practice managers, based upon the Phoenix Agenda (NHS Confederation, 1999). There were trained facilitators in each PCG to observe practice managers in relation to the achievement of competencies. In 2000, sixteen managers had undertaken the programme, and all were given feedback on their individual development. Practice managers were reported to have identified a need for an administrative competency programme in the following year.

Source: Regen et al (2001), p. 34.

The majority of groups within the HSMC study had examined or had plans to examine the training needs of practice nurses. As a first step, several groups had supported the development of practice nurse forums and some had been able to fund the backfilling of practice nurse time in order to facilitate attendance. Practice nurse forums were playing a key role in the production of training plans for practice nurses based upon core competencies and professional development issues for staff. The research revealed that the training needs of practice nurses included increased access to clinical supervision and preparation for new responsibilities with regard to the clinical priorities of the PCG/T, for example chronic disease management in the areas of coronary heart disease and diabetes. The training needs of non-clinical primary care staff were also being addressed by most groups within the study. The establishment of practice managers' groups, typically meeting on a monthly basis in order to promote networking and information sharing and to identify and meet training needs, was a feature of most of the case study sites (a practical example is set out in Box 10.2).

The Development of Practice-Based Services

All of the forty GP commissioning groups in the HSMC study in 1999 had carried out a stock take of practice-based services as a basis for deciding on future practice investment and development (Regen et al, 1999). These stock takes typically resulted in the development of new locally-based services for groups of practices, such as phlebotomy, physiotherapy or dietetics, and in specific practice investments to enable the provision of practice nursing, management and community pharmacy support in practices that had previously operated with little other than GP input. This again demonstrates the degree of importance attached by PCG/Ts to the area of primary care development, deploying scarce management resources in focused practice audit and planning activity. In contrast to the relatively slow start and lack of progress made by many PCG/Ts in their commissioning activity (see Chapter 11), primary care development was approached as an immediate and core priority. This is not surprising since PCGs had boards that comprised a majority of GPs who would be expected to view practice service development as a priority, and the early PCTs similarly had a clear clinical and practice focus to much of their development work.

Sustaining a strategic and practical focus on the development of practice-based services has been more of a challenge for PCTs post-2002 and the implementation of the policy of 'Shifting the Balance of Power' (Department of Health, 2001a). This is because wider responsibilities and the complexity and political importance of the targets to which PCTs became expected to work shifted the emphasis of priorities away from primary care development issues towards wider public health and service development objectives. The implementation of the new General Medical Services (GMS) contract in general practices in 2004 has however given a new impetus to the area of practice-based service development, entailing the specification of services provided by practices, within a Quality and Outcomes Framework that seeks to link financial incentives with the achievement of service quality indicators (see Chapter 8).

Chronic Disease Management

Apart from the extension of some practice-based services, the other main development within practices following the introduction of PCG/Ts was the establishment of new services and standards in relation to chronic disease management, most typically coronary heart disease, stroke and diabetes. Driven by clinical governance objectives and given further impetus by the publication of National Service Frameworks (NSFs) these health improvement activities were reported by almost two-thirds of the groups in the HSMC study (Regen et al, 2001). While chronic disease management services were being delivered in individual practices, PCG/Ts played a central role in the setting of standards and the monitoring of performance in this area, again demonstrating a new degree of management of primary care practitioners and their staff by the wider health system.

This early focus by PCG/Ts on improving the management of chronic disease within practices paved the way for PCTs to implement the new General Medical Services contract in primary care in 2004. Without the earlier analysis of services and staffing and the development of practice-based chronic disease management carried out by PCG/Ts, implementation of the new contract, with its focus on local negotiation of levels and quality of practice-based services, would have been much more problematic.

Chronic disease management is an area of increasing importance with NHS national plans. A whole chapter of the NHS Improvement Plan (Department of Health, 2004b) is devoted to the topic, and new policy guidance on long-term conditions, as this area of health care is increasingly described, was published in January 2005 (Department of Health, 2005), a reflection of the emerging policy focus on the need for PCTs to commission new and more sophisticated forms of care and support for people living with chronic disease. Analysis of the activity in acute hospitals attributable to chronic disease has been powerful in highlighting why PCTs need to focus on chronic disease management beyond primary care (indeed, across the whole spectrum of care) for evidence suggests that 5 per cent of hospital inpatients account for 42 per cent of overall inpatient days, namely those with complex and multiple health needs (Ham et al, 2003). There is every reason to expect that chronic disease management will increasingly form a core part of the commissioning activity of PCTs, moving out of the specific domain of practice-based care into the mainstream arena of service design and procurement.

The Department of Health has further emphasized its desire for a stronger management and policy focus on the care of people living with long-term conditions by means of the implementation of two pilot programmes of integrated models of care management, drawn from the experience of managed care in the USA. The first of these programmes is Evercare, a care management programme that seeks to improve the care of vulnerable older people by means of using specially trained nurses to identify, monitor and review the treatment of older people deemed to be at risk of hospital admission or other emergency episodes (Evercare, 2003). There are ten Evercare pilots in the NHS in England and they are subject to evaluation by the National Primary Care Research and Development Centre at the University of Manchester. Early claims have been made by the provider organization for significant reductions in hospital admissions for older people within Evercare programmes (Evercare, 2004) but health services researchers have urged caution as to the effectiveness of such approaches, suggesting that further evidence is required by means of high quality studies before such conclusions can be drawn (Hutt et al, 2004). The second tranche of pilots focusing on the care of people with long-term conditions are those known as Kaiser programmes, these eight pilots being intended to replicate the following:

> Kaiser (a US non-profit health care organization) is committed to a whole system approach to healthcare in which primary and secondary care are closely integrated…there are close links between GPs and hospitals and specialists, supported by electronic health records. Patient self-education is a priority, especially in Kaiser's approach to the management of chronic disease. Significant features of Kaiser hospitals are the relatively short lengths of stay, careful care planning and quite aggressive approach to discharging patients (Department of Health, 2004f, p. 17).

Patient management approaches such as Evercare and Kaiser will inevitably involve GPs, community nurses and others within primary care practices in the planning and commissioning of packages of care for individual patients within defined client/ chronic disease groups. As the English NHS introduces a new form of practice-based commissioning with effect from April 2005 (Department of Health, 2004a), it is these new practice-based commissioners (groups of GPs and their teams) who will in many instances take on the budgets for providing care for people with long-term conditions. In so doing, it can be expected that these commissioners will use managed care models as routes for providing such care, hoping to reduce hospital costs and thus release resources for reinvestment in intensive home and community support services. Hence, understanding and utilizing methods of chronic disease management will be a vital primary care development need for PCTs and practice-based commissioners to learn and employ in the future.

Initiatives to Promote Alternative Primary Care Provision

Research carried out in PCG/Ts revealed that many were participating in initiatives aimed at establishing new forms of primary care provision (Regen et al, 2001; Wilkin et al, 2001). For example, PCG/Ts were involved in the development of bids for NHS Walk-In Centres, and Healthy Living Centres and others were participating in the Department of Health's Primary Care Collaborative Programme aimed at improving access and service quality in primary care. The involvement of PCG/Ts in these initiatives was an early sign of primary care organizations becoming engaged in their role as planners and commissioners of primary care, a role that is now enshrined in statute for PCTs who, since 2002, hold and manage the contracts of local GPs, dentists, pharmacists and optometrists. The PCT's role in commissioning primary care gained further momentum following the introduction of the new General Medical Services Contract in 2004, for as noted earlier, this requires PCTs to work with practices to specify the range, level and quality of primary care services to be provided in return for payments fixed by a national tariff.

PCTs do not only commission primary care services from practices. In line with Department of Health policy to encourage greater patient choice and diversity of provision (Department of Health, 2003), PCTs are increasingly entering into contractual arrangements with private and voluntary sector providers of primary and community services as part of their overall strategy for commissioning primary care. Indeed, the policy of Patient Choice requires PCTs in England to ensure that every patient is offered a choice of at least five hospital providers by December 2005, with one of these providers being from the private or voluntary sector (Department of Health, 2004e). A further example of this desire to encourage greater plurality of NHS provision is in the area of out-of-hours care, where PCTs are turning to private companies and GP-owned co-operatives to provide services. Similarly, it is anticipated that PCTs will use private and not-for-profit third sector providers of chronic disease management services to design and provide care for specific client groups, these providers filling gaps in service provision where the NHS lacks the capacity, experience or initiative to operate (Department of Health, 2004b).

The Use of Incentives

The progress made by PCG/Ts in developing primary care in practices, and in improving the management of prescribing and implementing clinical governance as reported below, has been underpinned by an approach to the management of change that is firmly based on the use of financial (and other) incentives. For example, the achievement of PCG/T practice development targets related to coronary heart disease, diabetes, and prescribing have typically been supported by local incentive schemes where the attainment of certain targets attracts a financial payment to a specific GP practice. Clinical governance and training and development activities have frequently been supported by non-financial incentives such as the provision of locum and other staff 'backfill' support during PCG/T training workshops, and the offering of staff training and support in return for GP involvement in clinical governance activities. The importance for PCOs of aligning incentives with local objectives for change in primary care and other services is well documented in the research literature (LeGrand et al, 1998; Dudley et al, 1998; Dowling, 2000; Kralewski et al, 2000; Croxson et al, 2001; Spooner et al, 2001; Propper et al, 2002). This evidence demonstrates that GPs can be motivated to improve service quality and make better use of resources, given the appropriate application of incentives (Smith et al, 2004).

Primary Care Development – Summary

Research demonstrates that newly formed primary care organizations focus on achieving improvements in practice infrastructure and the development of new services within primary care. With regard to practice developments, research in NHS PCOs highlights a strong emphasis upon the pursuit of equitable provision and achieving conformity by practices to minimum standards using a range of financial and other incentives. PCOs clearly represent an important vehicle through which health systems can take stock of the level and quality of primary care provision as well as using the professional networks that underpin such organizations as a mechanism for bringing about changes to existing services and the development of new provision. The existence of a strategic framework through which to address issues of equity and quality, combined with sensitivity to individual circumstances, and the application of appropriate incentives, appears to have produced real changes in the range of primary care services available. What is however lacking in the wider literature is evidence about the quality of such expanded and new services, and the degree to which they attract greater patient satisfaction or otherwise (Smith et al, 2004).

The Management and Development of Prescribing

The management of quality and cost-effective prescribing has been an important objective for primary care organizations in the NHS and other health care systems throughout the 1990s and the early years of the 21st century, given its significance in terms of proportion of overall PCO budgets (Malcolm et al, 1999; Dowling and Glendinning, 2003). In the 1990s, GP fundholders held a cash-limited budget for prescribing, as did GPs in the GP commissioning pilot projects established in 1998. Research evidence on fundholding (Dixon and Glennerster, 1995; Coulter, 1995) and GP commissioning (Regen et al, 1999; McLeod et al, 2000) supports the view that primary care organizations can develop their practices to become more cost-effective prescribers, typically through increasing usage of generic (as opposed to brand name) drugs and reducing the incidence of repeat prescribing. There is however some debate in the literature as to whether such savings on practice-level drugs budgets are sustainable beyond the first year or two (Stewart-Brown et al, 1995; Audit Commission 1996; Goodwin 1998). As is described in the analysis of PCG/T experience below, approaches to the management of prescribing that have been based on locality or wider organizational approaches appear to have had a greater degree of success in bringing about demonstrable improvements in the quality of prescribing, typically by use of peer review and group incentives. Overall, it appears from the evidence that PCOs in the 1990s initially attempted to manage prescribing expenditure by introducing strategies to limit the prescribing costs of their practices, turning their attention to prescribing quality issues in subsequent years (Regen et al, 2001).

In a similar vein, PCG/Ts have continued to focus on prescribing as an important financial and service quality issue. Research reveals that PCG/Ts have used a range of initiatives when seeking to manage and develop prescribing performance at a practice level (Smith et al, 2000; McLeod et al, 2000; Regen et al, 2001; McLeod, 2001). A summary of the prescribing initiatives put in place by the 12 PCG/Ts in the HSMC national evaluation study is set out in Table 10.1 below.

Table 10.1 reveals that in 2000-2001 the sharing of prescribing data among GPs continued to be viewed as an important prescribing management strategy. Incentive schemes were being used by all PCG/Ts in the HSMC study who responded to a survey of PCG prescribing advisers, indicators for prescribing had been applied in eleven of the groups, and all bar two of the case study PCG/Ts were using pharmacists to review prescribing patterns. HSMC's analysis of the prescribing activity of the 12 case study PCG/Ts in 1998-1999 and 1999-2000 revealed that groups' performance varied considerably across a range of prescribing indicators. Four of the case study PCG/Ts (A, D, E and G) stood out as having performed comparatively well in terms of limiting the overall growth of prescribing costs in both 1998-1999 and 1999-2000. These case studies experienced a significantly smaller increase in weighted prescribing cost than that predicted on the basis of the experience of other practices in the host health authority areas. A summary of the weighted prescribing cost in 1998-1999 and 1999-2000 for the case study PCG/Ts and comparators is set out in

Towards Managed Primary Care

Table 10.2. When considering the performance of the case study PCG/Ts in relation to non-financial prescribing indicators, HSMC's research revealed that experience had been mixed (see Table 10.3). Only two of the best performing case studies in terms of non-financial indicators were also those that experienced a significantly lower than predicted level of total weighted cost in 1999-2000.

Table 10.1 Case study PCGs' prescribing initiatives in 1999-2000*

Initiative	Case study PCG												Total
	A	B	C	D	E	F	G	H	I	J	K	L	
Share prescribing data. N = named, A = anonymous	✓ N	✓ A	✓ A	✓ N	✓ N	✓ N	✓ A	✓ A	✓ N	✓ N	✓ A	✓ A	12
Use an incentive scheme	✓	✓	✓	✓	✓	✓	✓	✓	✓	✓	✓	✓	12
Use prescribing indicators to measure performance	✓	✓	✓	✓	-	✓	✓	✓	✓	✓	✓	✓	11
Use pharmacists to review practice prescribing patterns	✓	✓	✓	✓	✓	✓	✓	-	✓	✓	-	✓	10
Develop a local formulary	✓	✓	✓	-	✓	-	-	✓	✓	-	✓	-	7
To control the shifting of drug costs from secondary care	-	-	✓	-	✓	-	✓	✓	✓	-	-	✓	6
Establish special arrangements for nurse prescribing	-	✓	✓	-	✓	-	✓	✓	-	-	✓	-	6

* Data derived from postal questionnaire to PCG prescribing advisors with non-respondents followed up by telephone in the HSMC National Evaluation of PCG/Ts.

Source: Regen et al (2001), p. 36.

Table 10.2 All prescribing: weighted cost in 1998-1999 and 1999-2000 for case study PCGs and comparators

| | Net ingredient cost per ASTRO(97)PU (£) | | | | | | | | |
| | Case study PCG | | | Comparator | | | % difference between case study and comparator | Case study PCG | |
Case study PCG	1998-1999	1999-2000	% change	1998-1999	1999-2000	% change		Predicted value for 1999/00	Difference actual and predicted value
A	22.19	24.17	8.9	20.48	23.01	12.3	-3.4	24.79	0.63*
B	19.25	21.83	13.4	20.22	22.81	12.8	0.6	21.82	-0.002
C	19.38	21.26	9.7	19.11	21.01	10.0	-0.3	21.28	0.02
D	21.72	23.85	9.8	20.99	23.32	11.1	-1.3	24.29	0.45*
E	19.03	21.13	11.0	19.66	22.11	12.5	-1.5	21.48	0.35*
F	21.45	24.88	16.0	22.35	25.52	14.2	1.8	24.62	-0.26*
G	19.71	21.49	9.0	19.56	21.66	10.8	-1.8	21.96	0.47*
H	19.99	22.86	14.4	18.50	21.07	13.9	0.5	22.71	-0.16
I	24.44	27.01	10.5	25.29	27.90	10.3	0.2	27.03	0.02
J	23.29	24.91	7.0	22.43	25.22	12.4	-5.4	26.28	1.37*
K	21.44	24.22	12.9	22.61	25.04	10.8	2.1	24.05	-0.17

* $p < 0.05$. A significant positive difference between actual and predicted values in 1999/00, on the basis of the case studies' experience in 1998/99 and the experience of all other practices in the host health authority in 1998/99 and 1999/00, indicates a comparatively advantageous outcome for the case study PCGs. This occurred for five PCGs: A, D, E, G and J. One case-study PCG was omitted from the analysis because its population changed greatly on becoming a PCG. See McLeod (2001) for information about the analysis.

Source: Regen et al (2001), p. 37.

Qualitative research carried out as part of HSMC's evaluation of PCG/T prescribing performance, in particular data gathered in interviews with PCG/T chairs, pharmaceutical advisers and other board members, highlights the fact that relatively successful case studies were notable for having proactive pharmaceutical advisors. The availability of such prescribing expertise, in conjunction with committed and effective GP leadership, was reported as crucial. Similarly, a 'hands on' approach to using practice-based pharmacists was viewed as an important facilitator of change in prescribing behaviour, providing that such an approach was based on mutual trust and respect between GPs and pharmacists (Regen et al, 2001). A further lever for change in prescribing behaviour was the sharing of prescribing activity data,

Towards Managed Primary Care

a particularly effective approach when accompanied by communication from the PCG/T about good practice in prescribing, and the establishment of robust and respectful systems of peer review among local GPs. This analysis supports the conclusions of a recent analysis of primary care organization governance (Sheaff, 2004), namely that prescribing and clinical governance activities work best where they are managed across practices through peer support arrangements and the sharing and agreeing of protocols. Prescribing activity has thus been fundamentally more 'managed' across localities in PCG/Ts than it ever was in individual fundholder-based incentive systems where performance was found to be variable (Goodwin, 1998). This suggests that peer support networks based on quality/cost discussions do rather better in standardizing and controlling drug budgets and drug use than rather blunt and unmanaged financial incentives.

Table 10.3 Non-monetary prescribing indicators: summary of case study performance in 1999-2000

	Case study PCGs										
Prescribing indicators	A	B	C	D	E	F	G	H	I	J	K
Benzodiazepines (weighted DDD)	✓	-	-	✓	-	✓	✓	✗	✗	-	✓
Inhaled corticosteroids (weighted DDD)	-	✗	✗	✗	✗	✓	✗	-	-	-	✓
Antibacterials (weighted items)	✓	-	✗	✗	✓	✓	✓	-	✓	✓	-
Ulcer healing drugs (weighted DDD)	✓	✓	-	✓	✗	-	✓	-	✓	-	✗
Oral NSAIDS (weighted DDD)	✓	✗	-	-	✗	-	-	✓	-	✓	-
Hormone replacement therapy (DDD per patient)	✗	-	✗	-	✗	✗	-	✓	✓	✗	✓

DDD: Defined daily dose, NSAIDS: non-steroidal anti-inflammatory drugs.
Performance in 1999/00: ✓ significantly better than; ✗ significantly worse than; - not significantly different from that predicted on the basis of the case studies' experience in 1998/99 and the experience of all other practices in the host health authority in 1998/99 and 1999/00. One case study PCG was omitted from the analysis because its population changed greatly on becoming a PCG. See McLeod (2001) for information about the analysis.

Source: Regen et al (2001), p. 37.

The Management of Prescribing – Summary

At the conclusion of the HSMC PCG/T study, board members in the case study groups were asked what they saw to be the key areas of prescribing management that would require attention within PCTs. The most commonly expressed concerns in this regard were the need for more equitable budget setting processes at a practice level, and the importance of improving the interface between primary and secondary care prescribing (Regen et al, 2001). The variation in prescribing performance as revealed by the application of indicators within the HSMC study suggests that there is further potential for PCG/Ts to improve prescribing behaviour. It should however be pointed out that respondents in the research expressed concern about the considerable cost associated with continuing to try and improve quality within prescribing, especially in relation to implementing many of the recommendations of the National Institute for Clinical Excellence (NICE) – the body that issues guidance to the NHS about the use of drug therapies and other health care interventions). As Goodwin (2002) reveals, far from being a body that rations drug use across the NHS, NICE has actually raised the overall cost burden to the NHS rather than reduced it.

What is clear, however, is that prescribing, like primary care development within practices, has been an area in which NHS primary care organizations have achieved real and demonstrable change. It has been the ability of PCOs to harness GP and other clinical expertise and enthusiasm that has presented a new opportunity to develop prescribing practice according to agreed PCO-wide standards. This degree of professional scrutiny and challenge, whereby individual GPs and practices have been willing to subject their personal clinical practice to detailed review by peers, has been a notable achievement on the part of PCG/Ts and their predecessor PCOs. Whilst it is easy to always look for what has not yet been achieved, in the area of prescribing, as with practice primary care development, significant strides have been made in just a few years, strides that would not have been possible without the structures, focus and support of PCG/Ts.

The Development of Clinical Governance

A third and important strand of primary care development activity within PCG/Ts has been the implementation of clinical governance in NHS primary care. Clinical governance was introduced into the English health system as part of the incoming Labour government's overall health service reforms focused on improving quality within a stronger national framework. The concept of clinical governance was initially announced in the NHS White Paper the 'New NHS. Modern. Dependable' of 1997 (Department of Health, 1997a) and further clarified in guidance in 1998, 'A First Class Service: Quality in the New NHS' (Department of Health, 1998a). In this latter guidance, clinical governance was defined as being: 'a framework through which NHS organizations are accountable for continually improving the quality of their services, and safeguarding high standards of care by creating an environment in which excellence in clinical care will flourish' (Department of Health, 1998a, p. 33).

For English PCTs, the duty to implement clinical governance requires that the following are in place:

- arrangements for agreeing clear standards and responsibilities;
- a system of multidisciplinary clinical audit and follow-up;
- a programme of work aimed at improving the quality of clinical data;
- a clinical management strategy that supports evidence-based practice and the implementation of national guidelines;
- arrangements for the dissemination of good practice;
- a system for dealing with poor clinical practice;
- management systems that ensure that adverse events are investigated and lessons applied; and
- programmes to reduce clinical risk (Audit Commission, 2000).

HSMC's interim report on the development of PCGs (Smith et al, 2000) found that groups had made steady progress in terms of the implementation of clinical governance in line with national guidance (NHS Executive, 1999). Initial activities had focused on logistical and organizational issues such as appointing clinical governance leads at PCG and practice level, establishing sub-groups and carrying out baseline assessments. These findings are confirmed by other published research in the area (Audit Commission, 2000; Preston and Baker, 2000; Wilkin et al, 2000). Research covering the period April-September 1999 identified examples of quality improvement work in the form of standard setting and audit (Smith et al, 2000). Such developments were generally focused upon local health improvement priorities such as coronary heart disease, and half of the groups within the study reported that their clinical governance assessment activity and implementation strategies comprised an integrated work programme covering clinical governance and health improvement (Smith et al, 2000).

Establishing an Infrastructure for Clinical Governance

In establishing a clinical governance infrastructure within primary care, PCG/Ts typically set up a sub-group to focus on the implementation and oversight of clinical governance, with this usually being a formal sub-committee of the PEC and/or the PCT board (Wilkin et al, 2002; Regen et al, 2001). The lead for clinical governance was in most cases a medically qualified clinician, although there were often nurse clinical governance leads working in partnership with medical colleagues. The extent to which groups have drawn lay and social services colleagues into clinical governance sub-groups alongside clinical colleagues is clearly variable, although where lay members were engaged in such work, it was seen as a positive development by stakeholders (Regen et al, 2001). One of the main issues identified in HSMC's interim PCG/T evaluation report (Smith et al, 2000) was the lack of dedicated staff available to PCGs to undertake clinical governance work. Subsequent research highlighted progress in this area with just over half of HSMC's case study groups having appointed clinical governance support staff (Regen et al, 2001). There is clearly no room for complacency however. Research published by Sweeney and colleagues in 2002 described some clinical governance leads as feeling 'beleaguered' without adequate support (Sweeney et al, 2002). What is clear from the available evidence (Wilkin et al, 2002) is that most PCG/Ts came to view clinical governance as a core area of activity, requiring specific targeted management and clinical input and time, although some PCTs had struggled to put that support in place to the satisfaction of the clinicians leading this area of work.

Agreeing Clear Standards and Responsibilities

As part of the process of agreeing clear PCG/T-wide standards and responsibilities for clinical governance, PCG/Ts carried out initial baseline assessments of practices and other PCG/T services covering capacity and capability in relation to quality. Data gathered, usually by means of questionnaires and practice visits, included:

• Access to and availability of services
• Chronic disease management, usually with particular reference to health improvement and national service framework priorities
• Education and training
• Risk management

The majority of groups within HSMC's study shared clinical data gathered as part of baseline assessments and had plotted the performance of each practice in relation to the group average (Regen et al, 2001). In most cases, these data were still being shared anonymously. While the main purpose of the baseline assessment was to identify weaknesses in relation to quality and to inform the clinical governance action plan, it was also seen as a mechanism for highlighting and sharing good practice (Walshe, 1999; NHS Executive, 1999).

Initiatives for Quality Improvement

PCG/Ts within the HSMC study developed a range of strategies for quality improvement within general practices, including plans for improving data quality, audit projects linked to new standards for practice-based services, the development of clinical guidelines, and proposals for new forms of education and training. These initiatives were found to be very much focused on national and local priorities for health improvement, with examples of quality improvement being located in areas such as coronary heart disease, stroke, diabetes, mental health, asthma, and immunizations and vaccinations. Indeed, all groups were carrying out quality improvement work related to coronary heart disease, reflecting the national emphasis being placed on this area. This focus on core health priorities was striking in its difference from what was found in studies of PCOs prior to 1997, when for example, a national mapping of PCOs noted that a key challenge facing new PCGs to be launched in 1999 was to develop greater consistency in the clinical areas addressed by groups, and in particular making sure that 'thorny' issues such as mental health, emergency admissions and continuing care received appropriate attention (Smith et al, 1998).

In some PCG/Ts, an organization-wide approach to clinical governance was developed. For example, some adopted the East Kent Primary Care Clinical Effectiveness (PRICCE) approach whereby up-front investment was made by the PCG/T in practices taking part in a three-year programme of evidence-based standard-setting, service development, staff training, and administrative/IT development. It should be noted that the one key area of difficulty faced by most groups in the HSMC study in relation to developing quality initiatives was that of information management and data collection. It was clear that further investment in IT systems, training, incentives and support at a practice level would be needed if practical clinical governance initiatives were to be taken to the next level of development.

Audit

Audit projects within PCG/Ts were likewise typically linked to health improvement objectives and the setting of standards for primary and community care services. In the area of coronary heart disease, over half of the groups in the HSMC study established PCG/T-wide standards for practice-based services aimed at managing coronary heart disease. Standards were based on the NHS national service framework for coronary heart disease, and covered areas such as the development of disease registers, the setting up of screening schemes, ensuring regular monitoring of blood pressure/body mass index/cholesterol, and the prescribing of aspirin.

Having set these standards, PCG/Ts were found by the HSMC study to have developed incentives for practices to participate in audit projects. There were two main approaches to the use of incentives for audit and clinical governance. Firstly, incentives in the form of financial support, extra staffing, and training and development were offered for infrastructure development which was intended to encourage practices to make best use of computer systems and to collect and share clinical data. Secondly, PCG/Ts used practice incentive schemes in order to reward practices that reached specific clinical governance targets in key areas such as heart disease and diabetes. Within such schemes, local standards were agreed and set by PCG/Ts for practices, specific targets set at a practice level, and incentive payments made according to progress towards meeting targets. In many ways this approach to incentivizing practices within a framework of service quality standards prefigured the new GMS contract for UK GPs that was introduced in to the NHS in April 2004.

Addressing Poor Performance

HSMC's research in 2000 highlighted the developmental approach being adopted by PCGs in relation to clinical governance activities and noted that issues of poor performance were not in most cases being addressed in a strategic sense, a fact noted by the National Tracker study of PCG/Ts (Wilkin et al, 2001). Whilst the rationale given by PCG/T clinicians and managers for this 'carrots rather than sticks' approach was the need to draw people into the concept of clinical governance as a positive rather than punitive development, researchers sensed a reluctance on the part of some clinical governance leads in relation to addressing issues of poor performance among peers (Regen et al, 2001) and a lack of levers at their disposal in this regard (Sweeney et al, 2002). In 2001-2001, half of the HSMC case study PCG/Ts had developed strategies to identify poor performance, but were yet to move into the arena of taking action based on such analyses (Regen et al, 2001). With the transfer from health authorities to PCTs in 2002 of responsibility for formal performance procedures for primary care practitioners (GPs, dentists, pharmacists and optometrists), PCTs were clearly allocated the responsibility for tackling poor practitioner performance in primary care. As Campbell and Roland (2003) have noted, it is likely that such formal mechanisms for quality improvement will be used more frequently in future, where supportive and developmental approaches to quality development have not achieved the required aims.

Risk Management and Adverse Events

HSMC's study of PCG/Ts highlighted a focus on risk management as part of overall clinical governance activity (Regen et al, 2001). Practice systems for risk management were reported to have been examined as part of PCG/Ts' baseline assessments of clinical governance and the study identified a number of key areas where PCG/Ts were asking practices to ensure appropriate clinical governance in respect of risk, namely:

- the organization, legibility and confidentiality of patient records;
- arrangements for the storage of confidential patient information;
- procedures for dealing with complaints;
- health and safety policies within practices; and
- systems for reviewing critical incidents.

Evidence suggests that PCTs have continued to develop their activity related to risk management. For example, 90 per cent of PCTs were found in 2002 to be using significant event reporting, a process by which the organization can investigate cases where things have gone wrong (Campbell and Roland, 2003). Similarly, PCTs have had to interpret and enact national guidance about introducing controls assurance into their organization (NHSE, 1999), a further reflection of the increasingly statutory and formal nature of PCTs and in turn of their clinical governance work. In addition to the statutory framework within which PCTs have had to operate, it is important to note that the broader policy context has been supportive of an ever greater focus on the assurance of quality of health services and of such approaches being increasingly transparent in their nature. Two main factors that have contributed to this more 'quality-aware' policy context, namely the major scandals and subsequent public inquiries that took place in Bristol in relation to paediatric heart surgery (Kennedy, 2001) and in Manchester in relation to the GP murderer Harold Shipman (The Shipman Inquiry, 2004). In both cases, serious concerns were raised by the inquiry teams into the degree to which medicine as a self-regulating profession and the NHS as a health system failed to properly safeguard patients from inadequate care or (in the case of Shipman) criminal activity.

Training and Education

As explored earlier in this chapter, PCG/Ts have viewed the training and development needs of practice staff as being a key priority in their work to develop and improve primary care. Analyses of training needs and the development of programmes of activity to meet those requirements have been acknowledged by PCG/Ts as being a critical part of clinical governance and performance improvement work, as well as more general primary care development (Regen et al, 2001). In the early phases of development of PCG/Ts, education and development were seen as key levers for securing the engagement of GPs and other primary care staff in PCG/Ts (see Chapter 6). Whilst we have already noted the risk for PCTs in overly focusing on 'softer' development approaches to clinical governance at the expense of time spent on 'harder' issues such as tackling poor performance, it is clear that a training and development strategy for all staff and services is something that effective PCTs, as with all organizations, would be expected to have in place. Education and training have been seen by PCT/Gs as vehicles for bringing about wider cultural change and organization development. PCG/T-wide training events have been held, drawing together staff from across localities and disciplines, arrangements put in place for funded and protected time for training, and networks of professional groups within PCTs established (Regen et al, 2001). This use of education as a tool for clinical governance has been noted in a number of other studies (Malcolm and Mays, 1999; Sweeney et al, 2001, 2002; Campbell and Roland, 2003), thus demonstrating the way in which clinical governance as a strategic approach has drawn together a number of management and clinical activities into an overall approach focused on improving the quality of health care.

The Development of Clinical Governance – Summary

In relation to the implementation and development of clinical governance, the challenge for PCTs is to now build on the foundations that have been laid (the establishment of clinical governance infrastructure and support, the setting of standards for services, the investment in staff training and development) and demonstrate in a publicly accountable manner clear improvements in the quality of care delivered to patients. Aligned with this is the challenge explored in detail in Chapter 12, namely that of maintaining and growing the engagement of clinical professionals in the work of PCTs, and of finding incentives for professionals to achieve local and national health objectives. If clinical governance is to become more sophisticated and effective as an overall approach to quality improvement in primary care, it is vital that practitioners and staff value the overall aims of the organization, the managers it employs and the techniques being used as part of clinical governance. PCTs, as with all PCOs, disengage their clinical constituents at their peril. Conversely, PCOs with active and enthusiastic clinicians focused on improving patient care, adequate management support, and locally agreed plans and strategies underpinned with staff training have the necessary ingredients for a clinically governed organization that has the quality of patient care at its heart.

Conclusions: Lessons for Research and Practice

Practice-based primary care development, together with the management of prescribing and the development of clinical governance, is an area where researchers and analysts concur that sound and early progress was made by PCG/Ts and their forerunner primary care commissioning organizations (LeGrand et al, 1998; Regen et al, 2001; Wilkin et al, 2002; Dowling and Glendinning, 2003; Smith et al, 2004). In contrast with areas such as health improvement and the commissioning and development of secondary care services, these primary care-based activities have been a major early focus for PCG/Ts and appear to have captured the imagination and hence management attention of many if not all organizations. Crucial to the progress made in developing and improving primary care has been the development by PCOs of a much more 'corporate' culture within NHS primary care, where practices accept more readily that they should work towards local and NHS service objectives, and where the overall focus is less on the individual practice and more on the local health community and its needs (Smith and Walshe, 2004). That is not to say however that the unit of the general practice no longer has relevance. Indeed, it is the ability of general practice to innovate and change in a relatively rapid manner that has been a crucial factor in enabling PCG/Ts to make such striking progress in developing primary care. As such, the significant progress made by PCG/Ts in developing and improving primary care offers important lessons to other PCOs seeking to forge such changes to local primary care and community health services.

Lessons for Research

- There is little evidence as yet about how effective PCOs are at sustaining their early focus on primary care development at a practice level.
- Evidence is lacking about the quality of new and expanded services in primary care as developed by PCOs, who tend to assume such developments to be a

'good thing'.
- Research evidence suggests that PCOs can develop their practices to become more cost-effective prescribers. What is not yet clear is if this has been sustained within PCTs as they have become more complex organizations with apparently lower levels of clinical engagement.
- More evidence is required about the actual impact of the clinical governance strategies employed by PCTs in terms of impact on the quality of patient care.
- The impact of practice-led commissioning and the use and effectiveness of chronic disease management strategies employed by PCTs needs urgent examination to understand the best methods through which to control activity in secondary care and keep costs manageable.

Lessons for Practice

- Baseline assessment of primary care resources, facilities and services is a vital prerequisite to primary care development and clinical governance activity within PCOs.
- Further development of the primary infrastructure is likely to be an early action for PCOs, due to the need to address the priorities of primary care clinicians and to establish a robust basis for more extensive service improvement work across primary and secondary care.
- Information management and technology is a difficult area for many PCOs, incorporating the need to develop compatible and up-to-date systems at practice level with the strategic development of information sharing and systems across practices, localities and secondary health care providers.
- Analysis of local primary care workforce capacity and demography is a vital prerequisite to a PCO's planning for future service development.
- PCOs are increasingly seeking to use the development of new premises and buildings as a way of creating new and innovative forms of service delivery.
- The strengthening of practice-based teams and services, according to agreed PCO minimum standards, is a core part of PCO activity.
- The introduction of a new national contract for general practice, based on a quality and outcomes framework, gives renewed impetus to PCTs' primary care development and chronic disease management work.
- The development of primary care and chronic disease management are increasingly viewed as a fundamental part of a PCT's overall commissioning of care for the local population.
- PCTs are using the new GMS contract as a tool to enable them to be commissioners *of* primary care.
- PCOs offer an appropriate managerial and clinical infrastructure for the development of higher quality and cost-effective prescribing, by means of a range of incentives and strategies at practice and locality level.
- PCOs take their clinical governance responsibilities seriously and have

adopted multiple strategies in order to achieve improvements in the quality of care.

- The setting of minimum standards for service provision within NHS primary care is now accepted as the norm, testimony to the extensive cultural change brought about by PCOs working with their semi-autonomous practices.
- PCOs inevitably focus on developmental 'carrot' approaches to clinical governance in their early days, but need to demonstrate their preparedness to use 'sticks' where developmental techniques have failed to deliver improvements in care.
- PCOs provide a framework and organizational arrangements for the management of risk across general practice and community health providers, including the assurance of health and safety, confidentiality of records, and appropriate handling of complaints and untoward events.
- Training and development is a key mechanism for the development and change of culture related to primary care development and clinical governance within PCOs.

Chapter 11

Making a Reality of the Commissioning Function in PCG/Ts

Since the introduction of the internal market into the NHS in 1991, the terms 'contracting', 'purchasing' and 'commissioning' have been variously used to describe the process whereby funders (health authorities until 2002 and primary care trusts thereafter) allocate resources to health care providers, and in so doing, specify levels of activity and quality expected in return for this investment. This process of assessing needs and securing services to meet those needs on behalf of the local population (i.e. commissioning is one of three core functions of primary care trusts in England, the others being health improvement and the integration of health and social care (Department of Health, 2000). Commissioning is however the area in which PCTs' progress has been most questioned, with a widespread view emerging, both in research and practitioner circles, that this function has yet to 'deliver the goods' for the NHS (Audit Commission, 2004; IPPR, 2004; Smith et al, 2004).

In this chapter, an assessment is made of the experience of primary care groups and trusts in developing the commissioning function and in bringing about changes to clinical services in intermediate and secondary care. As context to this, the emergence of commissioning in the NHS is explored, along with the lessons to be gleaned from an assessment of the available research evidence on primary care led commissioning.

The Emergence of Commissioning in the NHS

The NHS White Paper of 1989 (Department of Health and Social Services, 1989) set out the internal market reforms of the NHS, including the fundamental change of separating the purchasing function from the provision of health services. This 'purchaser-provider split' was intended as a means of improving value for money, rewarding efficient and high quality providers, and encouraging greater responsiveness of services to patients (Dixon, 1998). As such, the purchasing of care and services emerged as a specific function within the NHS, a function that was initially the preserve of health authorities and GP fundholders, and as was noted in Chapter 2, one which subsequently evolved into a range of different forms and organizations in the late 1990s. The logic underpinning the development of NHS purchasing was that if money did not automatically flow from purchaser to provider, providers would have to compete for business and hence this competition would encourage providers to be more efficient, responsive and offer better quality of care (Dixon, 1998).

The term 'commissioning' entered the NHS vocabulary in the mid-1990s, as GPs who were ideologically opposed to GP fundholding set up their own parallel 'GP commissioning groups' as a way of seeking to influence local planning and purchasing of health services by working closely with health authorities. For a few years in the mid-1990s, the term 'commissioning' was synonymous with approaches to purchasing that were explicitly non-fundholding, and it was gradually taken up by the Labour opposition as a declared policy that would provide an alternative to GP fundholding. The defining features of commissioning at this point in time appeared to be a commitment to a population-based, as opposed to a practice-based approach, a focus on equity rather than competition, the collaborative working of GP or locality commissioning groups with their health authority, and a closer relationship with trusts based on long-term service agreements rather than contracts.

On coming to power in 1997, the Labour Government quickly declared its intention to fulfill its manifesto pledge to abolish GP fundholding, at the same time emphasizing its commitment to alternative primary care-led commissioning approaches by announcing a series of GP commissioning pilot projects (Department of Health, 1997b). The ensuing policy of primary care groups and trusts as announced in the 1997 NHS White Paper (Department of Health, 1997), underlined the Labour Government's retention of the purchaser-provider split whilst embedding this within its principles of population-based purchasing, equitable and more national approaches, and partnership and collaboration rather than competition. The term 'commissioning' quickly replaced any mention of 'purchasing', the latter being seen as associated with the internal market of the previous government. Thus it was that 'commissioning' took the place of purchasing within NHS policy and management.

Definitions of Commissioning

Independent analysts of health policy have likewise tracked the development of commissioning within the NHS, also noting the subtle changes of language along the way. Övretveit (1995) suggests that the terms can be distinguished as follows. 'Contracting' refers to the narrow process of negotiating, writing and monitoring annual contracts with providers, whilst 'purchasing' can be described as buying the best value for money services to achieve maximum health gain for those most in need. 'Commissioning' however is a more inclusive and far-reaching process whose purpose is: 'to maximize the health of a population and minimize illness, by purchasing health services and by influencing other organizations to create conditions which enhance people's health' (Övretveit, 1995, p.18).

Commissioning in the English NHS is not just concerned with the purchasing of services from secondary care providers. PCTs commission from a range of NHS, private and voluntary sector providers across the health care spectrum, including primary and community health services, secondary and specialist tertiary care. Some commentators take an even broader perspective, suggesting that commissioning in its true form encapsulates all four functions of PCTs, namely health improvement, the integration of health and social care, the development of primary care, and the purchasing of other health services (Wade, 2004). In the context of policy developments that include a new focus on managing care for people with chronic disease (Department of Health, 2004b) and increasing interest in the relevance for the NHS of the Kaiser Permanente model of managed care in the USA (Ham et al, 2003), a move away from the traditional understanding of commissioning as a form of contracting secondary care services towards a system focused on pathways of care for defined client groups seems to be both inevitable and highly desirable.

Overview of the Research Evidence Related to Primary Care-Led Commissioning

There is an increasing body of research evidence in the UK concerning the effectiveness of commissioning by primary care-based organizations. Much of this evidence is of particular relevance to PCTs, highlighting as it does a set of core messages related to what facilitates and inhibits effective commissioning. A review of this evidence (Smith and Goodwin, 2002) distilled six key themes:

- The significance of context;
- The need to identify levels of commissioning appropriate to the nature of the specific service;
- The importance of securing clinical involvement in commissioning;
- The challenge of developing adequate capacity for commissioning;
- The nature of budget holding and contestability; and
- The requirement for effective long-term relationships between key commissioning stakeholders.

The Significance of Context

Many studies highlight the significance of context in relation to the effectiveness or otherwise of commissioning carried out by primary care-based organizations (LeGrand et al, 1998; Audit Commission, 1999; Regen et al, 1999; Smith et al, 2000; Wilkin et al, 2000; Regen et al, 2001). There are two dimensions to this, the national and the local.

The national context has been noted as being of prime importance in relation to enabling or prohibiting stability in the policy environment within which commissioning organizations operate. Studies of PCG/Ts have highlighted the destabilizing impact that regular NHS organizational change can have on the performance of groups, as managerial staff face uncertainties, and GPs' willingness to initiate developments is compromised (Regen et al, 1999; Smith et al, 2000; Regen et al, 2001; Wilkin et al, 2000; Wilkin et al, 2001). These studies suggest that commissioning performance is particularly vulnerable to changes in the wider health care system. It appears that this vulnerability on the part of commissioning stems from three main factors. Firstly, as noted in Chapter 10, primary care organizations seem to focus mainly on primary care development in their first year of operation (Regen et al, 1999; Smith et al, 2000; Wilkin et al, 2000). Secondly, it is well documented in the literature that organizational change and merger will inevitably divert time and attention away from core business (including commissioning) towards organizational development and infrastructure issues (Cartwright and Cooper, 1992; Bosanquet et al, 2001; Fulop et al, 2002). Thirdly, evidence suggests that effective commissioning is dependent on the development of stable longer-term relationships between commissioners and providers (Flynn and Williams, 1997; Mays et al, 2001).

The national evaluation of total purchasing projects (TPP) in the NHS revealed the importance of local context in shaping and effecting innovations (Mays et al, 2001). Much depended on an environment conducive to service-led change yet this environment was often disrupted by a wide range of mitigating local contexts, some 'receptive' and others 'unreceptive', such as local professional cultures and relationships (Goodwin et al, 2000). This link between local context and progress made by primary care commissioners was also a feature of Audit Commission studies of PCGs (Audit Commission, 1999; Audit Commission, 2000). These studies suggested that groups comprising GPs who had previous experience of collaborative models of commissioning (e.g. multifunds and some forms of GP commissioning) were more likely to have the expertise required for successful PCG commissioning than groups made up of former fundholders.

Research studies examining the success of primary care organizations have provided insight into the significance of national and local contexts in influencing outcomes (Mays et al, 2001; Regen et al, 2001). Performance appears to have been variable since TPPs and PCGs made a difference only for some (mainly primary care and community health) services and in some contexts. What is clear is that variation in the progress made by different PCTs in commissioning is both necessary and legitimate given that these primary care organizations vary greatly in their history and experience of the process. Given that the timescale for developing mature commissioning is known to be several years, it is not surprising that some primary care organizations have made more progress than others.

Appropriate Levels of Commissioning

There is a continuing debate within the research literature concerning the organizational level at which the commissioning function should best be located within the NHS. Some, such as Dowling (2000), suggest that elective surgery (and perhaps most health care services) should be purchased by general practices with referral freedoms allowed by primary care organizations to promote provider contestability. Others (Mays et al, 2001; Regen et al, 2001; Dopson and Locock, 2002) highlight the potential to combine GP involvement in commissioning with the size, budget and credibility to mount an effective challenge to providers.

Indeed, early primary care organizations such as TPPs and GP multifunds acted as a 'bridge' between practice-level budget-holding and the development of a group-level collective approach to commissioning (Smith et al, 1997; Mays et al, 2001). Their focus was ostensibly on the commissioning of hospital and community health services, especially secondary care, and the assumption was that the ability to wield larger budgets would enable leverage over providers. In practice, these primary care organizations were a far more influential vehicle for developing a wider range of primary and intermediate care services outside hospital.

The research evidence suggests that services may best be purchased directly from GP settings where flexible, individual patient-focused responses are desirable. Services requiring population-based perspectives, however, seem better dealt with at a higher-level (Ham, 1996; Smith et al, 2004). For example, when discussing the appropriate size of a purchasing or commissioning unit, LeGrand et al (1998) proposed that different services were best purchased at different levels and that neither a fully centralized nor fully devolved system appeared appropriate. They identified a number of trade-offs involved in the level chosen such as the ability to minimize management costs; the richness of specialist knowledge, having an appropriate pattern of purchasing sensitive to needs; the level of financial risk; and ensuring the quickest access to care provision.

The dilemma as to whether to commission on a geographical locality basis, or using specialist service areas as the main focus, is also highlighted in the literature. Research by Dopson and Locock (2002) revealed a preference amongst providers to deal with clinically-informed specialist commissioners who understood the nature of the complexity of secondary care services. There is, however, evidence that primary care clinicians favoured a locality approach as a way of ensuring adequate 'grassroots' clinical involvement in the process (Smith and Shapiro, 1996; Regen et al, 2001; NHS Alliance, 2003). Many PCG/Ts have attempted to develop such locality structures, with devolved commissioning responsibilities, though this has clearly added to their overall management cost burden (Regen et al, 2001).

A comprehensive review of the literature concerning the effectiveness of primary care-led commissioning concluded that primary care-led commissioning should not be considered in isolation from other approaches to commissioning and planning, but rather seen as part of a continuum of models to be selected and used by funding and commissioning bodies such as PCTs, as appropriate to local needs and service configuration (Smith et al, 2004). The review concluded:

> Primary care-led commissioning may be effective as part of a continuum of commissioning models, and particularly appropriate for 'simple' and community-based chronic disease management and primary care services. Other models of commissioning are required for more specialized and complex services, including the development of more integrated forms of service provision based on managed care techniques and approaches together with care pathways. The challenge for funding organizations is rigorously to select an appropriate blend of approaches and to be clear about how and for what reasons that selection has been made (Smith et al, 2004, p. 38).

Thus the importance of adopting a pluralistic, rather than a single 'ideal' approach to the level and nature of commissioning is underlined. The continuum of models of commissioning proposed by Smith et al (2004) is set out in Figure 11.1 below.

Figure 11.1 The continuum of commissioning levels in the UK

Source: Smith et al (2004), p. 6.

Securing Clinical Involvement in Commissioning

The need to secure adequate and active clinical involvement is the most frequently cited factor in the research evidence related to effective health care commissioning by primary care organizations. Without exception, all research studies concluded that effective commissioning requires clinicians from both primary and secondary care and emphasizes the importance of clinician to clinician dialogue in the planning, improving and reconfiguring of services (LeGrand et al, 1998; Audit Commission, 2000; Mays et al, 2001; Regen et al, 2001; Dopson and Locock, 2002). The importance of clinicians to the process of commissioning is argued to be threefold: first, their *insight* into required service developments due to their clinical knowledge and expertise; second, their greater abilty to *influence* clinical directors within secondary care providers due to their professional status (compared with managers); and third, the greater likelihood that grass-roots clinicians within primary care organizations would implement and support commissioning decisions if the process had been led by respected peers, for example, to the adoption of demand management initiatives in primary care (Audit Commission, 2000; Regen et al 2001; Dopson and Locock, 2002; Lewis, 2004).

It is a cause for concern in the commissioning process, therefore, that one of the key observable trends in recent years in the English NHS has been the growing disenfranchisement of GPs with the work of PCTs as they perceive 'their' organization being 'taken over' by managers and becoming distant from the concerns of grassroots staff in practices and primary care teams (Regen et al, 2001; Regen,

2002; NHS Alliance, 2003; Smith and Walshe, 2004). Indeed, the final report of one national study of PCG/Ts suggested that commissioning was increasingly being led by managers rather than by GPs and secondary care clinicians (Regen et al, 2001). A study published by the National Clinical Governance Support Team and the NHS Alliance in 2004 revealed that the greatest influence within PCTs was deemed to reside with the chief executive and the management team rather than with the clinically-led PEC, the board, or the local community (NHS Alliance and CGST, 2004). This failure to engage GPs and other primary care colleagues in commissioning was prefigured by the Audit Commission's earlier warning of limited GP and consultant involvement in commissioning processes (Audit Commission, 2000).

Securing clinical involvement in commissioning is by no means straightforward. Levels of control exerted by GPs in English primary care organizations have, as noted in Chapter 2, become far more indirect over time. One cannot therefore assume that GPs will have the motivation or incentive to deliver benefits in the same way that self-selected GPs in GP commissioning, fundholding or total purchasing did. Importantly, service improvements now accrue to the PCT as a corporate body rather than to specific practices or groups of GPs. As LeGrand et al (1998) discuss, there is a need to develop incentives that relate both to the 'knavish' self-interest of GPs and also to their 'knightly' or altruistic nature. Therefore, a key lesson is the need to develop incentive structures that act at both corporate (PCT) and individual practice level.

Developing Adequate Capacity for Commissioning

Successive studies of English primary care organizations have pointed to the fact that organizational development and infrastructure issues inevitably dominated in the first year of the organization's life, diverting time and attention from core business such as commissioning (Mays et al, 1998; Goodwin et al, 2000; Smith et al, 2000; Wilkin et al, 2000; Regen et al, 2001; Wilkin et al, 2001). Moreover, the evidence reveals that new primary care organizations can be expected to spend their early months addressing fundamental organizational issues such as recruiting staff, and developing local priorities such as a clinical governance strategy, performance management framework, and primary care development plans. Developing these necessary functions has meant not only that the capacity of primary care organizations to address commissioning has remained limited, but that commissioning itself became regarded as a function to be tackled 'further down the line'. The securing of appropriate and adequate expertise for commissioning is widely reported as being problematic (Audit Commission, 1999; Abbott and Gillam, 2000; Audit Commission, 2000; Regen et al, 2001; Weiner et al, 2001). Areas cited as being particularly difficult have included recruitment of staff with the appropriate level of experience and expertise such as commissioning specialists (in particular within collaborative models of commissioning); public health commissioning experts; and information analysts.

One of the assumptions of the move away from small primary care purchasers to larger primary care organizations was that management costs per capita would reduce through economies of scale and reduced task duplication (Department of Health, 1997). However, the TPP evaluation revealed that the reduction in costs of negotiating contracts with a range of small purchasers (i.e. fundholders) were *exceeded* by the co-ordinating costs involved in TPPs in facilitating the more relational requirements of commissioning. As a result, no obvious economies of scale were present in the larger pilots (Posnett et al 1998, Mays et al 2000). In PCG/Ts, paying professionals (GPs) to ensure their involvement has proved a significant new cost since the large amount of uncosted time provided within voluntary pilots has eroded as primary care organizations became statutory (Audit Commission, 2000; Mays et al, 2001).

The evidence from primary care-led commissioners does suggest that greater spending on management leads to greater achievement of commissioning objectives. For example, the TPP research clearly indicated that the performance of pilots (in terms of their ability to purchase services directly and make changes to the pattern of care provision) was strongly linked to organizational capacity that in turn was associated with the level of management resources in a project (Mays et al, 2001). This was borne out in the major PCG/T studies where the lack of sufficient management resources and/or skilled staff to fulfil functions such as commissioning contributed to PCG mergers and the sharing of management and commissioning functions between groups (Audit Commission, 2000; Smith et al, 2000; Wilkin et al, 2000).

Given the challenging agenda set out for the PCTs in the NHS Plan (Department of Health, 2000) and in 'Shifting the Balance of Power' (Department of Health, 2001a), there is a need to draw together the capacity for commissioning services with that related to organizational redesign and modernization (Smith and Goodwin, 2002). The management and organizational capacity of PCTs is by definition finite. The challenge is how to best allocate a scarce resource so that PCTs can achieve maximum leverage and influence in seeking to develop improved services for their local population.

The Requirement for Effective Long-Term Relationships

Studies of NHS contracting (Flynn and Williams, 1997), GP commissioning (Shapiro et al, 1996), total purchasing (Wyke et al, 1999a) and PCG/Ts (Audit Commission, 2000; Regen et al, 2001; Wilkin et al, 2001) all emphasize the crucial nature of developing effective long-term relationships between commissioners and providers as a key enabling factor to achieving objectives. Likewise, research points to the need for well-developed inter-agency collaboration at the local level (Audit Commission, 2000; Regen et al, 2001; Wilkin et al, 2001). In particular, studies have highlighted the need to build robust strategic and operational relationships with social services and local NHS trusts in order that work to implement national service frameworks and care pathway approaches to care could be achieved.

Within the TPP, GP commissioning and PCG research, a strong relationship with health authorities was noted as being of vital importance to success as it influenced the willingness of health authorities to devolve contracting power, budgets and management resources – all aspects that were associated with successful outcomes. Moreover, integrated approaches to maternity care (Wyke et al, 1999b), continuing and community care (Myles et al, 1998) and mental health (Lee et al, 1999) were only developed where inter-agency co-operation and shared goals had developed. Similarly, evaluations have pointed to the need for PCTs to develop strong and effective relationships with NHS trusts, local authorities, and user/carer groups, as a prerequisite to achieving their service and commissioning objectives.

A further point concerning the relationships required for effective commissioning is that of the dynamic between leaders and followers within primary care organizations. TPP research identified the vital importance of key leaders and opinion formers whose presence and role were considered essential to the achievement of project objectives. These leaders were identified as follows:

- Lead GPs willing to put additional time in to the organization and who can demonstrate the advantages to other GPs;
- Highly skilled managers with technical knowledge, respect and influence who help to co-ordinate an effective organization and present a good face to external agencies;
- Key leaders in the health authority willing to support new ideas and changes; and
- Provider groups, especially clinicians, who are willing to take an active interest in commissioning objectives and contribute to service developments (Wyke et al, 2001).

Unfortunately, the relative lack of clinical involvement in PCTs (see Chapter 6) suggests that the clear and robust links between GP leaders and their colleagues in the wider GP community may not be as strong as within earlier models of primary care commissioning (Regen, 2002; NHS Alliance, 2003; Smith and Walshe, 2004). There is also a concern about potential loss of influence amongst GP leaders in PCTs, which emphasizes the need for primary care organizations to work at clinical involvement and leadership as an ongoing priority. What is clear is that relationships underpin and support commissioning activity in PCTs suggesting strongly that the clinical community is of particular importance to the effectiveness of PCT commissioning.

The Nature of Budget Holding and Contestability

The balance between hospital and community services in the UK has shown a 'chronic tendency' to allow hospital services to attract unduly both resources and power (Killoran et al, 1999). One reason for developing PCG/Ts was to overcome this imbalance by increasing the strength, scope and coherence of a more integrated primary/community health care sector (Department of Health, 1997). The TPP evaluation concluded that small, GP-led, organizations had distinct limitations as purchasers of secondary care but that they had made a real difference in primary care by increasing the range and delivery of services outwith hospitals (Mays et al, 2001). This focus by PCOs on developing services in primary care and at the interface between primary and secondary care has emerged as a consistent finding in the different stages of the major evaluations of PCG/Ts (Smith et al, 2000; Wilkin et al, 2000; Regen et al, 2001; Wilkin et al, 2001).

The TPP research supported the principle of devolving budgets to groups of practices to contract independently for services since those that were given such freedoms tended to make the most progress against stated objectives (Mays et al, 2001). Moreover, it was suggested that these findings would be best applied in PCG/Ts if budgets could be devolved as far as possible to practice-level in order to develop appropriate incentive schemes to influence GP behaviour (Smith, 1999; Mays et al, 2000).

An important aspect to the development of new contracts or service agreements was the perception of having purchasing 'clout' and the practical ability to shift contracts to another NHS or private provider. However, holding a budget and having the freedom to commission services directly from a range of providers appears not sufficient of itself. As the previous section emphasized, establishing mature and robust relationships with providers has also been a pre-requisite to effective commissioning practice. For example, research into total purchasing (Mays et al, 2001) and health authority commissioning (Dopson and Locock, 2002) highlighted the importance for commissioners of developing good relationships with clinicians in local trusts. This was noted as being a far more effective strategy than approaches employed by 'hands-off' purchasers. Thus, the holding of a budget with freedom to purchase care has not been a 'magic bullet'.

A key issue is that the development of contestability is not easy since many PCTs are within what might be described as the natural monopoly territory of a local acute trust with few obvious alternative providers. Even in the context of the Patient Choice policy (Department of Health, 2003) that now enables patients to choose alternative providers of acute care, it can be difficult for PCTs to offer any realistic choice of accessible local provider. Nevertheless, the evidence suggests that effective commissioning requires contestability which implies that, in these situations, the use of private or independent providers may offer the only realistic route towards some contestability in the commissioning system.

The finding that commissioning needs both contestability between providers *and* long-term relationships appears problematic. However, it has been suggested that what is needed to address both requirements is a commissioning approach based on a model of 'contestable collaboration' (Smith and Goodwin, 2002). This approach to, commissioning is one that enables an appropriate degree of contestability for certain services (e.g. routine elective surgery and diagnostics) whilst focusing largely on the development of local integrated networks of care or programmes of chronic disease management, commissioned with significant clinical dialogue and involvement.

In their conclusions about the influence of commissioning within the NHS, Dopson and Locock (2002) suggested that PCTs might eventually become stronger commissioning bodies than either health authorities or PCGs. This conclusion was based on a belief in the potential for PCTs to combine GP involvement in commissioning with the size, budget and credibility to mount an effective challenge to acute providers. The same authors warned of the risk of PCTs losing the locality perspective and direct GP involvement in commissioning decisions, as layers of management increase to cope with spanning a larger number of practices, services and diverse interests. Subsequent research suggests that this forecast has indeed turned out to be correct (NHS Alliance, 2003; Smith and Walshe, 2004; NHS Alliance and CGST, 2004; Lewis, 2004).

Given the policy focus in the NHS Plan on developing more integrated local services based on care pathways and close partnerships between different providers, PCTs face a challenging conundrum. How do they commission services in a contestable manner, while at the same time developing new forms of integrated managed care across primary and secondary care organizations?

The Approach Taken by PCG/Ts in Developing Commissioning

Research evidence on the progress made by PCG/Ts in their first two years in commissioning health care has suggested that significant change had been brought about in the area of primary care, community services and intermediate care (Regen et al, 2001; Wilkin et al, 2001). Examples of change have included the development of what had been considered formerly acute services redeveloped in community settings (e.g. intensive rehabilitation services following stroke, extended community mental health teams) and initiatives focused on trying to reduce demand for hospital services (e.g. specialist GP screening of referrals for chronic back pain or dermatological conditions).

Evidence related to achievements by PCG/Ts over the period 1999-2001 in terms of bringing about changes to the quality and pattern of provision of acute services has painted a picture of much more limited progress (Smith and Goodwin, 2002). In this, PCG/Ts have much in common with the experience of their predecessor PCOs in the 1990s, where the bringing about of significant changes to acute services was again cited as a challenge too far for most groups and indeed health authorities (LeGrand et al, 1998). At this point in time, researchers suggested that PCTs needed to address some core issues of infrastructure and management if they were to start to have a real influence on the wider patterns of provision of health care (Regen et al, 2001; Wilkin et al, 2002). A summary of these issues is set out in Table 11.1.

Table 11.1 Key issues in the development of the PCT commissioning function

- A need for greater management support to the commissioning process.
- The importance of securing improved financial data for commissioning.
- The lack of activity data for commissioning, including analytical capacity.
- The need to continue and further enhance the involvement of clinicians (both primary and secondary) in the process of commissioning.
- The importance of developing a greater range of strategic partnerships to underpin the commissioning process.
- The lack of space for PCTs to develop local commissioning priorities and plans in the face of a potentially overwhelming national agenda.
- The destabilizing effect of regular organizational change on the long-term partnerships needed for effective commissioning.

Source: Adapted from Regen et al (2001) and Wilkin et al (2001).

Research exploring the third year of operation of PCG/Ts painted a bleak picture in terms of progress in achieving their commissioning objectives (Dowling et al, 2002). It was noted that PCTs had taken on a wider range of purchasing responsibilities previously undertaken by health authorities and that commissioning infrastructures were largely in place. Quality standards were starting to be introduced into service agreements, and steps were being taken to develop integrated care pathways across a range of services (Dowling et al, 2002). However, the researchers pointed to the primacy of the national policy agenda in shaping commissioning priorities, and a perception of a low degree of leverage by PCG/Ts over NHS providers. In summing up their findings in 2002, Dowling and colleagues noted:

> Overall, some progress has been made in the commissioning function. But as with other key PCG/T personnel, commissioning leads perceive a lack of resources as an important obstacle to the successful execution of the commissioning function. The apparently widening gap between the expectations on PCG/Ts and their capacity to meet them means that the signs of progress in the commissioning function must be tempered by caution as far as long-term prospects are concerned (Dowling et al, p. 87).

The Changing Policy Context for PCT Commissioners

The commissioning task facing PCTs is increasing in its scope and complexity. In April 2004, a new 'financial flows' regime was introduced into the NHS, a new form of contracting for acute care episodes whereby money theoretically follows the patient and NHS trusts are reimbursed on a cost per case basis for any activity above agreed contract levels, or likewise penalized at such a rate if they under-perform against targets (Department of Health, 2002c). The simultaneous introduction of a national standard tariff for some procedures may also act to restrain increases in costs.

In addition to the introduction of financial flows, the new 'Patient Choice' policy, whereby patients have the right to a greater say in their choice of health care provider and in other elements of their treatment plan (Department of Health, 2003), adds a further dimension to the complexity of the PCT commissioning challenge (Roland and Smith, 2003). If patients can choose their provider of secondary care in discussion with their GP, and financial flows means that the money to pay for this care follows the patient, what is the role of the PCT commissioner? A possible answer to this question is that the PCT increasingly becomes the manager of performance of providers, and the designer of new pathways and forms of care that can in turn be chosen by patients and their advisers.

The increase in the effective number of health care purchasers taking place through the introduction of Patient Choice in England (i.e. the placing of the patient at the centre of the purchasing decision) is matched by a desire to stimulate greater diversity in terms of care providers. This increase in plurality of provision is occurring through the implementation of a policy aimed at greater devolution of hospitals, namely the introduction of self-governing foundation hospitals run on a mutual/friendly society model. These two parallel policy developments on the one hand offer PCTs an unrivalled opportunity to stimulate new and creative forms of care that are more responsive to the needs of users, and on the other hand threaten to destabilize and overwhelm an already overburdened PCT commissioning function.

Much of the research on commissioning by PCTs has to date focused on their activity in relation to purchasing secondary and intermediate care services, and to a lesser extent, the development of services in primary care. A function that has received relatively little policy and management attention has been the commissioning of primary care in its own right. The development in the late 1990s of a programme of local schemes where primary care was delivered through local, as opposed to national GP contract – personal medical services (PMS) schemes – was an important signal of a desire to develop more sophisticated and locally flexible contracts for primary care (see Chapter 8 for more details). This approach has now been given national expression in the negotiation and implementation of a new general medical services contract for NHS general practices whereby PCTs hold practices to account for their performance through a contract based on a quality and outcomes framework. Thus PCTs are now clearly the commissioner of primary care in the NHS, and are vested with an important new tool to use in their purchasing and performance management of services across the spectrum of health care. PCTs now have to make sense of this and other policy developments, whilst at the same time seeking to create, implement and performance manage new networks of and approaches to care. PCTs are thus at once both providers and commissioners of care. This represents a blurring of the boundaries of a simple purchaser-provider split and heralds the arrival of new, more complex forms of integrated providing/commissioning organizations. Such organizations share features with health maintenance organizations (HMOs) in the United States, including the responsibility for allocating health funding to service providers on behalf of a registered or enrolled population, along with the provision of local health and social care services within overall integrated care pathways. In their review of the literature of primary care-led commissioning in 2004 that included a consideration of how PCTs could learn from the USA experience of developing integrated providing/commissioning bodies (HMOs), Smith et al (2004) cited six possible future models of commissioning and service integration that might appear in the UK NHS:

1. Professionally owned and run primary care based commissioning organizations providing primary care services.
2. Community owned and run commissioning organizations with or without direct provider responsibilities.
3. Commercially owned and run commissioning organizations with or without provider responsibilities for primary care.
4. Vertically integrated NHS primary-secondary commissioning and providing organizations.
5. Vertically integrated, professionally owned and run commissioning and providing organizations providing primary and secondary care.
6. Vertically integrated, commercially owned and run commissioning and providing organizations providing primary and secondary care.

All of these six possible models would have radical implications for NHS policy and management if implemented, and Smith et al noted in particular the challenge in relation to accountability and regulation within an overall framework of a publicly funded NHS. The authors concluded:

> Collectively, they represent the sorts of organizations that might be invited to take over all or part of the commissioning and/or provision role in the NHS under a franchising regime in which the NHS contracts with the agent best placed to ensure the provision of high quality, efficient and equitable services to NHS patients within budget. They are perhaps most likely to enter the NHS as a response to major, irremediable performance failures stemming from management, governance or both levels in PCTs, LHBs [local health boards] and the like (Smith et al, 2004, p. 36).

Conclusions: Lessons for Research and Practice

The assessment in this chapter of the evidence related to commissioning by primary care organizations suggests that PCTs have the potential to be stronger commissioners than their predecessor health authorities or PCGs, but that to date it is just that – potential not reality. There is a need for PCTs and equivalent funding bodies rigorously to select a sophisticated blend of commissioning and service integration approaches, as dictated by local needs and service configuration (Smith et al, 2004). There is clear evidence to support the effectiveness of primary care organizations as commissioners of primary and intermediate care. However, there is little research that suggests progress in bringing about significant change in secondary care services, other than in relation to some increased responsiveness in elective care brought about via GP fundholding (Propper et al, 2002; Dusheiko et al, 2003). The challenge facing PCTs is to capitalize on their potential strength to become well-supported and effective local commissioners who work in close partnership with local primary and secondary care clinicians in developing new forms of redesigned services within a context of managed integrated care. The inherent paradox in the challenge posed for PCTs is summed up by Weiner et al (2001, p. 43) as follows:

> Balancing community-controlled planning, co-ordination and commissioning, with the flexibility of locally responsive alternative models of care delivery is, at the same time, a major strength and an Achilles heel of the reforms.

Lessons for Research

- Research into commissioning requires methods that are able to take account of changes in the wider policy context whilst still enabling the tracking of longer term service and health outcomes.
- Context is all when assessing the effectiveness of commissioning – a range of qualitative as well as quantitative methods will be needed to catch the key contextual subtleties and to complement the tracking of routine data re service changes.
- Evaluation of commissioning approaches needs to seek to track changes at different levels of the health system – in primary care, intermediate care and within secondary care services.
- Direct surveying of the views of GPs (or other health professionals) lends a valuable counter-balance to the opinions expressed by clinical and managerial leaders of PCTs.
- Research that is able to link inputs (e.g. management capacity) with outputs or outcomes, is particularly powerful in relation to influencing policy makers.
- Increasingly complex forms of commissioning, e.g. through networks and managed care, will call for more sophisticated approaches to monitoring and evaluation.

Lessons for Practice

- If PCTs are to have time and space to develop effective commissioning based on robust local relationships with providers and other stakeholders, there is a need for a degree of stability in the policy context.
- Given the range of local contexts and experience of commissioning, policy makers must avoid the temptation to impose structural approaches to commissioning at a local level.
- It is likely that a number of different levels will be used within a PCT commissioning process, with each level entailing a different approach to involving clinicians, relating to providers, budget-holding, and access to management support.
- Strong and effective clinical involvement from colleagues in primary and

secondary care is crucial to effective PCT commissioning.

- Engaging clinical colleagues requires funding and protected time, within an overall framework of incentives that recognizes the particular characteristics of general practice.
- Evidence from research highlights the importance of securing adequate management and organizational capacity for commissioning in PCTs, for this links directly with ability to achieve commissioning objectives.
- Specific issues likely to need attention include the recruitment, retention and development of a larger cadre of commissioning staff with specialist skills, with commissioning specialists being developed as a professional group in their own right.
- Skills increasingly required as part of commissioning capacity include redesign and the development of integrated managed care.
- Budget holding at practice and locality level makes a real difference to primary, community and intermediate care services.
- The implied contestability of budget holding lends 'clout' to primary care commissioners.
- PCTs need to develop and nurture robust and long-term relationships with local health and social care partner organizations, focusing on the development of pathways of care.
- Collaborative working with neighbouring PCTs is required if PCTs are to commission effectively across larger populations.
- The internal relationships between GP leaders and their constituency within PCTs are crucial to effective clinical involvement in commissioning, and there is evidence to suggest that these may need attention in some PCTs.

Note

This chapter draws upon a review of the evidence concerning effective commissioning by primary care trusts previously published as a monograph by the University of Birmingham in 2002 and funded by the Department of Health's Policy Research Programme. We are grateful to the Policy Research Programme for granting us permission to use this material as a basis for further analysis within this book.

Chapter 12

Sustaining Effective Clinical Engagement in Primary Care Trusts

Primary care professionals in England have experienced a rapid journey following the evolution of PCTs alongside policies which have sought to develop new and more specialist roles for nurses and doctors. The rise of new local contracts with salaried options of employment has also challenged traditional independence as the NHS system has sought to bring professionals under its wing (Smith and Walshe, 2004). In the process, the involvement of clinicians, particularly GPs, in shaping and leading these new developments has been encouraged. Successive government policies have asserted the role of frontline staff in taking managerial power within a context of working to national standards and accountabilities (Department of Health, 2000, 2001a). However, whilst health professionals were attracted by the prospect of greater local autonomy, the sustainability of professional engagement becomes questionable if they must adhere to nationally-based targets and procedures (Dowling et al, 2003). Moreover, although clinicians are integral to the leadership and management of PCTs, their involvement has often been compromised by a conflict of interest between professional and organizational interests (Croxson et al, 2003).

As Chapters 6 and 7 revealed, there has been growing disengagement in clinical involvement in PCG/T decision-making as the growth in the size and function of primary care organizations in England has led to greater influence and leadership from professional managers. This chapter concentrates on the issues faced by PCG/Ts in attracting clinicians to work within a more 'managed' system and considers the extent to which GPs, nurses, allied health professionals and other primary care practitioners feel engaged with these primary care organizations. The chapter examines the potential approaches that PCTs need to employ if they are to engage the wider constituency of primary care professionals, including the development and potential of new local contracts between PCTs and primary care practitioners as a method of sustaining effective clinical engagement in the future. The chapter concludes with some lessons for sustaining effective clinical engagement in future primary care organizations.

The Changing Role of Primary Care Professionals in England

Primary care organizations in England have developed at a time when the roles of primary care professionals are being redefined. For example, the GP as an 'expert generalist' (Starey, 2003) working in professional partnerships and as the gatekeeper to NHS services is changing to that of a care manager whereby GPs co-ordinate complex care packages for patients. As Gillam and Meads (2001) suggest, the move is in the direction of becoming a clinical care director in which the GP directs the care package of each patient from referral to design and implementation (see Table 12.1). As PCTs are developing, the concept of the GP as patient service facilitator, rather than universal gatekeeper, is being further encouraged by new methods of access such as walk-in centres, diagnostic treatment centres, and NHS Direct. Similarly, the roles of nurses and allied health professionals have been undergoing significant 'professionalization', or 'liberation', to become alternative providers of medical care and to have more strategic and managerial influence within PCTs and their professional executive committees (see Chapter 7).

Table 12.1 From expert generalist to clinical care director: the changing role of the GP within PCG/Ts

General Practitioner	Clinical Care Director
• Assessment of complaint	• Assessment of presenting issue
• Diagnosis	• Definition and description
• Investigation	• Supporting evidence
• Referral	• Seeking specialist advice
• Delegation	• Team-working
• Letter writing	• Negotiation of a care package
• Pick up the pieces	• Co-ordination of care provision
• Recipient of others' problems	• Control of resources

Source: Starey, 2003, p. 196.

For many primary care professionals, this movement away from their traditional areas of expertise has been tantamount to deprofessionalization, especially in cases where professionals become more like technicians through the use of protocols and prescribed care pathways and procedures. In tandem with these changes, increased affiliation to new primary care organizations is requiring primary care professionals to work more to the benefit of organizational goals rather than directly to the needs of individual patients. For the new agenda to be acceptable, such potential losses to both professional status *and* autonomy have needed to be offset by the overall retention of clinical power and authority by ensuring that professionals themselves take on influential management positions (Kitchener, 2000). Hence, devolution of power, budgets and responsibilities to front-line professionals for the delivery and commissioning of care through primary care groups and trusts was imbued with clinical leadership.

As Friedson (2001) argues, there are grounds to believe that individual professionals, especially GPs, are not only seeing their professional freedom and status erode, but that collective professional control of PCG/Ts has become severely diluted, particularly in the face of new regulatory pressures from the centre to scrutinize clinical practice and performance. The principle of local responsibility has become increasingly at odds with new national targets, potentially doing down professionals' estimates of the trustworthiness of PCTs (Bond and LeGrand, 2003). Yet, the extent to which PCTs will succeed in developing effective primary and community care services locally, whilst simultaneously encouraging corporate responses to governance and clinical quality, will be a key factor in their success.

Developing Corporacy in PCG/Ts

The development of primary care organizations in England has provided primary care with a corporate identity that was previously unimaginable. As Starey (2003) suggests, this 'corporacy' has several key features:

- A more *planned* approach to service development – taking a longer term view;
- A more *accountable* service – manifest in clinical governance requirements;
- A *safer home* for managing finances and providing support to staff and their careers; and
- A more *efficient* and *effective* approach to care provision – such as through the rolling-out GP co-operatives, integrated nursing teams and the development of intermediate care (Starey, 2003, p. 23).

Sustaining effective clinical engagement in the new regime is a key challenge since managers have had to apply their expertise to a largely disparate group of GPs and nurses who have been subject to little external management in the past. For example, relatively few community-based doctors are salaried employees (mostly in community paediatric, geriatric and psychiatric services) leaving managers and GP leaders in PCG/Ts in a weak position to regulate and govern. Applying evidence-based medical procedures that are underpinned by guidelines is more problematic in locations where local clinicians are not receptive to what they consider are managerial norms, or priorities that do not tally with perceived local or practice needs.

In the absence of hierarchical power, PCG/Ts have had to adopt locally-negotiated 'relational' contracts within their organizational network of primary care suppliers (Bennett and Ferlie, 1996). A new approach to governance has had to be developed that mixes demonstrable accountability with long term development of trust, and which mixes elements of competition with collaboration. Thus, managers of primary health care professionals need to be highly skilled in persuasion, negotiation, bargaining and conflict resolution (Hudson and Hardy, 2001).

These new forms of governance have been observed in the work of Sheaff et al (2003, 2004) which found that PCG/Ts were populated by a 'core' of strongly professionalized networks of GPs that exerted a powerful influence in PCG Boards and the professional executive committees of PCTs (see Chapter 5). However, there was also a large 'periphery' of nurses and other health care professionals detached from the inner network of GPs that were often difficult to influence (see Chapters 6 and 7). Reflecting on the development of clinical governance activities at practice-level, Sheaff et al's (2004) empirical review suggested that:

- contracts and hierarchies played little role in clinical governance which was administered through semi-formal networks;
- GP and nurse compliance was achieved partly by discursive appeals to the legitimacy of clinical governance;
- a range of methods for medical self-surveillance were used; and
- the practical consequences of clinical governance were limited and uneven.

Such research findings reflect those from other investigations into the management of clinical governance by PCG/Ts in which peer-pressure was complemented by subtle methods of coercion, for example by persuading GPs that PCT policies were acting as a 'buffer' to the vague threat of more heavy-handed government-led alternatives (Wilkin et al, 1999, 2001; Smith et al, 2000; Regen et al, 2001; Dixon and Sweeney, 2000; and see Chapter 10).

Similar lessons arise from the experience of corporatization of primary care practices in New Zealand where IPAs have seemingly performed better than PCG/Ts in persuading participants to change clinical behaviour by developing 'relational' approaches to governance manifest in the use of clinical leaders and the minimization of bureaucracy (Malcolm and Mays, 1998). In the USA, organizations such as Kaiser Permanente have been highly effective in attracting and managing care professionals due to its medical leadership and coherent sense of collective ownership amongst physicians (Feacham et al, 2002; Ham et al, 2003; Shapiro, 2003). For PCG/Ts, engendering such professional ownership and commitment has been more problematic since such organizations were not created directly on behalf of primary care professionals (as in IPAs), nor through the use of exclusive salaried employment of staff (as in Kaiser Permanente), but mandated through top-down NHS reform.

Developing Legitimacy and the Mandate to Manage

A key lesson for PCTs in sustaining clinical engagement arising from this body of evidence is the need for 'soft governance' techniques to enable a degree of line-management. More crucially, it suggests that the ability of PCG/Ts to manage clinicians results from a mandate from the clinicians themselves. As Sheaff et al (2003) concluded, primary care professionals were more willing to legitimize a local medical leadership and renounce some of their power to it, but not to the leadership of NHS managers.

This finding reflects a key conclusion from research into clinical networks that suggest that the most effectively managed networks are those in which professionals provide the mandate to be governed by a set of negotiated rules (Goodwin et al, 2004a). Inducing skeptics to adopt PCT objectives and guidelines, therefore, requires the development of professional legitimation. This suggests that local professional leaders need to adopt increasingly active forms of medical self-regulation whilst avoiding managerial 'encroachment'.

Since PCTs remain network organizations based on non-hierarchical relationships, the extent to which future primary care organizations can sustain professional engagement will rely on relational governance techniques. However, as Chapter 6 and 7 reported, a growing number of GPs, nurses and allied health professionals have become disengaged with their PCTs to the point where they offer passive resistance to collective approaches. It has been suggested, therefore, that relational governance techniques have failed within the current context of NHS reforms in primary care. Consequently, there has been a growing call to make clinicians more truly accountable to PCG/Ts, perhaps in vertically-integrated managed networks of care. Policy direction in England, encompassing new local contracts and a greater proportion of salaried employment, appears to be moving in this direction.

Developing Effective 'Grassroots' Engagement

> It is unthinkable that PCTs could achieve significant or sustainable progress in any of the areas of their core business without full and wholehearted participation from general practitioners, the wider independent contractor community, nurses and other AHPs, and without effective leadership from the PEC (NHS Alliance, 2004, pp. 60-61).

As Chapters 6 and 7 reported, the extent to which constituent GPs and other primary care clinicians feel 'engaged' is clearly linked to specific factors such as bureaucracy; workload, remuneration and morale. Moreover, resistance to engagement has been fuelled by a general resentment to the wider 'modernization' process and centrally imposed 'must-dos'. If PCTs are to plan and improve health services, the evidence suggests that PCTs must engage more directly with the clinical workforce, and at the earliest opportunity (Commission for Health Improvement, 2004).

In developing management strategies to 'engage' the grass-roots, the perceived wisdom from Chapters 6 and 7 pointed to the need for a developmental process built on promoting the 'relational' characteristics for good networking, such as leadership by peers and good levels of communication, sprinkled with funding to oil the wheels of participation. More fundamentally, there is a perceived need for PCTs to develop a positive *and empowered* culture where an effective front-line voice is present to participate and lead service design and provision. This would precipitate the role for peer-elected GP and nurse leaders, but also the need for a stronger professional executive committee with the power to influence PCT decisions. As the NHS Alliance (2004) argues, the 'high performing' PCT is one in which boards and PECs make best use of their aggregated individual talents through effective clinical engagement yet remain significantly 'challenged' such that professional 'cohesion' does not degenerate into complacency or collusion (see Figure 12.1).

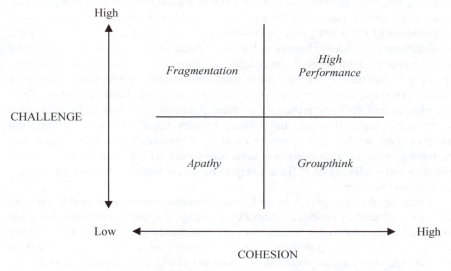

Figure 12.1 The relationship between cohesion and challenge to maximize performance in PCTs

Source: NHS Alliance (2004).

Incorporating health care professionals into 'corporate' PCT-based planning, decision-making and leadership activities appears essential to the health of the organization. However, a key challenge to PCTs is the sheer breadth of potential stakeholders which, other than GPs and nurses, might include other primary care practitioners (such as dentists, optometrists and pharmacists) and a plethora of activity under the umbrella heading of allied health professionals, such as dieticians, occupational therapists, physiotherapists, podiatrists, speech and language therapists, psychologists and counsellors. Furthermore, the formal relationship between PCTs and professional stakeholders varies considerably with some being direct employees, others working to independent contracts, and many working to sub-contracting arrangements to both NHS and independent organizations. The question arises, therefore, why should PCTs engage with the wider range of professionals and, if so, how should this be undertaken?

According to the NHS Alliance (2003), engaging frontline professionals is necessary at a strategic level to ensure that PCTs understand the practical experiences of patients to services provided across the spectrum of care. In particular, logging the wider experience of primary care professionals should enable PCTs to draw on a bank of untapped knowledge, not least for understanding practical ways to work across boundaries with social and voluntary care providers. It can also be argued that engaging frontline professionals is a priority task for meeting key outcome targets, for example, in the ability to reduce GP workloads through task substitution and/or reducing inappropriate referrals to hospital by providing better assessment processes (such as the use of counsellors for assessing mental health patients). Moreover, such engagement of the wider group of frontline professionals might enable the greater management of patients at home (such as through the flexible use of physiotherapists and occupational therapists); the greater treatment and management of chronic diseases in community settings; more community-based interventions (such as in pharmacies); and better screening and preventative public health activities. Thus, approaches that integrate professional stakeholder activities potentially have great merit in meeting PCT targets for reducing hospital admissions and securing local access to care. As the NHS moves to a system of 'payments by results', this ability to manage patients in primary and community care settings will be crucial since the financial wellbeing of PCTs is likely to be sorely tested in the face of income-maximizing providers.

Engaging the 'grassroots' in such ways, however, has proven problematic to-date for a number of reasons. Within PCTs, engaging wider stakeholders has often appeared to be more of a burden than an opportunity due to time and capacity constraints. Moreover, the continued development of a GP-nursing model of medicalized care does not create an environment in which other professions fit very comfortably (NHS Alliance, 2003). For the professional stakeholders, any incentive to participate is often offset by the additional demands placed on their time and fears related to PCT bureaucracy, reduced professional freedom, and cynacism as to whether they will really be 'valued' and 'listened to' as well as 'used' (NHS Alliance, 2003, 2004 and see Chapters 6 and 7).

Finding the Right Incentives

A key challenge for PCTs is to develop the 'right' set of incentives that enable professionals to participate actively, rather than passively, in PCTs within corporate structures such as professional executive committees and task groups. Moreover, such professionals need to be engaged at a practical level such that their activities compliment and reflect PCT service development objectives. To do this, PCTs need to adopt a 'dual' approach of 'empowerment and influence'. Top foster empowerment, the evidence suggests that PCTs must try to avoid the dangers of tokenism by embracing allied health professions and primary care practitioners as valued members of their organization manifest in their ability to exert demonstrable influence and leadership. In so doing, leaders in PCTs from the various professional fields have a greater opportunity to influence professional behaviours on the ground. This reflects the 'mandate to manage' principle that is so important to the success of network organizations such as PCTs, a concept encapsulated in the recommended actions for change emanating from a joint review of clinical engagement in PCTs undertaken by the National Clinical Governance Support Team (a part of the NHS

Modernization Agency), the NHS Alliance and NatPaCT (NHS Alliance, 2003; see Table 12.2).

Table 12.2 Engaging clinicians in PCTs: key action points for change

• There needs to be an effective clinical and front-line voice within PCT governance. The CEO and Chair and the PCT itself should be performance managed to ensure this happens
• PCT boards should agree a clear PEC remit and the two groups should work closely together if they are to serve the collective needs of local communities
• PCT structures need to be flat and organic rather than bureaucratic
• PECs should set their own priorities and agendas
• Front-line clinical staff should be effectively involved in redesign, service provision and in ensuring services are used cost effectively
• PECs need to provide visible and effective leadership for front-line colleagues and ensure clinicians feel empowered, valued and engaged
• Intelligent information is needed for all this to happen
• Significant investment will need to be targeted at PEC members and front-line clinical staff for real change to be generated and sustained

Source: Adapted from the NHS Alliance (2003), p. 91.

Whether the 'mandate to manage' principle can be effective depends on a range of contextual factors, not least the availability of time, management resources and capacity to enable the process of engagement. This may be problematic since research has often concluded that PCTs were unlikely to improve the level of clinical engagement because they simply had not been provided with the tools to establish the necessary incentives to enable them to engender a collective response (Regen et al, 2001, 2002; Locock et al, 2004). Indeed, research by Locock and colleagues on GP decision-making and relationships with PCG/Ts found that all GPs intended to do what they thought was in the best interest of their patient *regardless* of any PCT generated guidelines or protocols (Locock et al, 2004). Since most saw money as a just reward for the extra work involved, the use of financial incentives was generally reported as the most effective mechanism through which GPs would abide by collective policies. This research suggests that, at least for independent practitioners, sustaining clinical involvement requires additional financial incentives to draw from them the willingness to play an active part in PCT activities.

Developing Effective Clinical Leadership

One of the most important conclusions from the research evidence is the need for PCT and PECs to provide visible and effective leadership to front-line colleagues that ensures clinicians feel empowered, valued and engaged. In this regard, PCTs need to invest in the process of leadership development because the nature and personalities of clinical leaders representing front-line professionals at board/executive committee level has a major bearing on their willingness to engage. As Locock et al's (2004) research uncovered, not all professionals react positively to leaders, particularly to those clinical professionals promoted to management positions yet who are perceived as less competent than their peers in their 'real' job (i.e. nursing and/or general practice). Hence, if it is perceived that clinical leaders are 'beneath' their colleagues in terms of professional competence, part of a 'lowerarchy', such managers may not carry the respect of their peers and their leadership role becomes undermined.

As Locock et al (2004) uncovered, the perception from grassroots GPs as to what motivates their colleagues to engage in PCT management suggests that many have not been primarily motivated by either the best interest of patients or professionals (Table 12.3). If one accepts that clinical involvement and ownership are important pre-requisites in the effective organization of a PCT, the potential of 'lowerarchies' needs to be avoided. Thus, whilst funding and other clinical incentives to encourage participation are fundamental, so too is attracting the right kind of leader. Moreover, since benefits to participation can be perceived to accrue to the collective rather than individual practice, the incentive of independent contractors to be active players in PCTs is one driven more by personal choice rather than by mandate or financial advantage.

Table 12.3 The motives of general practitioners working in PCG/T management positions

1.	*The Politician:* those motivated by an urge to exercise power.
2.	*The Visionary:* driven by a will to innovate, improve patient care, work for the common good, and shape the future of primary care.
3.	*The Sufferer of the Middle Age Crisis:* those who are bored with general practice and direct patient contact, seeking an alternative source of job satisfaction. Doctors in this category were thought to be particularly unable to exercise authority over their frontline colleagues.
4.	*The Megalomaniac:* a compulsive workaholic who cannot say no and enjoy meetings.
5.	*The Beleaguered:* those with little motivation to do the job but who feel that somebody has to do it.

Source: adapted from Locock et al, 2004, p. 32.

As Locock et al (2004, p. 35) conclude:

> As it stands, unless PCTs are able to champion effectively some collective or common cause, they will find it difficult to gain the unwavering allegiance of the majority of their primary care professionals, since managerial control of a PCT can be contested whereas their ability to provide financial incentives is limited.

New Local Contracts as a Mechanism for Clinical Engagement

A mechanism for engaging clinicians more directly with PCTs has been the development of new local contracts with primary care professionals (see Chapter 8). Since the NHS (Primary Care) Act 1997, general practitioners, primary care dentists and community pharmacists have had the option to sign-up to pilots that enable them to negotiate a contract directly with their PCT. The purpose of the policy has been to help integrate and engage nurses and other primary care professionals with medical practitioners by promoting 'team-working' and skill-mix changes. For PCTs, professionals would supposedly become more responsive to governance issues as a result of a more directly accountability structure (Walsh et al, 2001).

Evaluation of PMS pilots suggest that early uptake tended to be in groupings of 'change junkies' or innovative practitioners that had been at the forefront of previous schemes such as fundholding and total purchasing pilots. Hence, it was not surprising that success in developing PMS schemes was related to strong clinical leadership, vision and a culture embracing change (PMS National Evaluation Team, 2002). However, innovator practices that took part in PMS pilots did so primarily to defend their own priorities from the corporateness of PCG/Ts and it was also observed how most PMS pilots had moved back to a medically-led model of provision with the absence of any real nurse, social service or public health voice (Walsh and Huntington, 2003).

As the study by Sheaff et al (2004) has shown, what is significant is how local contracts have *not* been used. For example, few respondents in their study viewed PMS contracts as a way of better managing the quality of clinical work. Indeed, activities within PMS pilots were still organized largely through professional networks rather than line-management systems. Even if PCTs wished to use more formal contractual arrangements, there is evidence to suggest that most lacked the information systems capable of monitoring much of the relevant data (Maddox, 1999). Thus, even under this apparently more managed and contractual process, PCTs have had to rely on the relational forms of engagement referred to earlier, with the use of some limited financial incentives for practice infrastructure or benefits in kind such as the provision of education and training.

The development of new local contracts has also been used as a mechanism to engage primary care dentists. Personal Dental Services (PDS) pilots, the dental equivalent of Personal Medical Services, were introduced to overcome the weakness of the previous dental item-of-service remuneration system that placed dentists on a 'treadmill' of activity-based practice leading to unnecessary treatments, inflated activity and reduced consultation times (Bloomfield, 1992). The system severely over-worked primary care dental providers and undermined NHS commitment leading to a haemorrhaging of NHS provision as dentists went private (Gollamy and Gorham, 1998). The use of locally-negotiated contracts based on either capitation funding or salaried employment was designed to overcome both issues. The evidence from pilots suggests it achieved some success in promoting dental 'teams', in which nurses and hygienists took on more clinical roles (mainly in preventative and diagnostic work). In turn, this freed-up the time of dentists to work on more urgent or complex cases and improved their working conditions (Goodwin et al, 2004). The apparent success of the PDS pilots, however, has not been shared by the wider dental profession who see the initiative as a mechanism to cap income and as a form of deprofessionalization.

The 2004 GP Contract

The 2004 GP contract builds upon a premise that a more direct PCT-practice contractual relationship allows primary care organizations greater managerial and financial leverage to shape service delivery. The new GMS contract has been designed to be administered by PCTs to primary care practices. Patients are no longer required to register with an individual GP, but to practices that are free to determine their own skill-mix to achieve a certain level of service. Each practice has that ability to opt-out of 'additional' service provision, such as cancer screening, vaccinations and immunizations, child health surveillance, minor surgery and out-of-hours coverage. Where certain practices opt-out they return funding for these elements to their PCT who must take responsibility for securing these services to the patients of these practices. For primary care organizations, therefore, the implication is the need to contract sessions of care from other existing practices, alternative (private) suppliers, or to maintain a range of full or part-time salaried nurses and practitioners themselves. According to Lilly (2003), making PCTs accountable for securing services under this new system of opt-outs will raise both the costs of service delivery and shift the key operational function of the primary care organization to that as a procurement agent for services via locally-held contracts.

An important element to the new GMS contract is that approximately half of a practice's income will be achieved through payments based on the achievement of performance and quality targets (NHS Confederation, 2003). The quality and outcomes framework stipulates a number of organizational and clinical standards to be achieved and includes payments based on patient experiences. Each standard in the framework is given a points value. A maximum of 1050 points is available of which just over half relate to clinical quality (Table 12.4). Providers can 'aspire' to achieve a certain level of points (say 900/1050) and are then paid one-third of the remuneration value in monthly installments with the remainder awarded at the end of the year following an annual visit and return by the PCT.

Linking remuneration directly to the attainment of a set of quality standards heralds a further trend in primary care towards greater managerial control and corporatism. Since the system places a considerable proportion of a practices income at risk it rewards cost-effective practice, the use of evidence-based principles, and systems of peer review. However, whether the new GMS contract will foster greater clinical engagement and integration, or further undermine the professional morale of GPs and nurses, remains to be seen. A heavier reliance on PCT financial incentives may make GPs less willing to respond in the best interests of patients when not directly rewarded (see LeGrand, 2003). To avoid the new contract being a 'constitution for knaves that crowd out civic virtues' (p. 26), engaging GPs in the new era requires well-designed contractual incentives (Smith and York, 2004). These key points about motivation, agency and contractual incentives are explored in more detail in Chapter 14.

Table 12.4 Clinical standards in the new GMS contract, 2004

Service Area	Points Value
Coronary Heart Disease	121
Hypertension	105
Diabetes	99
Asthma	72
Chronic Obstructive Pulmonary Disease	45
Mental Health	41
Stroke or TIAs	31
Epilepsy	16
Cancer	12
Hypothyroidism	8
Total	**550**

Source: Department of Health, 2004c.

The likelihood of primary care practices behaving in a more distant contractual relationship with PCTs appears to have been encouraged since the new contract allows primary care providers to create their own limited companies. This raises the prospect for the development of new organizations in England similar to IPAs in New Zealand that are owned and controlled independently by doctors, negotiate contracts and fees with budget holders (such as PCTs) and may become powerful corporate bodies protecting the professional autonomy of their members. These organizations might also be more successful in developing their own internal mechanisms to achieve quality targets, or in working to protocols and guidelines. Research undertaken by Barnett (2004), for example, has shown how professionals are far more supportive and engaged with independent organizations which represent what they perceive as their best interests compared to mandated or imposed organizations (such as PCTs) despite each employing very similar managed care techniques. It could be argued, therefore, that the degree of legitimacy a primary care organization has with its constituent professionals is potentially a more powerful tool in developing and sustaining clinical engagement than contracting or through monetary incentives.

Practice-Based Commissioning

The introduction of practice-based commissioning into the NHS in 2005 (Smith et al, 2004; Department of Health 2005b), in which budgets for elective care are devolved to groups of practices on a voluntary basis, has been promoted in an effort to re-engage GPs with their host PCTs through providing inherent incentives in the form of the reinvestment of 'efficiency savings' into practice and/or community-based services. Under the initial plans for practice-based commissioning (Department of Health, 2005b), PCTs will retain ultimate responsibility for the use of the funds, will be heavily involved in administration, whilst practice groups will need to base their commissioning activities on an agreed local development plan (LDP). The initiative is thus predicated on the need to develop a mature partnership between PCTs and those practices opting to take a budget, a scenario that may not be acceptable to many GPs and practice groups seeking to develop their local independence.

Conclusions: Lessons for Research and Practice

This chapter has stressed how effective clinical engagement is an essential ingredient to the successful working of primary care organizations. Most importantly, it has shown how the current disengagement of many primary care professionals with their PCT needs to be addressed such that clinicians can become central determinants directing care from within PECs yet with inter-dependence to other professionals working in primary care. The leverage needed to be developed by PCTs to facilitate this is their key challenge since it is clear that the future requires integrating the role of the clinician into the wider 'managed care system'. The introduction of practice-based commissioning may be one such mechanism that attracts primary care physicians and practice groups to work in partnership with PCTs in commissioning services, developing chronic disease management strategies and re-investing resources in primary and community care services. However, in terms of engaging clinicians, the success of the scheme will be dependent on whether this potential for investment is realized, and whether PCTs can tread the fine line between being facilitative and controlling of the local commissioning agenda.

The set of professional networks that characterize primary care makes highly complex this relationship between clinicians and PCTs. The 'third way' of organizing primary care through relational governance techniques and professional self-surveillance has considerable difficulties and it remains unclear whether the modernization agenda of the NHS can be delivered through such structures. As Bond and LeGrand (2003) suggest, there is a danger that new primary care organizations will combine the anarchy of market relations with the dictatorship of hierarchy.

The acceleration of new local contracts in England could be argued to be a new trend that moves away from the network-model towards a hierarchical and/or contractually controlled approach. Many commentators have suggested that the process of PCT mergers and new local contracts is a preliminary step to something more formal and vertically-integrated that in time may lead to a highly managed but clinically-led US-style of managed care organization, such as the likes of the Kaiser Permanente provider/purchaser organization (Pollock, 2001). Practitioners wishing to secure a locally-negotiated contract income in this model would be under greater pressure to synchronize clinical activity and respond directly to corporate and financial incentives.

As PCTs and primary care practitioners are drawn ever closer together, this may appear a logical conclusion. However, research into primary care organizations in the UK and USA suggests that looser network-based models are more likely to be successful in securing the medical engagement that is crucial to the overall achievement of clinical and service objectives as well as to the management of clinical practice (Smith and Walshe, 2004). Developing a new form of management hierarchy, therefore, is likely to lose professional ownership. Nonetheless, the new GMS contract and local contracts for other health professionals brings the prospect of 'managed primary care' closer to reality. Engaging primary care clinicians within such a system will as much require active PCT facilitation as new contractual arrangements:

> Simply introducing contracting for primary care, performance appraisal and review, career planning, etc, will not work any more than deciding that waiting lists will be abolished. Rather, PCTs will need to balance their approach by demonstrating that they understand the [professional's] role 'as a whole' and appreciate the dynamics of the 'system' that he or she works within and often conducts (Starey, 2003, p. 199).

Lessons for Research

- Research into sustaining clinical engagement needs to take into account the wider political context since negative attitudes towards political reform processes can inhibit relationships with primary care organizations.
- Groups of innovative GPs and professionals at the forefront of change have often been the focus for enquiry in order to 'learn lessons' for those where engagement has been less developed. However, research needs to be aware of the specific environment and status of innovator sites and ensure that research examines those areas where clinical engagement has proven more difficult.
- Future qualitative research examining clinical engagement needs to go beyond opinion surveys of managers and professionals to establish more in-depth observational methods of inquiry. Fruitful areas might include an analysis of the functioning of professional networks and how these respond to different forms of external governance.
- The nature and importance of clinical leadership in PCTs as a mechanism for ensuring clinical engagement is under-researched. There is an opportunity for research to examine both the importance of the background of clinical leaders as well as the effectiveness of different leadership styles. This would require direct surveying of GPs as well as an examination of the competencies and characteristics of effective clinical leaders.
- The introduction of the new GMS contract provides a new method through which PCTs and primary care clinicians will engage. There is the potential to examine a range of case studies to establish the different ways in which PCTs can, or have, used such contracts to enable effective clinical engagement at a

strategic level as well as to foster collective responses between practices.

- There are no studies that have examined head-to-head comparisons between different models of PCT-clinician engagement. Such an analysis could undertake a comparison across the spectrum of emerging PCT-provider relationships ranging from vertically-integrated and highly managed purchaser/provider models to networks of primary care providers based on a system of procurement.
- Regardless of the context within which professionals are placed, there is a need to examine the underlying motivations and responses of professional groups to different forms of governance and incentive arrangements.
- A potential consequence of the new GMS contract will be the development of limited companies which provide a range of primary care services to PCTs. The impact of such innovations on clinical engagement 'within' these new corporate bodies, as well as the relationship with PCTs, needs to be on the research agenda.
- PCTs will be have been tasked with developing closer operational relationships with primary care dentists, pharmacists and optometrists. Given that these professional groups have to-date remained outside the decision-making structure of PCTs, research might examine the development of these new relationships and the managerial techniques through which such professionals can be engaged.

Lessons for Practice

- Sustaining clinical engagement in PCTs is a key challenge since primary care professionals have not been subject to external management in the past.
- PCTs need to adopt a decentralized approach to decision-making to facilitate grass-roots support and need to find ways to let small organizational values and freedoms survive in the bigger corporate environment where centrally-determined standards of care must be met.
- PECs need to be given the authority and freedom to lead service development and change processes. Administrative control needs to be kept to a minimum whilst ensuring appropriate accountability.
- The facilitation of practice-based commissioning is one potential mechanism that may be used for this task, but PCTs must be willing to 'let go' its direct control of commissioning budgets and agendas to gain the support of practices and professionals.
- Network-based management models are more likely to be successful in securing professional engagement and ownership but they lack the managerial leverage needed to synchronize clinical activity. A mix of techniques is therefore required, both relational and contractual, if PCTs are to effectively manage professionals.
- 'Soft' governance techniques and financial incentives need to be retained alongside well designed local contracts that enable greater managerial control

by linking remuneration to the attainment of quality targets and cost-effective practice.

- If clinicians are to commit, they need to see the clinical merit in working to well developed clinical guidelines and protocols. This requires the technical evidence-base and information systems to facilitate the process of collective learning. PCTs need to establish network structures of peer groups to establish good relationships, a process requiring protected time and funding.
- Respected clinical leaders, and a new cadre of clinician manager, are required to create a symbiosis of professional and managerial leadership.
- PCTs cannot expect to gain compliance unless a mandate for governance is granted to the organization by the clinicians themselves. Legitimacy is more powerful than quality contracts and/or financial incentives in sustaining clinical engagement and engendering collective responsibility to PCT policies.
- Sustaining clinical engagement is likely to be presented with even greater challenges in the future as new initiatives, such as foundation hospitals, patient choice, practice-based commissioning, and the potential development of independent practitioner organizations, further complicate the PCT-clinician relationship.

Chapter 13

Conclusions: Evaluating the Progress Made by Primary Care Organizations

One of the main characteristics of the international research evidence on on primary care organizations is that relatively little independent evaluation of their activities has been undertaken. Even in the UK, where much has been written on PCOs, the emphasis has been placed on issues related to organizational processes rather than impact in terms of patient care or user experiences (Smith et al, 2004). In evaluating the progress made by PCOs, therefore, this chapter attempts to distil what is known in terms of their implementation, development and impact in order to take forward the lessons, and to develop an agenda, on how PCOs in the future should be evaluated.

Evaluating the International PCO Experience

This book has emphasized how the development of primary care organizations has been an international phenomenon in which the policies of different nations have seemingly undergone a process of cross-fertilization. It was reported how managed care techniques, in particular, have been widely adopted (Rosleff and Lister, 1995) whilst PCOs have also adapted themselves to tackle public health issues and health inequalities (see Chapter 3). Policy makers, however, have largely used the experiences from other countries as exemplars of processes, potentially out of context. A key lesson, therefore, is for international policy networks in this field to carry out a more systematic assessment of the available experience in order to derive specific lessons for the effective development of PCOs generally, and of methods of governing professionals and professional organizations more specifically. To enable PCO developments between international health care systems with different governance regimes and cultural contexts to be assessed, a specific set of PCO-based performance indicators needs to be developed. In the UK context, the impact of devolution in the four home countries of the UK is likely to be a fruitful area for comparative analysis of performance since devolution represents a natural policy experiment within which the relative performance of PCOs might be compared and the lessons shared (Smith et al, 2004).

Evaluating the Organization and Management of PCOs

Generating lessons to understand the most effective (and least effective) method of organizing and managing PCOs is an important issue for both policy makers and managers, particularly as many PCOs have developed into large and highly complex organizational forms. In the English context, finding the right structures and incentives that can be employed to engage professional partners and achieve best organizational outcomes has been a searching task. The evidence suggests that organizational and managerial approaches need to be 'appropriate' to the size of the organization as well as take into consideration 'soft' values such as local cultures, professional values and the propensity to work corporately (Bjoke et al, 2001). However, such 'findings' provide relatively little comfort to the manager since they offer little in the way of 'hard' evidence on best practice.

To an extent, the finding that the most appropriate organizational and management approaches will differ by PCO is important since it stresses that there is no 'one size fits all' policy that is workable. Hence, the PCO evaluations stress the need for non-structural solutions that are designed in a more bespoke manner. A key lesson for managers and practitioners is to continually evaluate managerial arrangements to explore the degree to which the organizational structure remains appropriate to its overall size and objectives. This is particularly important in the discussion of the implementation of new structurally-imposed solutions, such as mergers, since it is likely that trade-offs will apply in the process – for example, between increased managerialism and corporatism with the retention of professional leadership and ownership (Peck and Freeman, 2005).

One of the key lessons, therefore, is that PCOs should become 'learning organizations' to develop and use knowledge to change and improve themselves on an ongoing basis. The concept of the 'learning organization' is popular in the business literature as organizations, subjected to exhortations to become more adaptable and responsive to change, have attempted to develop structures and systems that nurture innovation (Peters and Waterman, 1982; Senge, 1990). The key characteristics of 'learning organizations' (see Table 13.1) show that it is particularly skilled at disseminating, acquiring and transferring knowledge and modifying its own organizational behaviour to get the best out of those 'in' the organization (Bloisi, Cook and Hunsaker, 2003).

The evidence from the organization and management of PCOs summarized in Chapter 5 concluded that PCOs should be encouraged to undertake and learn from their own organizational experiences. Carrying out non-participant observation of the public meetings of PCOs, for example, might offer valuable insights into the intra-board dynamics of the PCO team. Similarly, questioning PCO members about their perceptions of their own and others' influence on decision-making offers further important learning in terms of the relative power of different professional and lay groups within PCOs, and points to those actions required to address evident imbalances in influence. It is important that any PCO should return on a regular basis to assess the impact of its organizational and managerial arrangements, particularly since PCOs are in a seemingly continuous process of change. Armed with these characteristics, a PCO might be better equipped to deal with the traditional constraints of fragmentation, professional competition and reactiveness.

Table 13.1 Characteristics of a learning organization

- **Systems thinking**. Members perceive their organization as a system where any action taken will have repercussions on other variables in the system. It is important to see the 'big picture'.
- **Shared vision.** Belief and commitment toward a goal deeply desired by all.
- **Personal mastery.** Continual learning and personal growth by all organizational members helps them to give up old ways of thinking and embrace better ones for themselves and/or the organization.
- **Mental process models.** Willingness to reflect on the reasons underlying organizational changes, to challenge assumptions and to create a more appropriate process for doing things.
- **Team learning.** Members openly communicate across organizational and professional boundaries to help solve problems. The need for personal wins decreases as the search for the good of the team increases.

Source: Adapted from Bloisi, Cook and Hunsaker (2003), p. 732.

Evaluating the Process of Professional Engagement

If PCOs need to embrace the evaluation of their organizational and management processes as a way to improve performance, the specific issue of professional engagement is also a key source of enquiry. This is particularly necessary as the experience of PCTs has revealed a growing level of 'disengagement' from GPs, nurses and allied health professionals to the work of their host primary care organizations which they commonly perceive as 'controlled' by managers. The potential solutions to this debate that have been teased out in this book provide a lengthy list, but it is instructive to show the breadth of conclusions that have been drawn as follows:

- the need for clinical leadership and/or ownership;
- the need for a new breed of respected clinician-managers;
- the need for better communication and consultation processes between managers and professionals through forums;
- the need for the development of joint-working to promote understanding;
- the need for training and development opportunities;
- the need for professionals to feel their work is valued, makes a difference, and has influence;
- the need for professionals to see that there is clinical merit to activities through

    the availability of a sound technical evidence-base;
- the ability of professionals to debate and challenge priorities in PCOs;
- the need to reduce bureaucracy;
- the need to ensure sustainable workloads;
- the need for a common vision or common agenda;
- the need for 'decentralized' decision-making that is professionally driven, for example by providing professional executive committees with the power and authority to lead service developments;
- letting small organizational values survive within the bigger corporate environment;
- the need for local contracts and direct incentives based on the attainment of quality targets and cost-effective practices;
- the need for 'soft' governance techniques to be retained alongside financial incentives for participation; and
- the need to gain legitimacy in order to get compliance – the 'mandate to manage' principle.

Evaluations of primary care organizations have tended to view the level of professional engagement as a key contextual variable affecting the ability to achieve objectives rather than as a process that should be examined more closely to focus on the micro-processes and dynamics of manager-professional relationships and the incentives psyche of GPs and other clinicians. For example, since effective clinical leadership is reported as an important contributor to the level of engagement, research that identifies the core characteristics of effective clinical leaders and clinician-managers may prove to be helpful in identifying future leaders and generating a positive organizational culture in future PCOs. Monitoring levels of engagement alongside research that provides regular feedback on the motivation and reaction of professionals over time should also help PCOs understand better the issues in sustaining and developing engagement.

    In undertaking the research process into clinical engagement, evaluators need to go beyond opinion surveys of managers and professionals to establish more in-depth observational methods of inquiry. Fruitful areas might include an analysis of the functioning of professional networks and how these respond to different forms of external governance, or to reactions to recent initiatives such as the new GMS contract and practice-based commissioning. Regardless of the context within which professionals are placed, there is a need to examine the underlying motivations and responses of professional groups to different forms of governance and incentive arrangements. Research into sustaining clinical engagement also needs to take into account the wider political context since negative attitudes towards political reform processes can inhibit relationships with primary care organizations. Finally, research has tended to take its lessons from GPs and professionals at the forefront of change in order to 'learn lessons' for those where engagement has been less developed. However, such research needs to be aware of the specific environment and status of innovator sites and ensure that research examines those areas where clinical engagement has proven more difficult, including those PCOs considered to be late adopter's of change.

Evaluating the Performance of PCOs

As Chapter 8 reported, English PCOs have become subject to increasingly stringent and formal methods of external performance assessment to the point where PCTs are now a formally accountable NHS body. However, it was concluded that the research evidence on PCO performance as collected by external regulatory bodies such as CHI (now the Healthcare Commission) and the Audit Commission remained limited with significant gaps in terms of their relative impact on health outcomes and activity. Like many forms of evaluation, the body of research evidence that is available primarily relates to issues of process, context and structure with little detailed or sustained analysis on health outcomes and activity. This fact highlights a major deficiency in our knowledge of PCOs since there is relatively little comparative evidence on whether they have had a net positive or negative impact on the quality of services provided and health outcomes more generally. Whilst the continual reform of PCOs in England has often precluded this issue from being addressed in any comprehensive fashion, there is nonetheless an acute need for research that explores ways of assessing the real impact of PCOs, especially in relation to the analysis of routine data. The new GMS contract and its associated data collection and quality and outcomes framework offer a specific opportunity for researching and assessing the performance of PCTs.

Evaluating Partnership Working for Health Improvement

Partnership working for health improvement has been a problematic and developmental process for PCG/Ts. As Chapter 9 recounted, partnership working with social services and the wider local authority was reported as a lesser priority in most PCG/Ts and has been hampered by a triumvirate of organizational, financial and cultural barriers. Moreover, PCOs appear to have struggled to find the capacity, time and skills to develop effective public health teams and have only recently developed public health directorates. Links to the public and community groups have also generally been slow to materialize. The research suggested three recurrent issues in the ability of PCOs to make progress in these areas:

* the impact of constant organizational upheavals, making the development of new partnerships, or the retention of existing ones, problematic;
* capacity problems in PCTs in tackling new functions previously performed by health authorities resulting in the prioritization of other 'core' activities to the detriment of partnership activities; and
* health care professionals leading PCOs remaining medically-focused rather than keen to embrace wider strategies for improving health and wellbeing.

The key management task within future PCOs will be to break down remaining barriers to partnership working. To help PCOs better understand how to do this effectively, research needs to focus on the dynamics of professional relationships. Moreover, since the potential impact of new partnerships is unknown, research needs to establish the costs and benefits of such approaches on staff and patients. Research should also attempt to contribute to the development of the competencies for public health staff, and to professionals working in posts across institutions and assessment should be made of the impact and effectiveness of patient forums and other forms of community engagement to establish progress and derive lessons for PCTs and policy makers on how best to take forward this agenda.

Developing and Improving Primary Care Services

The evaluation of practice-based primary care developments set out in Chapter 10 suggests that this is an area where PCOs have achieved their greatest successes. However, there is little evidence to show whether or not the development of new primary care-based services has been sustained into the longer term. There is evidence to suggest, for example, that in the transition to PCG/Ts some of the gains in primary care service innovations at a practice level may have been lost though the removal of fundholding budgets (Street et al, 2001). No systematic analysis of this has ever been undertaken.

An issue that is perhaps of more concern is that the quality of new and expanded services in primary care has never been adequately analyzed (Smith et al, 2004). If PCOs are to establish more and more primary and community care alternatives to hospital provision as part of an overall strategy to manage chronic diseases in the community, it is clearly unsatisfactory that the evidence-base in terms of whether quality is retained in such a transition is lacking. More evidence is required on the feasibility and quality of community-based care and of the impact of clinical governance arrangements more generally on the quality of patient care. With the introduction of 'payment by results' and the emergence of practice-based commissioning in England, the impact this new environment has on disease management strategies needs urgent attention – not least to help future PCOs understand the most effective methods of controlling referrals to secondary care in order to keep within budget.

Assessing the PCO Commissioning Function

The most controversial PCO activity of all, in the English context, has been the continuation of the PCO's role as the principal commissioning agent of care services. Though the progress made by PCOs in this regard has attracted a great deal of attention from the research and practitioner community (see Audit Commission 2004; Smith et al, 2004), the results suggest that PCOs have failed, on the whole, to embrace the complexities of the commissioning function and to use the process to make a significant impact on care provided in hospitals – though PCOs have fared better in the development of primary, community and intermediate care services (see Chapter 11).

An emerging research agenda to evaluate the effectiveness of commissioning shows just how complex the activity is likely to be. Smith et al's (2004) review of commissioning, for example, revealed that a continuum of commissioning models existed such that a commissioning agency (such as a PCO) might select and use different approaches as appropriate to the context of the local health community. This might include devolving budgets to localities or practices, pooling budgets with other agencies to commission collectively, or indeed ceding budgets to other organizations that might commission on the PCO's behalf. The key research question to be posed is fundamental but complex – what is the most effective blend of commissioning approaches, and how can PCOs decide how to select that blend? The need for more systematic assessment of the impact of health commissioning, including the examination of a PCO's ability to achieve specific service and patient quality objectives in so doing, needs to be researched and monitored in a rigorous manner. Such evaluation needs to be contextually-specific (e.g. to policy changes) whilst still being able to track longer-term service change and outcomes. The links between key variables and outcomes also needs far greater in-depth study – such as the link between management capacity and/or clinical involvement and outcomes compared between PCOs nationally and internationally. All of these issues are complex evaluation tasks requiring a range of qualitative and quantitative methodologies to catch the meaning of the associations between commissioning models, contextual settings, commissioning dynamics, and changes in activity or services.

Undertaking Effective Evaluations of the Development of PCOs

Chapter 4 provided a review of the evaluation challenges faced by researchers in studying highly complex policy initiatives such as TPPs, PCGs and PCTs. It highlighted that evaluations examining the development of PCOs faced fundamental challenges for a number of key reasons, including:

- the fact they often have a strong political dimension and are subject to evolution and change over the study period;
- the problematic ability to make direct comparison between PCOs since there are few opportunities available to utilize control sites;
- the pragmatic nature of evaluations as a consequence of their contextually-specific nature; and
- the predominant objective from funding agencies of identifying lessons to inform the future implementation of PCO policies rather than to fundamentally assess impact and outcomes.

Despite these underlying difficulties, research into examining the development and impact of PCOs can be effective as long as the process follows a set of key research principles as follows:

1. *Clarify research objectives.* Evaluators of PCOs need to develop specific research objectives, questions and success criteria. Whilst some of these objectives and criteria may be generic to all PCOs, the experience of PCO evaluations in the UK has shown that each individual PCO needs to be assessed in terms of its ability to achieve its own specific objectives. To this end, the collection of baseline information on the individual objectives, strategies and contexts of PCOs is important to clarify research objectives. This process needs to be continually reviewed since it is in the nature of PCOs to develop over time and so change their priorities.

2. *Set the evaluation framework.* Though PCOs are complex organizations to examine, with the process requiring a healthy regard for pragmatism, evaluators need to establish clear evaluation frameworks based on an agreed set of research questions and hypotheses. Given the nature of PCOs, such a framework should enable a contextually aware analysis to be undertaken. Contextual analysis provides an important basis for investigation, but there is also a need to develop greater theory-based approaches to the design and implementation of evaluations.

3. *Select the most appropriate methods for the analysis.* Evaluations should be formative and iterative to ensure flexibility, but methodologies should employ a range of data collection methods to improve the validity of the results observed. In particular, evaluations of PCOs need to be led by multi-disciplinary teams since there is great value in having a mix of social scientists, health economists, and other disciplines involved in the evaluation process.

4. *Ensure reflexivity.* Evaluators should be aware of the changing policy context and employ a robust research design that is adaptable to change.

5. *Develop relationships with funders and research users.* Without losing focus on the longer-term issues, evaluations must meet the demands of policy makers and accepting that the evaluation will be undertaken in a political context. Evaluators need to 'manage upwards' to ensure good relationships through regular forms of feedback but retain their sense of independence. Similarly, research should attempt to engage the 'end user' to foster 'ownership' of the results.

6. *Employ a strategy to disseminate evaluation findings to influence policy and practice.* Since PCOs have developmental needs, researchers would be advised to develop a more interactive 'action research' model that engages practitioners and policy makers in training and development sessions to share research findings and learn about best practice and/or alternative approaches.

New Evaluation Approaches for 21st Century PCOs

Evaluation has an important role to play in informing policy options and guiding new policy initiatives. For example, in the future development of PCOs in England, knowledge needs to be gained, synthesized and disseminated on how best PCOs might tackle new arrangements such as the administration of new GMS contracts, practice-based commissioning (indeed, all forms of commissioning), out-of-hours arrangements and the development of chronic disease management strategies in a 'payment by results' regime. What is clear is that PCOs themselves need to be engaged in the research process as a part of a strategy linked to being a 'learning organization' manifest in their willingness to learn and potentially change working practices in the light of what is observed. Indeed, PCOs might be advised to develop 'research networks' in which feedback and learning from evaluation studies as well as shared experiences in development can be discussed and shared.

Such a network strategy appears to be at the heart of a current UK initiative for building research capacity into the NHS. The Research Capacity Development Programme, for example, aims to build a skilled workforce capable of undertaking 'high quality' research with the aim of maintaining and improving health with a knowledge-based, patient-centred health service. In line with 'learning organization' principles, the essential ingredient appears to be the creation of an environment where research and research findings are valued and acted upon. The creation of 'learning networks' has been heralded as a key mechanism for knowledge transfer in this regard (Davies, 2005). However, at present, such learning networks are being advanced in medically-dominated disease-based areas such as cancer, diabetes and mental health care. In many respects, this reflects the predominant paradigm in the way that most funding for research is made available – in silos of professionally-led medical areas rather than to organizational studies taking a wider and more holistic view of health services. If one accepts that the effective management of chronic disease in primary and community care settings has and will be the most pressing issue for the future management of health services in the 21st century (as opposed to the treatment of acute conditions) it is imperative that both research funders and the NHS recognize the importance of the issue and begin to invest in evaluation and learning processes that are more fit for purpose.

PCOs in England and the UK are, and will be, in great need of such help. The relationship between researchers, practitioners and policy-makers therefore needs to be redefined to ensure that findings are disseminated in the most effective way possible and that a 'learning' culture is developed. Independent research funding into PCO issues would help in this regard. However, what is particularly important is that research should not be undertaken simply to inform policy development, but should examine in more detail the costs and impact of innovations, as well as the processes that underpin them.

Assessing the Evaluation Process: Lessons for Policy Makers, Practitioners and Researchers

The evaluation of PCOs has been a complex process in the UK and previous research has highlighted the importance of developing contextually-aware frameworks for data collection and analysis, as well as to be responsive to the needs of policy-makers and research users. In the preceding sections of this chapter, the emerging research agenda on the different aspects of PCO developments has been highlighted. To improve the quality and relevance of such future work, this chapter concludes with a set of key lessons for influencing policy, practice and research.

Key Lessons for Policy Makers

- Policy makers need to prioritize research and development activities that move away from the predominant study of acute diseases to the effective organization of primary and community care services as a mechanism for integrating care for the treatment of long-term chronic diseases;
- Policy makers need to accept the role that independent evaluation can play as a mechanism for assessing impact, for challenging the status quo, and for developing policy options for the future development of PCOs;
- Policy makers have the opportunity to examine and fund a more systematic analysis of the international evidence on PCOs to help derive policy options, though the process should use a generic set of performance indicators;
- Policy makers need to fund research and development activities such that PCOs are better able to share learning and build managerial competencies;
- Policy makers might enable PCOs to embrace the value of research by providing direct incentives for PCOs to lead the process as well as to respond to findings.

Key Lessons for Practitioners

- PCOs, and the managers and professionals within them, need to develop themselves as 'learning organizations' that engage in the process of research and value outcomes such that implied changes to working practices are embraced;
- Learning networks for PCOs are required in which feedback and learning from evaluation studies, as well as shared PCO experiences, can be discussed and transferred;
- PCOs should develop incentives for practitioners and professionals to engage in the process of research as a natural part of their working lives.

Key Lessons for Researchers

- Effective learning from PCOs requires an in-depth understanding of context, but future evaluations need to pay more attention to the development of theory to avoid overly pragmatic responses;
- Researchers must undertake evaluations in a flexible yet robust manner that encourages rapid feedback to be provided to policy-makers and practitioners;
- Researchers need to develop a more interactive 'action learning' based model of evaluation that engages policy makers and practitioners more directly and contributes to their training and developmental needs;
- Researchers must move beyond analyses based on the qualitative examination of process issues, or the soliciting of opinions through surveys, to examine directly the impact of PCO activities in terms of their costs and outcomes.

Chapter 14

Conclusions: Primary Care Organizations in the Future

Primary care organizations have become increasingly important within many health systems as governments internationally have sought to integrate and co-ordinate primary and community care services in a more directly managed fashion. The experience of PCOs detailed in the preceding chapters shows consensus on their ability to improve quality, access and the cost-effectiveness of provision, particularly within the vertically-integrated systems such as Kaiser Permanente in the USA. Nonetheless, the international research evidence suggests that primary care organizations face a number of fundamental managerial challenges in fulfilling their functions, not least for English PCTs that have the unique (and as yet unproven) task of purchasing/commissioning care for their local population. This concluding chapter summarizes the challenges and the lessons for future policy and practice in developing primary care organizations in the UK and international context.

The Importance of PCOs in an International Context

Primary care reforms internationally have favoured the move towards 'managed primary care' not only to co-ordinate care provision but to take on responsibility for developing a public health role and for tackling health inequalities. The reasons for this shift in emphasis towards PCOs internationally are set out in the first chapter of this book and can be summarized are as follows:

- to improve health outcomes;
- to manage demands and control costs;
- to engage primary care physicians;
- to enable greater integration of health services;
- to develop more accessible services in community and primary care settings; and
- to enable greater scrutiny of primary care services.

These reasons reflect the fact that the burden of disease in developed countries has moved away from the need to treat acute illnesses, such as cancers and heart attacks, to the need to treat chronic diseases, such as diabetes, asthma and arthritis. As people live longer, it is chronic illnesses that are the most prevalent health problems in terms of both cost and impact. Consequently, the rise of the PCO and of managed care more generally has been a reflection of a system-response to develop a new paradigm of care. As Wagner (1998) describes, the challenge for health systems is the development of a chronic care model. The features of this model include the integration of primary and secondary care; the co-ordination of health and social care; the development of team-based services where the skills of nurses and doctors are used to their best advantage; and the need for patients to take expert control of the management of their conditions (Wagner, 1998).

The rise of the PCO in an international context, therefore, is strongly associated with the growing need to concentrate health service activities on chronic disease management. Indeed, research on outcomes underlines the essential contribution that primary care must play in this regard (Starfield, 1998). However, the international evidence reviewed in Chapter 2 showed how PCOs have faced a number of fundamental managerial challenges, particularly in engaging primary care professionals in corporate activities. This is because 'managed' primary care, and the chronic disease management model, threatens directly the traditional professional territory of primary care physicians by encouraging the growth of multi-professional teams and clinical governance regimes. Managers of PCOs, therefore, must be continually aware of, and address, the inherent tension between professional autonomy and organizational managerialism.

One of the most salient conclusions for the future development of PCOs to be drawn from Chapter 2 is the importance of two-way learning. With so many countries developing different models of managed primary care, there is surely much to be gleaned from their experiences. Indeed, in England, much learning in the late 1990s and the early 2000s was being drawn from the Kaiser Permanente managed care system in the USA due to its comparatively low hospital utilization rates (acute bed days for the eleven leading causes of bed use were shown to be 3.5 times lower than in the NHS) (Ham et al, 2003). Kaiser's focus on the chronic disease model of care, where an 'unplanned admission' to hospital is seen as a 'system failure', clearly provides some important lessons for all PCOs.

However, as with all comparative learning, understanding the context of developments is important. In Kaiser Permanente, for example, far from being 'not-for-profit' in the traditional sense, there is actually a strong commercial culture with many parts of the system acting as business corporations that are allowed to generate and distribute surpluses. Moreover, medical leadership and responsibility for managing care individually is encouraged greatly because physicians are shareholders in the system (Ham, 2005). For many health care systems such medical 'ownership' is not possible and there is thus a danger of importing policies that are 'out of context'. As Smee (1999) observed, in the context of the UK NHS, 'hanging international ideas, like Christmas tree decorations, on the NHS may not necessarily be either useful or relevant' (p. 10). In other words, international learning can only be relevant where a conscious effort has been made to identify its relevance to domestic issues. The development and ongoing evaluation of eight Kaiser 'pilots' in the NHS, for example, has been an intelligent response to discovering if the lessons can be transferred effectively between systems (Department of Health, 2004f).

A final conclusion for the future of PCOs that can be drawn from the international evidence is that physician integration and commitment is related to the development of incentives rather than on structures of compliance. PCOs in the future will need to adopt a combination of relational and contractual forms of governance in order to achieve commitment. These lessons are provided in more detail in the 'engaging stakeholders' section below.

Box 14.1 Key lessons for PCO policy and practice from the international experience

> - Managed primary care is a legitimate and effective method in primary and community health services delivery and is essential in the effective tackling of chronic diseases
> - The effectiveness of the PCO's role as commissioners of secondary care as yet remains unproven
> - All primary care organizations internationally face similar management challenges, particularly in engaging professionals in corporate activities
> - Physician integration and commitment within PCOs is related to the development of incentives rather than on structures of compliance
> - A process of two-way learning needs to be encouraged to learn the lessons from high performing PCOs in different health systems

The Principles of Developing Primary Care Organizations

The ability of managed primary care organizations to deliver the benefits described above is clearly related to how such organizations originate and how they are then subsequently developed. In Chapter 3, an assessment of the published research into the range of PCO models adopted in England since the early 1990s revealed a number of key principles that need to be observed if this process is to be tackled effectively and lead to best results. Perhaps the most fundamental factor in a PCO's ability to achieve this is to ensure that primary care professionals and other stakeholders become integrated into the PCO in a manner that facilitates a more corporate and coherent arrangement. Consequently, as Chapter 5 found, whilst the optimal size for a PCO remains the subject of ongoing debate, the more important fact was that it should not become unduly complex, bureaucratic and distant from its professional stakeholders.

One of the most striking features of Chapter 3's examination of PCO developments in England was the frequency with which certain messages and lessons recurred over time (see summary in Box 14.2). The research evidence showed that the experience of GP commissioning pilots, total purchasing pilots, and primary care groups is as relevant today as it was at the time of the original research. This is important for the future of English NHS policy and practice where continual reform of the 'demand-side' of the NHS system has led to the re-evaluation and development of new models of primary care organization every few years. The fact that there are *recurrent* lessons to the development of PCOs suggest that there is a pressing need for managers and policy makers to develop a more attuned corporate memory since it is clear that managers do not have to start from scratch in the face of a new policy initiative in this field. As Chapter 3 concluded, whilst the labels applied to the latest incarnation of primary care organization may change, the challenges of enabling GPs, nurses, managers and others to work together to achieve truly primary care-led commissioning, service developments, and chronic disease management processes remain constant.

Box 14.2 Key lessons for the development of primary care organizations in England

- PCOs take at least two years to become established and/or to emerge from the inevitable turmoil of organisational change
- Adequate levels of management and organisational support are crucial if PCOs are to properly discharge their functions
- The engagement of GPs to the strategic aims and objectives of a PCO is crucial, but is particularly challenging in larger and more complex PCOs where there is a tension between professional autonomy and managerialism
- Other primary care professionals, especially nurses, will struggle to gain influence at a strategic level in comparison with medical and managerial colleagues
- The involvement of service users and the public in the operation of PCOs is challenging and, for many, problematic
- The development of strategic partnerships with local authorities, social services and other NHS providers is an important but time-consuming activity
- PCOs can achieve service gains in primary care and community services, with clinical governance being a key lever in this process
- The jury is still out as to whether significant progress in commissioning secondary care by PCOs can ever be made effective
- A positive relationship between a PCO and its supervisory tier, manifest in a degree of devolution and freedom of operation, is important
- PCOs have the potential to combine sensitivity to the needs of individual patients with a population-based public health perspective

Clinical and Managerial Leadership

Primary care organizations internationally have in general developed into large and complex entities. A key tension during this evolution has been the relationship between clinical and managerial leadership and the impact this has had on the ability of PCOs to achieve their objectives. In particular, the original philosophy underlying the creation of primary care-based organizations in England was to imbue the system with clinical leadership from the 'frontline'. Hence, PCOs were intended to be led by professionals such that funding decisions could be made nearer to the needs and demands of patients. Within PCTs, the 'engine-room' of this process was to be the professional executive committee – a microcosm of local professional representation.

Chapter 5 examined the leadership debate within English PCTs in the context of their organizational and management arrangements. It showed how the leadership and governance of the PCT was split between three key groups: the board, the PEC and the management team. This had led to overlap, tensions and confusion in leadership roles between the three groups. Indeed, the evidence suggested that the leading influence on strategic as well as operational decisions was the executive management team, rather than the professional executive committee, and which was primarily made up of managers as opposed to clinicians. As a result, there was evidence of professionals feeling that 'their' organization had been 'taken over' by NHS managers resulting in further difficulties in engaging professionals to lead the work of PCOs. As Chapter 5 concluded, the tension between managerial and professional leadership reflects a paradox at the heart of PCTs – that they potentially represent real devolution of leadership to 'frontline professionals' and users, but that they are also a device to draw primary care professionals (and GPs in particular) into the mainstream of NHS organization under a managed care system. The key lessons for the leadership of PCOs in England are summarized in Box 14.3 below.

Box 14.3 Key lessons for the leadership of primary care organizations in England

- There is a risk of executive management teams overly influencing the strategy of PCOs. It is crucial that the clinician lead in this team is not 'squeezed out' by the more traditional chair/chief executive leadership model
- The respective roles of boards, professional executive committees, management teams and other constituencies need to be clearly articulated to avoid overlap and tensions
- The PCT must allow the PEC to provide visible and effective leadership so front-line colleagues feel empowered, valued and engaged
- PECs must evolve from being GP-led to enable lay members, nurses and other primary care professionals to play a truly influential role in the strategic decision-making and direction of PCOs. This requires considerable facilitation, attention to deep-seated cultural barriers to involvement, and overcoming the risk of tokenism regarding public involvement
- A proper locality focus is needed to avoid organizational leaders becoming distant from the general practices, health centres, and local communities they represent
- Engaging professionals in the leadership and operation of PCOs is time-consuming, but to neglect this is to abandon the spirit and strength of PCOs
- Respected clinical leaders, and a new cadre of clinician-managers, are required to create a symbiosis of clinical and managerial leadership

Evidence from the international experience warns against 'corporate' organizations led by managers because it threatens effective professional engagement (Smith and Walshe, 2004). The conclusion reached in the research evidence into PCTs was the need for PECs to provide visible and effective leadership to front-line colleagues to ensure clinicians feel empowered and engaged. Moreover, professional leaders needed to be those individuals respected and trusted by their peers to whose call for action others would more readily follow. However, whilst the effective leadership of PCOs is a key factor to their success, it needs to be developed alongside the provision of the right practical incentives in order for professionals to engage in an active rather than passive manner.

Accountability

As Chapter 5 discussed, one of the most frequent criticisms levelled at the GP-led primary care organizations in the NHS in the 1990s was the relative lack of corporate governance and professional accountability in comparison with that expected of NHS trusts and health authorities. However, as PCOs grew larger, good progress was reported to have been made by PCGs and PCTs with regard to issues of probity and corporate governance. This is, perhaps, not surprising since in PCTs such accountability arrangements have been more formally defined given the statutory nature of these organizations.

Perhaps the most significant and ongoing area of weakness regarding PCO governance concerns the issue of public accountability. As Chapter 5 uncovered, whilst PCG/Ts recognized accountability to the public as an important aspect of their role, few were successful in strengthening the process. Whilst progress has been made in terms of opening up the governance of primary care organizations in the NHS to both public involvement and scrutiny, fears have been voiced on the extent to which more formal processes of governance and accountability has stifled professional engagement.

Box 14.4 Key lessons for the development of accountability procedures in primary care organizations

- Statutory PCOs are required to take on formal public accountability, but there is a real risk in this process of disenfranchising those professionals who developed and shaped PCOs in the first place
- There is a need for greater dissemination of examples of good practice related to developing new forms of public accountability for PCOs, including those related to the purpose and conduct of public meetings
- PCOs need to implement more creative and varied approaches to public involvement and evaluate the effectiveness of such interventions

Engaging Stakeholders

The evidence drawn from studies of emerging PCOs in England as well as internationally shows that engaging professional stakeholders is fundamental to their effective functioning and success. It has already been concluded in this chapter that there are two fundamental criteria that enable this process to work:

first, that professional integration and commitment are related to the development of incentives rather than to structures of compliance; and second, that PCOs need to adopt a combination of relational and contractual forms of incentives (governance) in order to achieve such commitment.

Chapter 6 provided a review of the role and engagement of GPs within PCG/ Ts and reported a growing disenfranchisement of these professionals due to a fundamental tension between shifting power and responsibility to the frontline and the dual expectation that GPs would then prioritize national targets over local priorities. More fundamentally, it was suggested that GPs would continue to contest the managerial control exerted by PCTs unless the necessary synergies or incentives could be found to engender engagement. Similarly, Chapter 7's analysis of the engagement of nurses and allied health professionals with PCOs found that a number of key inhibiting factors were restricting stakeholder engagement, despite an underlying trend towards more active participation.

The key conclusion reached in Chapters 6 and 7 was that the current disengagement of primary care professionals with their PCT needs to be addressed such that clinicians can become central determinants directing care from within PECs yet with inter-dependence to other professionals working in primary care. The potential range of actions needed, as summarized in Box 14.5, reflect the highly relational requirements of a network-based organization that does not have direct power of control over its professional partners. However, for any professional stakeholder, an incentive to participate in PCOs is often offset by the additional demands placed on their time and fears associated with bureaucratic control and reduced professional freedoms. As discussed in Chapter 12, developing a new form of management hierarchy is not the answer, since research into primary care organizations in the UK and USA suggests that looser network-based models are far more likely to be successful in securing professional engagement (Smith and Walshe, 2004).

The key challenge for PCOs in *sustaining* engagement is to develop the 'right' set of incentives that enable professionals to take an active part in their organization. As the NHS Alliance (2003) concluded, a dual approach of 'empowerment and influence' is required that enables professional stakeholders to wield demonstrable influence and leadership which in turn should result in influencing professional behaviour on the ground. Hence, what appears crucial for sustained engagement is the need for PCOs to remain professionally-led, and even professionally-owned, since the systems that appear to work better internationally tend to focus on creating a stakeholder relationship with their professionals – for example as 'owners' of the system (such as in IPAs in New Zealand) or as 'shareholders' (such as in Kaiser Permanente in the USA). Within PCTs, where such direct ownership is unavailable, it would appear that the next best strategy is to develop a 'mandate to manage' in which professional stakeholders will adopt PCT strategies because they have implicitly given their authority to the managers to do so. This process explicitly requires PCTs to adopt professional rather than managerial leadership (see Box 14.6, see also Sheaff et al, 2003 and Chapter 12).

**Box 14.5 Key lessons in the practice of engaging GPs and nurses in
       primary care organizations**

GP engagement
- PCOs need to show GPs how their activities are designed to deliver improvements to
  patients and engage them via their clinical interests. Tangible improvements to services
  must be demonstrated
- GPs need the necessary capacity and competencies to take on managerial roles – GPs
  should be encouraged to take leadership of the agenda within PECs
- PCOs should strengthen channels of communication though GP representation and
  forums. The more GPs are informed about PCT activities, the more likely it is for them
  to become directly involved.
- A locality focus is likely to retain GP interest
- PCOs need to facilitate GP involvement by reducing bureaucracy to ensure that
  workloads are manageable and rewards are maximized; paying for locum cover; and
  provide access to training and education
- GP practices need to be fairly rewarded for meeting PCT expectations

Nurse engagement
- PCOs need to ensure that the workloads of nurses and AHPs engaged in organizational
  activities remain sustainable by providing resources for backfill
- Further efforts are needed to bring together the different nursing professions to promote
  understanding, joint working and the development of generic nurse roles
- Engaging nurses through professional nurse forums is a crucial mechanism for
  engendering support and participation. Views and ideas should not be 'tokenistic' but
  be seen to provide a worthwhile contribution that influences PCO strategy
- PCTs should provide opportunities for training and professional development. Lead
  nurses need to develop skills in clinical supervision, information technology, advice
  and mentoring if they are to facilitate educational and training opportunities
- Lead nurses in PCTs need to be of sufficient seniority to debate and challenge priorities
  within the PCT itself. PCTs should avoided an overly medical agenda and sustain an
  active interest in nursing roles

This debate has been encapsulated in LeGrand's (2003) theory of 'knights and
knaves' which examined the underlying motivation of professionals and their
interaction with the public sector. According to LeGrand (2003), both self-interested
('knavish') and more altruistic ('knightly') motivations co-exist within individuals
such that their reaction to incentives and rewards are complex. In his analysis of
the incentive structures in PCTs, LeGrand essentially argues that, to sustain clinical
engagement, a 'shareholder' relationship between GPs and PCTs should be created
such that financial 'surpluses' are shared (and potentially 'deficits' too) thus aligning
the interests of the professional to that of the PCT. However, whilst LeGrand saw
underlying merit to the approach, real problems existed in regulating PCTs and
practices to ensure they simply do not generate surpluses at the expense of patient
care. Moreover, unlike the 'stakeholder' systems described earlier, patients have no
ability to 'exit' the system as no competition exists for patient enrolment whilst
their ability to 'voice' opposition has traditionally been weak. Consequently, central
government may potentially impose stricter sanctions on the activities of PCTs in

order to regulate provision, arousing resentment and lowering morale in a system designed to improve it (LeGrand, 2003).

Box 14.6 Key lessons in sustaining professional engagement in primary care organizations

- PCOs cannot expect to sustain professional engagement unless a mandate for governance is granted to them by the clinicians themselves
- Legitimacy is more powerful than quality contracts and/or financial incentives in sustaining clinical engagement and engendering collective responsibility
- 'Soft' governance techniques and financial incentives need to be retained alongside well designed local contracts that enable greater managerial control by linking remuneration to the attainment of quality targets and cost-effective practice
- Professional stakeholders should lead service development and change processes
- Administrative control needs to be kept to a minimum whilst ensuring appropriate accountability
- PCOs need to adopt a decentralized approach to decision-making to facilitate grass-roots support
- PCOs need to find ways to let small organizational values and freedoms survive in the bigger corporate environment where centrally-determined standards of care must be met
- Sustaining clinical engagement in England is likely to be presented with even greater challenges in the future as foundation hospitals, patient choice, practice-based commissioning, and the potential development of independent practitioner organizations, further complicate the PCT-professional relationship

The option favoured by LeGrand, which reflects the views of Enthoven (1999) and is based on his interpretation of the fundholding experience in England, is to create a competitive system on the demand-side in which patients could choose their PCT. However, reflecting on the fundholding experience, whilst this *might* be a method of engaging and sustaining stakeholder involvement, the potential for cream-skimming and the likelihood of a two-tier system developing is highly likely. Consequently, this option for developing stakeholder involvement in the system has not been embraced (as of yet). However, what has been adopted is a policy of practice-based commissioning in which practices from April 2005 gained the 'right' to commission services from hospitals and reinvest 'efficiency gains' into primary and community care (Department of Health, 2005b).

Delivering Quality Services

The ability of PCG/Ts to deliver and commission services of high quality has faced a number of common challenges. In particular, constant organizational upheavals in the English NHS have created significant difficulties, none more so than in creating sustainable partnerships with other agencies for tackling key public health problems (Chapter 9). In order to avoid an over-medicalized approach to care, it could be argued that future PCOs need to make a priority of the public health agenda and work more closely with partner agencies and social care professionals. However, to do so, PCOs need to invest in their public health skills and competencies and look to reduce organizational fragmentations and to develop more holistic approaches to care. However, the external pressures on PCOs in England has meant their core activities have primarily related to achieving government-imposed targets rather than on the wider promotion of health and wellbeing to local populations. Hence, government targets for PCTs have tended to make priorities of other agendas leading to under-investment in the skills and time required for the public health and partnership agendas to flourish. Central expectations and targets for PCTs need to be revisited to help future PCOs focus and prioritize on these core functions of their activity.

Box 14.7 Key lessons for delivering quality services in primary care organizations

- PCOs can make a significant impact on the quality of primary and community care services, and are effective in managing prescribing and developing clinical governance mechanisms
- Further development of primary care infrastructure is need if PCOs are to develop more extensive service improvements
- PCOs need to strengthen and monitor the work of primary care-based teams to ensure that quality reaches set standards. A quality-based contract allows emphasis to be placed on primary care development and the management of chronic diseases
- PCOs need to make a priority of the public health agenda to avoid an over-medicalized approach to care and invest in public health skills
- Professional and organizational fragmentations limit the ability of PCOs to promote holistic approaches to care. Future PCOs need to address these professional and cultural barriers
- Government targets and expectations need to facilitate PCOs in addressing their core functions rather than divert them to address other priorities
- Community involvement remains limited – strategies need to be advanced that engage user groups and create influential patient forums

Despite the fluctuating policy environment, PCOs in England have made significant gains in the management of prescribing, the development of clinical governance, and in developing practice-based primary care services. The lessons from the evidence in this regard (see Box 14.7) are important for future PCOs seeking to improve the accessibility and quality of primary care-based services to their local communities. Of particular importance is the ability of PCOs to strengthen primary care-based teams and services to the point where accessible and viable local alternatives to a hospital referral are created, thus improving the quality of services to patients and enabling effective chronic disease management strategies to be introduced. In order to achieve this position, significant investment in the primary care workforce is required and specifically investment in new premises and buildings to enable new forms of service delivery to flourish. Within the current English system, the introduction of a new national contract for general practice, based on a quality and outcomes framework, gives renewed impetus to PCTs' primary care development and chronic disease management work, whilst practice-based commissioning may act as a lever for diverting and investing resources in primary and community care.

Commissioning Services

The *potential* of PCOs to use commissioning as a lever to improve service quality in primary, community and intermediate care services is backed up by the evidence – particularly from the most innovative sites where significant investments in such services were enabled by devolving budgets to a community or locality level. Moreover, historical evidence shows that commissioning at this level also enabled significant reductions in waiting lists, lengths of stay and elective admissions as alternatives to care in hospitals were advanced (Propper et al, 2002; Mays et al, 2001; Dusheiko et al, 2003). As Chapter 11 revealed, the fact that the commissioning function in PCGs and PCTs has been relatively ineffective reflects a number of inhibiting factors:

- the lack of a truly contestable market – both in terms of provider competition for contracts, but also in the availability of community-based alternatives;
- the lack of management capacity, expertise and commissioning skills;
- the lack of clinical involvement and leadership;
- the lack of data sources on which to base sound commissioning decisions.

If future PCOs are to address the commissioning function effectively, all of these key weaknesses need to be addressed. More specifically, for commissioning to be successful, future PCOs need to provide the incentives for clinicians to become re-engaged in the process. The re-emergence of practice-based commissioning in 2005 in England, alongside a 'payment by results' system of paying for clinical activity, is potentially one way in which this might be fostered since the scenario potentially has a dual benefit of directly rewarding investment in, and the provision of, primary care alternatives but also may act as a key lever in the armoury of PCTs in tackling rising provider costs. Indeed, since 'payment by results' rewards providers based on their volume of activity, practice-based commissioning is likely to be a vital tool that PCOs can use to combat rising provider costs through investment in primary care alternatives and chronic disease management practices. Indeed, the system suggests that there is significant potential for PCOs to invest in primary and community care.

However, whether PCO-based commissioning in the future will work is contestable for a number of reasons. Firstly, the process needs strong and mature co-operative agreements between PCOs and constituent practices, but history suggests that practices prefer the autonomy to work independently. Developing a new era of partnership may require significant degrees of brokering to create win-

win scenarios or a more direct 'shareholder'-based agreement related to contractual rewards for achieving system-wide outcomes. Secondly, PCOs and practices need to invest in community and practice-based infrastructure and services in order to create the physical preconditions necessary to engender contestability – but this will require significant sunk costs. Thirdly, IT systems and data sources, chronically under-developed at the beginning of 2005, are needed for the effective planning and forecasting of demand. Fourthly, investment in commissioning skills and capacity remains essential since the necessary cadre of staff has been in short supply since PCG/Ts were formed. Finally, and the key paradox to the system as a whole, PCOs need to be able to 'shake up' the system to develop alternative models of care delivery, yet must also ensure that services to local people are not compromised in the process. It is clearly problematic for a PCO to disinvest in a large acute hospital if this threatens its financial viability.

The Implications for Future Policy

The international evidence is clear – that by investing in strong and effective primary care so health care systems are more likely to show improvements in terms of both health outcomes as well as in managing demand and controlling costs. The realization that such overwhelming advantages can be gained by investing in a primary care-led approach has led the governments of many countries to try and manage more directly the activities of primary care professionals and to develop a range of community-based services. This has led to the phenomenon of 'managed primary care' and to the creation of primary care organizations for this purpose. In this book, the story of the development of PCOs in England has been told, revealing in some detail the trials and tribulations of successive organizational iterations and their impact on professional activity and care service provision.

What is revealed in these pages is that a PCO, in its function as the coordinator of primary and community care services, should remain a key component of the English health system (indeed, one might argue, any Western health system). This is especially true when one considers that its greatest potential strength is in the innovation of primary, community and intermediate care services that should better enable the management of chronic diseases in the most appropriate care settings. Indeed, since the burden of disease now lies primarily in tackling the comorbidities of the frail elderly, the existing acute disease paradigm (centred on hospital-based medical interventions) has become untenable. The more appropriate and effective model of care is now the coordination and integration of services at a primary care-level amongst teams of primary care professionals. The English story of PCO development has revealed the struggle and many barriers associated with making this paradigm shift.

In taking the PCO agenda forward, policy makers need to ensure that the process of change is facilitative rather than disruptive. In this regard, a weakness in English health policy has been the continual pre-occupation with demand-side reform in the search for a system that can achieve best results. It is clear, however, that continuous structural reforms have not brought with them the desired benefits in terms of a primary care-led system to effectively challenge the acute service paradigm. Nonetheless, some great strides have been made in terms of improving standards through clinical governance, managed prescribing practices and, more recently, the introduction of quality-based contracts that focus on tackling chronic diseases. These latter gains suggest a truism in the process of achieving desired change – that it should be based on creating the right incentives on those within the system rather than on changing the structures within which they work.

Creating the right incentives for professionals to take a 'stake' in their PCO is perhaps the most important conclusion for future policy. What has been revealed as crucial is the need for PCOs to remain professionally-led, and even professionally-owned, since PCOs work better if a stakeholder relationship is formed. This process explicitly requires future PCOs to adopt professional rather than managerial leadership.

One of the unmet challenges in the PCO policy is whether they can effectively work as a commissioning agency. The many problems associated with this activity revealed in Chapter 11 highlight the fact that PCOs have struggled to make a reality of the 'contestable collaboration' model of commissioning, primarily because they lack the capacity and power to change the way secondary care providers go about their business. Since former health authorities were no better at this process, calls to merge PCOs in order to develop some form of 'critical mass' in the commissioning function would seem an unsound policy solution – the more so since it might undermine the many positive influences a PCO has on managing primary and community care activities locally.

The introduction of policies related to foundation trusts, payment by results, patient choice and provider plurality would suggest that English health policy in 2005 is intent on developing institutional capacity in order to provide speedier access to hospital-based care. As a consequence, PCTs may continue to find it problematic to integrate and manage care as these NHS reforms reinforce divisions and fragmentations. Practice-based commissioning may be one mechanism that PCOs can employ to help invest in primary and community care alternatives, and develop chronic disease management systems, but the incentives inherent in a 'payment by results' system risk creating a battleground for patient referrals between primary and secondary care providers. Moreover, unless primary care professionals are provided with the necessary incentives to participate in the process, then the battle is likely to be one-sided. Current policies need to be scrutinized closely to ensure that the potential advantages of PCOs in managing primary care activities are not undermined.

This book has shown that PCOs are effective in the management and integration of primary and community care services and can improve the quality of prescribing and care provision through effective clinical governance procedures and quality-based contracts. Moreover, PCOs are likely to be a key mechanism for investing in a chronic disease model of care that provides more appropriate, and more cost-

Bibliography

Abbot, S. and Gillam, S. (1999), 'Health Improvement', in D. Wilkin, S. Gillam, and B. Leese (eds.), *The National Tracker Survey of Primary Care Groups and Trusts 1999/2000: Progress and Challenges*, The University of Manchester, Manchester, pp. 47-50.

Abbott, S and Gillam, S, (2001), 'Health Improvement', in D. Wilkin, S. Gillam, and A. Coleman (eds.), *The National Tracker Survey of Primary Care Groups and Trusts 2000/2001: Modernising the NHS?*, The University of Manchester, Manchester, pp. 60-65.

Adamiak, G. and Karlberg, I. (2003), 'Situation in Sweden', in A. Van Raak, I. Mur-Veenan, B. Hardy, M. Steenbergen and A. Paulus (eds.), *Integrated Care in Europe: Description and Comparison of Integrated Care in Six EU Countries*, Elsevier Gezondheidszorg, Maarssen, The Netherlands, pp. 41-72.

Alborz, A., Wilkin, D. and Smith, K. (2002), 'Are Primary Care Groups and Trusts Consulting Local Communities?', *Health and Social Care in the Community*, Vol.10(1), pp. 20-27.

Anderson, W. and Florin, D. (2000), *Involving the Public – One of Many Priorities. A Survey of Public Involvement in London's Primary Care Groups*, King's Fund, London.

Anderson, W. and Florin, D. (2002). *Every Voice Counts: Primary Care Organisations and Public Involvement*, King's Fund, London.

Antrobus, S. and Bailey, J. (1998), 'Feature', *Nursing Times*, Vol. 94, p. 45.

Appleby, J. and Dixon, J. (2004), 'Patient Choice in the NHS', *British Medical Journal*, Vol. 329, pp. 61-62.

Ashton, T. (1998), 'Contracting for Health Services in New Zealand: a Transactional Cost Analysis', *Social Science and Medicine*, Vol. 46(3), pp. 357-367.

Audit Commission (1996), *What the Doctor Ordered: A Study of GP Fundholders in England and Wales*, HMSO, London.

Audit Commission (1999), *PCGs: An Early View of Primary Care Groups in England*, Audit Commission, London.

Audit Commission (2000), *The PCG Agenda: Early Progress of Primary Care Groups in the New NHS*, Audit Commission, London.

Audit Commission (2004), *Transforming Primary Care: The Role of Primary Care Trusts in Shaping and Supporting General Practice*, Audit Commission, London.

Baggot, R. (2000), *Public Health: Policy and Politics*, Palgrave-MacMillan, Basingstoke.

Ball, J. and Pike, G. (2003), *Stepping Stones: Results from the RCN Membership*

Survey 2003, Royal College of Nursing, London.

Barnes, M. and McIver, S. (1999), *Public Participation in Primary Care*, Health Services Management Centre, University of Birmingham.

Barnett, P. (2004) *The Formation and Development of Independent Practitioner Associations in New Zealand, 1991-2000*, PhD thesis, University of Otago, Dunedin, New Zealand.

Bate, P. and Robert, G. (2003), 'Where Next for Policy Evaluation? Insights from Researching NHS Modernization', *Policy and Politics*, Vol. 31(2), pp. 249-262.

Beecham, L. (2001), 'Most GPs Would Consider Resigning from the NHS', *British Medical Journal*, Vol. 322, p. 1381.

Benaim, R. (2001), 'Getting to Grips with Social Services', in G. Meads and T. Meads (eds.) *Trust in Experience: Transferable Learning for Primary Care Trusts*, Radcliffe Medical Press, Abingdon, pp. 89-102.

Bennett, C. and Ferlie, E. (1996), 'Contracting in Theory and Practice: Some Evidence from the NHS', *Public Administration*, Vol. 74(1), pp. 49-66.

Benson, L. and Wright, J. (2002), 'Primary Care Groups: What Are They and Why Are They Here?', in R. Rushmer, H. Davies, M. Tavakoli and M. Malik (eds.), *Organisational Development in Health Care. Strategic Issues in Health Care Management*, Ashgate, Aldershot.

Berk, R. and Rossi, P. (1990), *Thinking About Program Evaluation*, Sage, Newbury Park, California.

Bjoke, C., Gravelle, H. and Wilkin, D. (2001), 'Is Bigger Better for Primary Care Groups and Trusts?', *British Medical Journal*, Vol. 322, pp. 599-602.

Bloisi, W., Cook, C. and Hunsaker, P. (2003), *Management and Organisational Behaviour*, McGraw Hill, Maidenhead.

Bloom, A. (ed.) (2000), *Health Reform in Australia and New Zealand*, Oxford University Press, Melbourne.

Bloomfield, K. (1992), *Fundamental Review of Dental Remuneration: Report of Sir Kenneth Bloomfield KCB*, London.

Bond, M. (2001), 'Pharmacists and the multi-disciplinary health care team', in K. Taylor and G. Hardy (eds.), *Pharmacy Practice*, Taylor and Francis, London, pp. 249-269.

Bond, M., Irving, L. and Cooper, C. (2001), *Public Involvement in Decision Making in Primary Care Groups*, School of Health and Related Research, University of Sheffield.

Bond, M. and LeGrand, J. (2003), 'Primary Care Organizations and the "Modernization" of the NHS', in B. Dowling and C. Glendinning (eds.), *The New Primary Care: Modern, Dependable, Successful?*, Open University Press, Maidenhead, pp. 21-39.

Bosanquet, N., Dixon, J., Harvey, T., Hunter, D., Pollock, A., Sang, B., Wall, A. and Webster, C. (2001), 'Across the Great Divide: Discussing the Undiscussable', *British Journal of Healthcare Management*, Vol. 7(10), pp. 395-400.

Brennan, J., Fennessey, E. and Moran, D. (2000), *The Funding of Primary Health*

Care, The Society of Actuaries of Ireland.

Broadbent, J. (1998), 'Practice Nurses and the Effects of the New General Practitioner Contract in the British NHS: The Advent of a Professional Project?', *Social Science and Medicine*, Vol. 47, pp. 497-506.

Busse, R. (2002), 'The Netherlands', in A. Dixon and E. Mossialos (eds), *Health Care Systems in Eight Countries: Trends and Challenges*, European Observatory on Health Care Systems, Copenhagen, pp. 61-73.

Campbell, S. and Roland, M. (1999), 'Clinical Governance', in D. Wilkin, S. Gillam and B. Leese, B. (eds.), *The National Tracker Survey of Primary Care Groups and Trusts: Progress and Challenges 1999/2000*, The University of Manchester, Manchester.

Campbell, S. and Roland, M. (2000), 'Clinical Governance', in D. Wilkin, S. Gillam and A. Coleman. (eds.), *The National Tracker Survey of Primary Care Groups and Trusts 2000/2001: Modernising the NHS?*, The University of Manchester, Manchester.

Campbell, S. and Roland, M. (2003), 'Improving the Quality of Health Care through Clinical Governance', in B. Dowling and C. Glendinning (eds.), *The New Primary Care: Modern, Dependable, Successful?*, Open University Press, Maidenhead, pp. 101-122.

Cartwright, S. and Cooper, C. (1992), *Mergers and Acquisitions: The Human Factor*, Oxford, Butterworth Heinemann.

Charles, C. and DeMaio, S. (1993), 'Lay Participation in Health Care Decision-Making: A Conceptual Framework', *Journal of Health Politics, Policy and Law*, Vol. 18(4), pp. 881-904.

Clarence, E. and Painter, C. (1998), 'Public Services under New Labour: Collaborative Discourses and Local Networking', *Public Policy and Administration*, Vol. 13, pp. 8-22.

Coleman, A. and Glendinning, C. (2001), 'Partnerships', in D. Wilkin, S. Gillam, and A. Coleman (eds.), *The National Tracker Survey of Primary Care Groups and Trusts 2000/2001: Modernising the NHS?*, The University of Manchester, Manchester, pp. 54-59.

Commission for Health Improvement (2004), *What CHI Has Found in Primary Care Trusts*, Sector Report, Commission for Health Improvement, London.

Cornish, Y. (2001), 'Owning Up to the Public Health Agenda', in G. Meads and T. Meads (eds.) *Trust in Experience: Transferable Learning for Primary Care Trusts*, Radcliffe Medical Press, Abingdon, pp. 69-88.

Coulter A. (1995), 'General Practice Fundholding: Time for a Cool Appraisal', *British Journal of General Practice*, Vol. 45(392), pp. 119-120.

Croxson, B., Ferguson, B. and Keen, J. (2003), 'The New Institutional Structures: Risks to the Doctor-Patient Relationship', in B. Dowling and C. Glendinning (eds.), *The New Primary Care. Modern, Dependable, Successful?*, Open University Press, Maidenhead, pp. 70-82.

Croxson, B., Propper, C. and Perkins, A. (2001), 'Do Doctors Respond to Financial Incentives? UK Family Doctors and the GP Fundholder Scheme', *Journal of*

Public Health Economics, Vol. 79, pp. 375-398.

Cumming, J. (2000), *Management of Key Purchaser Risks in Devolved Purchasing Arrangements in Health Care,* Treasury Working Paper, Wellington, New Zealand.

Dash, P., Gorman, N. and Traynor, M. (2003), 'Increasing the Impact of Health Services Research', *BMJ*, Vol. 327, pp. 1339-1341.

Davies, C. (2005), *R&D for the NHS – Delivering the Research Agenda*, paper presented to How to Build Research Capacity in the NHS, Church House, London, Tuesday 22nd February, 2005.

Davis, P. and Ashton, T. (eds.) (2001), *Health and Public Policy in New Zealand*, Oxford University Press, New Zealand.

Dent, M. and Burtney, E. (1997), 'Changes in Practice Nursing: Professionalism, Segmentation and Sponsorship', *Journal of Clinical Nursing*, Vol. 6, pp. 355-363.

Department of Health (1989), *Working for Patients*, White Paper. Cm 555, HMSO, London.

Department of Health (1994), *Developing NHS Purchasing and GP Fundholding*, EL [94] 79, NHS Executive, Leeds.

Department of Health (1996), *Choice and Opportunity*, Department of Health, London.

Department of Health (1997), *The New NHS. Modern. Dependable*, Department of Health, London.

Department of Health (1997b), *GP Commissioning Groups*, EL 1997/37, Department of Health, London.

Department of Health (1998a), *Modernizing Social Services: Promoting Independence, Improving Protection, Raising Standards*, Cm 4169, The Stationery Office, London.

Department of Health (1998b), *Partnership in Action*, The Stationery Office, London.

Department of Health (1998c), *A First Class Service: Quality in the New NHS,* Department of Health, London.

Department of Health (1999), *Health Act 1999*, The Stationery Office, London.

Department of Health (2000), *The NHS Plan. A Plan for Investment. A Plan for Reform*, The Stationery Office, London.

Department of Health (2001a), *Shifting the Balance of Power within the NHS: Securing Delivery*, The Stationery Office, London.

Department of Health (2001b), *Involving Patients and the Public in Health Care: Response to the Listening Exercise*, The Stationery Office, London.

Department of Health (2001c), *Health and Social Care Act*, The Stationery Office, London.

Department of Health (2002a), *Liberating the Talents. Helping Primary Care Trusts and Nurses to Deliver the NHS Plan*, The Stationery Office, London.

Department of Health (2002b), *A Guide to NHS Foundation Trusts*, Department of

Health, London.

Department of Health (2002c) *NHS Foundation Trusts: Eligibility Criteria and Timetable*, Department of Health, London.

Department of Health (2002d), *Options for Change*, The Stationery Office, London.

Department of Health (2003) *Building on the Best: Choice, Responsiveness and Equity in the NHS*, Department of Health, London.

Department of Health (2004a), *Practice Based Commissioning: Engaging Practices in Commissioning*, Department of Health, London.

Department of Health (2004b), *NHS Improvement Plan: Putting People at the Heart of Public Services*, The Stationery Office, London.

Department of Health (2004c), *Investing in General Practice: The New GMS Contract*, Department of Health, London.

Department of Health (2004d), *Reconfiguring the Department of Health's Arm's Length Bodies*, Department of Health Publications, London.

Department of Health (2004e), *'Choose and Book': Patients' Choice of Hospital and Booked Appointment: Policy Framework for Choice and Booking at the Point of Referral*, Department of Health, London.

Department of Health (2004f), *Configuring Hospitals Evidence File: Part Two*, Department of Health, London.

Department of Health (2005a), *Supporting People with Long Term Conditions. An NHS and Social Care Model to Support Local Innovation and Integration*, Department of Health, London.

Department of Health (2005b), *Making Practice-Based Commissioning a Reality: Technical Guidance,* Department of Health, London.

Department of Health Research and Development Directorate (1995), *National Evaluation of Total Purchasing Pilot Schemes: Research Brief*, Department of Health, London, mimeo.

Department of Health and Social Security (1988), *Promoting Better Health*, DHSS, London.

Department of Health and Social Security (1989), *Working for Patients*, DHSS, London.

Department of Health and Social Security (1990), *GP contract*, DHSS, London.

Department of Health and Social Services (1998), *Fit For the Future: A New Approach,* The Stationery Office, London.

Dixon, J. (1998), 'The Context', in LeGrand, J., Mays, N. and Mulligan, J-A. (eds.), *Learning from the NHS Internal Market: A Review of the Evidence*, King's Fund, London, pp. 1-14.

Dixon, J. and Glennerster, H, (1995), 'What Do We Know About Fundholding in General Practice?', *British Medical Journal,* Vol. 311, pp. 727-730.

Dixon, M. and Sweeney, K. (eds.) (2000), *A Practical Guide to Primary Care Groups and Trusts*, Radcliffe Medical Press, Abingdon.

Dixon J., Goodwin N. and Mays N. (2001). 'Holding Total Purchasing Pilots to Account', in N. Mays, S. Wyke, G. Malbon, and N. Goodwin (eds.), *The*

Purchasing of Health Care by Primary Care Organisations. An Evaluation and Guide to Future Policy, Open University Press, Buckingham, pp. 208-229.

Dixon, M. and Sweeney, K. (eds.) (2000), *A Practical Guide to Primary Care Groups and Trusts*, Radcliffe Medical Press, Abingdon.

Donabedian, A. (1980), *Explorations in Quality Assessment and Monitoring. Volume 1: The Definition of Quality and its Approaches to Assessment*, Health Administration Press, Ann Arbor, Michigan.

Dopson, S., Locock, L. (2002), 'The Commissioning Process in the NHS: The Theory and Application', *Public Management Review*, Vol. 4(2), pp. 209-230.

Dowling, B. (2000), *GPs and Purchasing in the NHS: The Internal Market and Beyond*, Ashgate, Aldershot.

Dowling, B., Coleman, A., Wilkin, D. and Shipman, C, (2002), 'Commissioning', in D. Wilkin, A. Coleman, B. Dowling and K. Smith (eds.), *The National Tracker Survey of Primary Care Groups and Trusts, 2001/2002: Taking Responsibility?*, National Primary Care Research and Development Centre, University of Manchester, Manchester, pp. 73-87.

Dowling, B. and Glendinning, C (eds.) (2003), *The New Primary Care, Modern, Dependable, Successful?*, Open University Press, Berkshire.

Dowling, B., Wilkin, D. and Smith, K. (2003), 'Organizational Development and Governance of Primary Care', in B. Dowling, and C. Glendinning (eds.), *The New Primary Care: Modern, Dependable, Successful?*, Open University Press, Maidenhead, pp. 85-100.

Dowswell, G., Harrison, S. and Wright, J. (2002), 'The Early Days of Primary Care Groups: General Practitioner's Perceptions', *Health and Social Care in the Community*, Vol. 10(1), pp. 46-54.

Dowswell, T., Wilkin, D. and Banks-Smith, J. (2002), 'Nurses and English Primary Care Groups: Their Experiences and Perceived Influence on Policy Development', *Journal of Advanced Nursing*, Vol. 37(10, pp. 35-42.

Doyal, L. and Cameron, A. (2000), 'Reshaping the NHS Workforce. Necessary Changes are Constrained by Professional Structures from the Past', *British Medical Journal*, Vol. 320, pp. 1023-1024.

Dudley, R., Miller, R., Korenbrot, T. and Luft, H. (1998), 'The Impact of Financial Incentives on Quality of Health Care', *Milbank Quarterly*, Vol. 76(4), pp. 649-86.

Dushiesko, M., Gravelle, H., Jacobs, R. and Smith, P. (2003), *The Effect of Budgets on Doctor Behaviour: Evidence from a Natural Experiment*, Centre for Health Economics Technical Paper No. 26, University of York.

Elbers, M. and Regen, E. (2001), *Public and User Involvement in Primary Care Groups and Trusts*, Health Services Management Centre, University of Birmingham.

Enthoven, A. (1999), 'America's Experience with Managed Health Care and Managed Competition', in N. Goodwin (ed.), *The New NHS: What Can We Learn from Managed Care in New Zealand and the US?*, Seminar Briefing No.1, Office of Health Economics, London.

Evans, D., Mays, N. and Wyke, S. (2001), 'Evaluating Complex Policies: What Have We Learned from Total Purchasing?', in N. Mays, S. Wyke, G. Malbon and N. Goodwin (eds.), *The Purchasing of Health Care by Primary Care Organisations. An Evaluation and Guide to Future Policy*, Open University Press, Buckingham, pp. 230-252.

Evercare (2003), *Adapting the Evercare Programme for the National Health Service: Background, Principles, Components, Pathway, Consistency with NSF, Benefits, Adapting the model*, United Health Group.

Evercare (2004). *Implementing the Evercare Programme: Interim Report*, United Health Group.

Exworthy, M. (2001), 'Primary Care in the UK: Understanding the Dynamics of Devolution', *Health and Social Care in the Community*, Vol. 9(5), pp. 266-278.

Exworthy, M. and Peckham, S. (1998), 'The Contribution of Coterminosity to Joint Purchasing in Health and Social Care, *Health and Place*, Vol.4(3), pp. 233-243.

Exworthy, M. and Peckham, S. (1999), 'Collaboration between Health and Social Care: Coterminosity in the New NHS', *Health and Social Care in the Community*, Vol. 7(3), pp. 229-232.

Farhan, F. (2003), 'LPS – a one-year progress report', *The Pharmaceutical Journal*, Vol. 270, pp. 361-362.

Feacham, R., Sehkri, N. and White, K. (2002), 'Getting More for their Dollar', *BMJ*, Vol. 324, pp. 135-143.

Fisher, B. and Ellis, D. (1990), *Small Group Decision Making: Communication and the Group Process*, McGraw Hill Publishing Company, New York.

Flynn, R. and Williams, G. (eds.) (1997), *Contracting for Health: Quasi-Markets and the National Health Service*, Oxford University Press, Oxford.

French, S., Old, A. and Healy, J. (2001), *New Zealand, Health Care in Transition,* Vol. 3, No. 19, European Observatory on Health Care Systems, Copenhagen.

Friedson, E. (2001), *Professionalism: Third Logic*, Polity Press, Cambridge.

Fulop, N., Protopsaltis, G., Hutchings, A., King, A., Allen, P., Normand, C. and Walters, R. (2002), 'Process and Impact of Mergers of NHS trusts: Multicentre Case Study and Management Cost Analysis', *BMJ*, Vol. 325, p. 246.

Gabel, J. (1997), 'Ten Ways HMOs Have Changed During the 1990s', *Health Affairs*, Vol. 16 (3), pp. 134-145.

Gillam, S. and Meads, G. (2001), *Modernisation and the Future of General Practice*, King's Fund, London.

Glasby, J. and Peck, E. (eds.) (2004), *Care Trusts: Partnership Working in Action,* Radcliffe Medical Press, Abingdon.

Glendinning, C. (1999), 'GPs and Contracts: Bringing General Practice into Primary Care', *Social Policy and Administration*, Vol. 33(2), pp. 115-131.

Gollamy, J. and Gorham, J. (1998), 'Improving Access to NHS Dentistry?', *Community Dental Health*, Vol. 15, pp. 129-131.

Goodman, C. (2000), 'Integrated Nursing Teams: In Whose Interests?', *Primary*

Health Care Research and Development, Vol. 1, pp. 207-215.

Goodwin, N. (1996), 'GP Fundholding: A Review of the Evidence', in A. Harrison (ed.), *Health Care UK 1995/6*, King's Fund Policy Institute, London.

Goodwin, N. (1998), 'GP Fundholding', in LeGrand, J., Mays, N. and Mulligan, J-A. (eds.), *Learning from the NHS Internal Market: A Review of the Evidence*, King's Fund, London, pp. 43-68.

Goodwin, N. (ed.) (1999), *The New NHS: What Can We Learn From Managed Care in New Zealand and the US?*, Seminar Briefing No.1, Office of Health Economics, London.

Goodwin, N. (2001), 'The Long Term Importance of English Primary Care Groups for Integration in Primary Care and Deinstitutionalisation of Hospital Care', *International Journal of Integrated Care*, March 2001.

Goodwin, N (2002), 'Creating an Integrated Public Sector? Labour's Plans for the Modernisation of the English Health Care System', *International Journal of Integrated Care*, Vol. 2(1).

Goodwin, N., 6, P., Peck, E., Freeman, T. and Posaner, R. (2004), *Managing Across Diverse Networks of Care: Lessons from Other Sectors: Policy Report*, Health Services Management Centre, University of Birmingham.

Goodwin, N., Abbott, S., Baxter, K., Evans, D., Killoran, A., Malbon, G., Mays, N., Scott, J. and Wyke, S. (2000), *The Dynamics of Primary Care Commissioning: Analysis and Implications of Eleven Total Purchasing Pilot Case Studies*, King's Fund Publishing, London.

Goodwin, N., Morris, J., Hill, K., McLeod, H., Burke, T. and Hall, A. (2004), 'National Evaluation of Personal Dental Services (PDS) Pilots: Main Findings and Policy Implications', *British Dental Journal*, Vol. 195, pp. 640-643.

Goodwin, N. and Peet, S. (2004), 'Intermediate Care', in J. Glasby and E. Peck (eds.), *Care Trusts: Partnership Working in Action*, Radcliffe Medical Press, Abingdon, pp. 51-62.

Goodwin, N. and Pinch, S. (1995), 'Explaining Geographical Variations in the Contracting Out of NHS Hospital Ancillary Services: A Contextual Approach', *Environment and Planning A*. Vol. 27, pp. 1397-1418.

Goodwin, N. and Shapiro, J. (2001), *The Road to Integrated Care Working*, Health Services Management Centre, University of Birmingham.

Green, J. and Thorogood, N. (1998), *Analysing Health Policy: A Sociological Approach*, Longman, London.

Green, J. and Tones, K. (1999), 'Towards a Secure Evidence-Base for Health Promotion', *Journal of Public Health Medicine*, Vol. 21, pp. 133-139.

Greenbaum, T. (1998), *The Handbook for Focus Group Research*, Sage, London.

Greer, S. (2001), *Divergence and Devolution*, The Nuffield Trust, London.

Griffiths Report (1988), *Community Care: Agenda for Action*, HMSO, London.

Groenewegen, P., Dixon, J. and Boerma, W. (2000), 'The Regulatory Environment of General Practice: An International Perspective', in R. Saltman, R. Busse and E. Mossialos (eds.), *Regulating Entrepreneurialism in Health Care*, Open University

Press, London.

Guillemin, J. and Holmstrom, L. (1986), *Mixed Blessings: Intensive Care for Newborns*, Oxford University Press, Oxford.

Ham, C. (1996), 'Population Centred and Patient Focused Purchasing: The UK Experience', *Milbank Quarterly*, Vol.74 (2), pp. 191-214.

Ham, C. (2004), *Health Policy in Britain*, sixth edition. Palgrave-MacMillan, Basingstoke.

Ham, C. and Alberti, K. (2002), 'The Medical Profession, The Public and Government', *BMJ*, Vol. 324, pp. 838-842.

Ham, C., Robinson, R. and Benzeval, M. (1990), *Health Check: Health Care Reform in an International Context*, King's Fund Institute, London.

Ham, C., Smith, J. Temple, J. (1998), *Hubs, Spokes and Policy Cycles: An Analysis of the Service Implications for the NHS of Changes to Medical Staffing*, King's Fund, London.

Ham, C., York, N., Sutch, S. and Shaw, R. (2003), 'Hospital Bed Utilisation in the NHS, Kaiser Permanente, and the US Medicare Programme: Analysis of Routine Data', *BMJ*, Vol. 327, pp. 1257-1260.

Harrison, J., Innes, R. and van Zwanenberg, T. (2001), *The New GP: Changing Roles and The Modern NHS*, Radcliffe Medical Press, Abingdon.

Harrison, M. and Calltorp, J. (2000), 'The Reorientation of Market-Oriented Reforms in Swedish Health Care', *Health Policy*, Vol. 50, pp. 219-240.

Harrison, S. and Wood, B. (1999), 'Designing Health Service Organization in the UK, 1968 to 1998: From Blueprint to Bright Idea and "Manipulated Emergence"', *Public Administration*, Vol. 77, pp. 751-768.

Harrison, S., Hunter, D., Marnoch, G. and Pollitt, C. (2004), 'General Management in the NHS: Assessing the Impact', in A. Clarke, P. Allen, S. Anderson, N. Black, and N. Fulop (eds.), *Studying the Organisation and Delivery of Health Services: A Reader*, Routledge, London.

Hart, C. (2004), 'The Politics of Nursing', *Health Management*, May, pp. 14-16.

Hazell, R. and Jarvis, P. (1998), *Devolution and Health*, Nuffield Trust Series No. 3, Nuffield Trust and University College London.

Healy, J. (2002), 'New Zealand', in A. Dixon and E. Mossialos (eds.), *Health Care Systems in Eight Countries: Trends and Challenges*, European Observatory on Health Care Systems, Copenhagen, pp. 75-88.

Hennessy, D. and Spurgeon, P. (eds.) (2000), *Implications of Policy Development for the Nursing Profession*, MacMillan, London.

Henwood, M. (2001), *The Health and Social Care Interface: From Partnership to Integration?*, Paper to Health and Social Care in Britain and Europe Conference, London School of Economics, 10 January 2002, London.

Hill, K., Goodwin, N., Morris, J., Hall, A., McLeod, H. and Burke, T. (2003), *Personal Dental Services (PDS) Pilots: Final Report of the National Evaluation*, School of Dentistry and Health Services Management Centre, University of Birmingham, 2003.

Himmelstein, D. and Woolhandler, S. (1998), 'The NHS at 50: An American View',

Lancet, Vol. 352 (9121), pp. 54-55.

Hjortsberg, C. and Ghatnekar, O. (2001), *Health Care Systems in Transition: Sweden*, European Observatory on Health Care Systems, Copenhagen.

Hudson, B. (1999), 'Primary Health Care and Social Care: Working Across Professional Boundaries', *Managing Community Care*, Vol. 7(2), pp. 15-20.

Hudson, B. (2002), 'Integrated Care and Structural Change in England: The Case of Care Trusts', *Policy Studies*, Vol. 23(2), pp. 77-95.

Hudson, B. and Hardy, B. (2001), 'Localization and partnership in the "New National Health Service": England and Scotland compared', *Public Administration*, vol. 79, no. 2, pp. 225-315.

Hudson, B. and Henwood, M. (2002), 'The NHS and Social Care: The Final countdown?', *Policy and Politics*, Vol. 30(2), pp. 153-166.

Hudson, B., Callaghan, G., Exworthy, M. and Peckham, S. (1999), *Locality Partnerships: The Early PCG Experience*, Report to Northern and Yorkshire NHS Executive.

Hudson, B. and Hardy, B. (2001), 'Localization and Partnership in the "New National Health Service": England and Scotland Compared', *Public Administration*, Vol. 79(2), pp. 225-315.

Hudson, B., Hardy, B., Glendinning, C. and Young, R. (2002), *National Evaluation of Notifications for Use of the Section 31 Partnership Flexibilities in the Health Act 1999. Final Project Report*, National Primary Care Research and Development Centre, University of Manchester.

Hutt, R., Rosen, R. and McCauley, J. (2004), *Case-Managing Long Term Conditions: What Impact Does It Have in the Treatment of Older People?*, King's Fund, London.

Jacobs, K. (1997), 'A Reforming Accountability: GPs and Health Reform in New Zealand', *International Journal of Health Planning and Management*, Vol. 12, pp. 169-185.

Jenkins-Clarke, S. and Carr-Hill, R. (2001), 'Changes, Challenges and Choices for the Primary Health Care Workforce: Looking to the Future', *Journal of Advanced Nursing*, Vol. 34, pp. 842-849.

Jenkins-Clarke, S., Carr-Hill, R. and Dixon, P. (1998), 'Teams and Seams: Skill Mix in Primary Care', *Journal of Advanced Nursing*, Vol. 28, pp. 1120-1126.

Judge, K. and Bauld, L. (2004), 'Strong Theory, Flexible Methods: Evaluating Complex Community-Based Initiatives', in A. Clarke, P. Allen, S. Anderson, N. Black, and N. Fulop (eds.), *Studying the Organisation and Delivery of Health Services: A Reader*, Routledge, London, pp. 304-314.

Kaner, E., Haighton, C. and McAvoy, B. (1998), 'So Much Post, So Busy with Practice, So ... No Time!: A Telephone Survey of General Practitioners' Reasons for not Participating in Postal Questionnaire Surveys', *British Journal of General Practice*, Vol. 48, pp. 1067-1069.

Keen, J. and Packwood, T. (1996), 'Case Study Evaluation', in N. Mays and C. Pope (eds.), *Qualitative Research in Health Care*, BMJ Publishing Group, London, pp.

59-67.

Kennedy, I. (2001), *The Report of the Public Inquiry into Children's Heart Surgery at the Bristol Royal Infirmary 1984-1995*, Cm 5201(1), The Stationery Office Limited, Norwich.

Killoran, A., Abbott, S., Malbon, G., Mays, N., Wyke, S. and Goodwin, N. (1999), *The Transition from TPPs to PCGs: Lessons for PCG Development*, King's Fund, London.

Kinnersley P., Anderson, E., Parry, K., Clement, J., Archard, L., Turton, P., Stainthorpe, A., Fraser, A., Butler, C. and Rogers, C. (2000), 'Randomised Controlled Trial of Nurse Practitioner versus General Practitioner Care for Patients Requesting "Same Day" Consultations in Primary Care', *British Medical Journal*, Vol. 320, pp. 1043-1048.

Kitchener, M. (2000), 'The "Bureaucratisation" of Professional Roles: The Case of Clinical Directors in UK Hospitals', *Organization*, Vol. 7(1), pp. 129-154.

Klein, R. (1995), 'From Evidence-Based Medicine to Evidence-Based Policy', *Journal of Health Services Research and Policy*, Vol. 5(2), pp. 65-66.

Klein, R. (2001), *The New Politics of the NHS*, Pearson Education, Harlow.

Klein, R. (2003), 'Governance for NHS Foundation Trusts', *British Medical Journal*, Vol. 326, pp. 174-175.

Klein, R. (2004), 'The First Wave of NHS Foundation Trusts', *British Medical Journal*, Vol. 328, pp. 1332.

Kmietowicz, Z. (2001), 'Quarter of GPs Want to Quit', *British Medical Journal*, Vol. 323, pp. 887.

Kralewski, J., Rich, E., Feldman, R., Dowd, B., Bernhardt, T., Johnson, C. and Gold, W. (2000), 'The Effects of Medical Group Practice and Physician Payment Methods on Costs of Care', *Health Service Research*, Vol. 35(3), pp. 591-613.

Krueger, R. (1994), *Focus Groups: A Practical Guide for Applied Research*, Sage, London.

Lee, J., Gask, L., Roland, M. and Donnan, S. (1999), *Total Purchasing and Extended Fundholding of Mental Health Services. Final Report to the Department of Health*, National Primary Care Research and Development Centre, University of Manchester, Manchester.

LeGrand, J. (2003), *Motivation, Agency and Public Policy. Of Knights & Knaves, Pawns & Queens*, Oxford University Press, Oxford.

LeGrand, J., Mays, N. and Mulligan, J-A. (1998), *Learning from the NHS Internal Market: A Review of the Evidence*, King's Fund, London.

Leon, S. and Rico, A. (2002), 'Sweden', in A. Dixon and E. Mossialos (eds.), *Health Care Systems in Eight Countries: Trends and Challenges*, European Observatory on Health Care Systems, Copenhagen, pp. 91-102.

Lewis, R. (2004), *Practice Led Commissioning: Harnessing the Power of the Primary Care Frontline*, King's Fund, London.

Lieverdink, H. (2001), 'The Marginal Success of Regulated Competition Policy in the Netherlands', *Social Science and Medicine*, Vol. 52, pp. 1183-1194.

Light, D. (2001), 'Cost Containment and the Backdraft of Competition Policies',

International Journal of Health Services, Vol. 31(4), pp. 681-708.

Lilly, R. (2003), *The New GP Contract. How To Make The Most Of It*, Radcliffe Medical Press, Abingdon.

Locock, L., Regen, E. and Goodwin, N. (2004), 'Managing or Managed? Experience of General Practitioners in English Primary Care Groups and Trusts', *Health Services Management Research*, Vol. 17, pp. 24-35.

Loudon, I., Horder, J. and Webster, C. (1998), *General Practice Under the National Health Service 1948 - 1997*, Clarendon Press, Oxford.

Lupton, C., Peckham, S. and Taylor, P. (1998), *Managing Public Involvement in Healthcare Purchasing*, Open University Press, Buckingham.

Macinko, J., Starfield, B. and Shi, L. (2003), 'The Contribution of Primary Care Systems to Health Outcomes within Organizations for Economic Cooperation and Development (OECD) Countries, 1970-1998', *Health Services Research*, Vol. 38(3), pp. 831-865.

Malcolm, L. and Mays, N. (1999). 'New Zealand's Independent Practitioner Associations: A Working Model of Clinical Governance in Primary Care?', *British Medical Journal*, Vol. 319, pp. 1340-1342.

Malcolm, L., Wright, L. and Barnett, P. (1999), *The Development of Primary Care Orgnanisations in New Zealand*, Ministry of Health, Wellington, New Zealand.

Malcolm, L., Wright, J., Seers, M. and Guthrie, J. (1999), 'An Evaluation of Pharmaceutical Management and Budget Holding in Pegasus Medical Group', *New Zealand Medical Journal*, Vol. 112, pp. 162-164.

Martin, S. and Sanderson, I. (1999), 'Evaluating Public Policy Experiments: Measuring Outcomes, Monitoring Performance, or Managing Pilots?' *Evaluation*, Vol. 5(3), pp. 245-258.

Maynard, A. (2004), 'Entrepreneurial spirit', *Health Services Journal*, Vol. 114(5907), pp. 16-17.

Maynard, A., Bloor, K. and Freemantle, N. (2004), 'Challenges for the National Institute of Clinical Excellence', *BMJ*, Vol. 329, pp. 227-229.

Mays, N. and Dixon, J. (1996), *Purchaser Plurality in UK Health Care: Is a Consensus Emerging and Is It The Right One?*, King's Fund Publishing, London.

Mays, N. and Goodwin, N. (1998), 'Primary Care Groups in England', in Klein, R, (ed.). *Implementing the White Paper: Pitfalls and Opportunities*, King's Fund Publishing, London, pp. 1-18.

Mays, N., Goodwin, N., Killoran, A. and Malbon, G. (1998), *Total Purchasing: A Step Towards Primary Care Groups*, King's Fund, London.

Mays, N., Goodwin, N., Malbon, G. and Wyke, S. (2001), 'Health Service Development: What Can Be Learned From The UK Total Purchasing Experiment', in N. Mays, S. Wyke, G. Malbon and N. Goodwin (eds.), *The Purchasing of Health Care by Primary Care Organisations: An Evaluation and Guide to Future Policy*, Open University Press, Buckingham, pp. 1-25.

Mays, N. and Mulligan, J-A. (1998), 'Total Purchasing', in LeGrand, J., Mays, N. and Mulligan, J-A. (eds.), *Learning from the NHS Internal Market: A Review of the Evidence*, King's Fund, London, pp. 84-99.

Mays, N., Mulligan, J-A. and Goodwin, N. (2000), 'The British Quasi-Market in Health Care: A Balance Sheet of the Evidence', *Journal of Health Services Research and Policy*, Vol. 5(1), pp. 49-58.

Mays, N. and Pope, C. (1995), 'Observational Methods in Health Care Settings, *British Medical Journal*, Vol. 311, pp. 182-184.

Mays, N. and Pope, C. (1996) (eds.), *Qualitative Research in Health Care*, BMJ Publishing Group, London.

Mays, N. and Wyke, S. (2001), 'Designing the Evaluation of the Total Purchasing Experiment: Problems and Solutions', in N. Mays, S. Wyke, G. Malbon, and N. Goodwin (eds.), *The Purchasing of Health Care by Primary Care Organisations. An Evaluation and Guide to Future Policy*, Open University Press, Buckingham, pp. 253-277.

Mays, N., Wyke, S., Malbon, G. and Goodwin, N. (eds.) (2001), *The Purchasing of Health Care by Primary Care Organisations: An Evaluation and Guide to Future Policy*, Open University Press, Buckingham.

Mays, N., Wyke, S. and Evans, D. (2001), 'The Evaluation of Complex Health Policy. Lessons from the UK Total Purchasing Experiment, *Evaluation*, Vol.7(4), pp. 405-426.

McCay, C. and Donnelly, M. (2000), *Northern Ireland Primary Care Commissioning Group Pilots: Interim Report*, Health and Social Care Research Unit, Queen's University of Belfast.

McLeod, H. (2001), *Prescribing in Twelve Case Study PCGs: Results from 1999/2000*, Health Services Management Centre, University of Birmingham.

McLeod, H., Baines, D. and Raftery, J. (2000), *Prescribing in the Commissioning Groups: Results from 1998-1999*, Health Services Management Centre, University of Birmingham.

Meads, G., Killoran, A., Ashcroft, J. and Cornish, Y. (1999), *Mixing Oil and Water: How Can Primary Care Organisations Improve Health as Well as Deliver Effective Health Care?*, Health Education Authority, London.

Milewa, T., Harrison, S. and Dowswell, G. (2003) 'Public Involvement and Democratic Accountability in Primary Care Organisations', in B. Dowling and C. Glendinning (eds.), *The New Primary Care: Modern, Dependable, Successful?*, Open University Press, Maidenhead, pp. 179-195.

Miller, R. and Luft, H. (1994), 'Managed Care Plans – Characteristics, Growth and Premium Performance', *Annual Review of Public Health*, Vol. 15, pp. 437-459.

Ministry of Health, Welfare and Sport (2001), *Vraag Aan Bod, 2002*, The Hague.

Moon, G. and North, N. (2000), *Policy and Place: General Medical Practice in the UK*, Macmillan, London.

Mulligan, J-A. (1998), 'Locality and GP Commissioning', in LeGrand, J., Mays, N. and Mulligan, J-A. (eds.), *Learning from the NHS Internal Market: A Review of the Evidence*, King's Fund, London, pp. 69-83.

Murphy, E. (2001), 'Micro-Level Qualitative Research', in N. Fulop, P. Allen, A. Clarke, and N. Black (eds.), *Studying the Organisation and Delivery of Health*

Services. Research Methods, Routledge, London, pp. 40-55.

Myles, S., Wyke, S., Popay, J., Scott, J., Campbell, A. and Girling, J. (1998), *Total Purchasing and Community and Continuing Care: Lessons for Future Policy Developments in the NHS*, King's Fund, London.

NERA (2005), *New Commissioning Roles in the New NHS Framework*, National Economic Research Associates Consulting, London.

Newman, K. and Maylor, U. (2002), 'The NHS Plan: Nurse Satisfaction, Commitment and Retention Strategies', *Health Services Management Review*, Vol. 15, pp. 93-105.

NHS Alliance (2002), *NHS Alliance Survey of PEC Clinical Chairs*, NHS Alliance, Retford.

NHS Alliance (2003), *Engaging GPs in the New NHS*, NHS Alliance, Retford.

NHS Alliance (2004a), *A Guide to Practice-Led Commissioning*, NHS Alliance, Retford.

NHS Alliance (2004b), *Engaging Nurses in the New NHS*, NHS Alliance, Retford.

NHS Alliance and Clinical Governance Support Team (2004), *Making a Difference: Engaging Clinicians in PCTs*, NHS Alliance, Retford.

NHS Alliance and Primary Care Report (2003), *Clinician Engagement: A National Survey*, NHS Alliance, Retford.

NHS Appointments Commission (2002), *Welcome to the NHS: Induction Guide for Chairs and Non-Executive Directors*, NHS Appointments Commission, London.

NHS Confederation (2003a), *The New Structure of the NHS in Wales*, Briefing 83, NHS Confederation, June 2003.

NHS Confederation (2003b), *The New Structure of NHS Scotland*, Briefing 84, NHS Confederation, June 2003.

NHS Confederation (2003c), *The Structure of Health and Social Services Provision in Northern Ireland*, Briefing 85, NHS Confederation, June 2003.

NHS Confederation (2003d), *The Role of Nurses under the New GMS Contract*, NHS Confederation, London.

NHS Confederation (2003e), *Investing in General Practice: The New General Medical Services Contract*, Briefing 79, NHS Confederation, London.

NHS Executive (1994), *Developing NHS Purchasing and GP Fundholding*, EL 1994/79, NHS Executive, Leeds.

NHS Executive (1997a), *Changing the Internal Market*, EL 1997/33, NHS Executive, Leeds.

NHS Executive (1997b), *GP Commissioning Groups*, EL 1997/37, NHS Executive, Leeds.

NHS Executive (1998a), *Developing Primary Care Groups*, HSC 1998/139, NHS Executive, Leeds.

NHS Executive (1998b), *A First Class Service*, NHS Executive, Leeds.

NHS Executive (1998c), *Information for Health*, HSC 1998/168, NHS Executive, Leeds.

NHS Executive (1999a), Primary Care Trusts – Establishing Better Services, NHS

Executive, Leeds.

NHS Executive (1999b), Quality and Performance in the NHS: High Level Performance Indicators, NHS Executive, Leeds.

North, N., Lupton, C. and Khan, P. (1999), 'Going with the Grain? General Practitioners and the New NHS?', *Health and Social Care in the Community*, Vol. 7(6), pp. 408-416.

North, N. and Peckham, S. (2001), 'Analysing Structural Interests in Primary Care', *Social Policy and Administration*, Vol. 35(4), pp. 426-440.

O'Connor, D. and Peterson, C. (2002), 'General Practice in Australia: The Effects of Reforms and the Process of Privatisation', in H. Gardner and S. Barraclough (eds.), *Health Policy in Australia*, 2nd edition, Oxford University Press, Oxford, New York.

Olesen, F., Jensen, P., Grinsted, P. and Henriksen, J. (1998), 'GPs as Advisors and Co-ordinators in Hospitals', *Quality in Health Care*, Vol. 7, pp. 42-47.

Övretveit, J. (1995), *Purchasing for Health*, Open University Press, Buckingham.

Övretveit, J. (1998), *Evaluating Health Interventions*, Open University Press, Buckingham.

Patton, M. (1990), *Qualitative Evaluation and Research Methods*, 2nd Edition, Sage, Newbury Park, California.

Pawson, R. and Tilley, N. (1997), *Realistic Evaluation*, Sage, London.

Peck, E. and Freeman, T. (2005), *Reconfiguring PCTs: Influences and Options*, NHS Alliance and Health Services Management Centre, Retford and Birmingham.

Peckham, S. (2003), *Improving Local Health*, in B. Dowling, B. and C. Glendinning (eds.), *The New Primary Care: Modern, Dependable, Successful?*, Open University Press, Maidenhead, pp. 159-178.

Peckham, S. and Exworthy, M. (2003), *Primary Care in the UK: Policy, Organisation and Management,* Palgrave-MacMillan, Basingstoke.

Peters, T. and Waterman, R. (1982), *In Search of Excellence*, New York, Harper and Row.

Pettigrew, A., Ferlie, E. and McKee, L. (1992), *Shaping Strategic Change*, Sage, London.

Pettigrew, A., Ferlie, E. and McKee, L. (2004), 'Receptive and Non-receptive Contexts for Change', in A. Clarke, P. Allen, S. Anderson, N. Black, and N. Fulop (eds.), *Studying the Organisation and Delivery of Health Services: A Reader*, Routledge, London, pp. 249-259.

PMS National Evaluation Team (2002), *National Evaluation of First Wave NHS Personal Medical Services Pilots – Summaries of Findings from Four Research Projects*, National Primary Care Research and Development Centre, Manchester.

Pollock, A. (2001), 'Will Primary Care Trusts Lead to US-style Health Care?', *British Medical Journal*, Vol. 322, pp. 964-967.

Pollock, A., Prince, D., Talbot-Smith, A. and Mohan, J. (2003), 'NHS and the Health and Social Care Bill: End of Bevan's Vision?', *British Medical Journal*, Vol. 327, pp. 982-985.

Popay, J. (2001), *Evidence to House of Commons Select Committee on Health*, The

Stationery Office, London.

Posnett, J., Goodwin, N., Griffiths, J., Killoran, A., Malbon, G., Mays, N., Place, M. and Street, A. (1998), *The Transaction Costs of Total Purchasing*, King's Fund Publishing, London.

Preston, C. and Baker, R. (2000), 'Survey of the Development of Clinical Governance in England and Wales NHS', *Journal of Clinical Governance*, Vol. 8, pp. 118-123.

Propper, C., Croxson, B. and Shearer, A. (2002), 'Waiting Times for Hospital Admissions: The Impact of GP Fundholding', *Journal of Health Economics*, Vol. 21, pp. 227-252.

Raine, R. (1998), 'Evidence-Based Policy: Rhetoric and Reality', *Journal of Health Services Research and Policy*, Vol. 3(4), pp. 2251-2253.

Regen, E. (2002), *Driving Seat or Back Seat? GP's Views on and Involvement in Primary Care Groups and Trusts*, Health Services Management Centre, University of Birmingham.

Regen, E. and Smith, J. (2000), *Getting on Board: A Study of the Appointment and Induction of PCG Board Members in the West Midlands*, Health Services Management Centre, University of Birmingham.

Regen, E., Smith, J.A., Goodwin, N., McLeod, H. and Shapiro, J. (2001), *Passing on the Baton: Final Report of a National Evaluation of Primary Care Groups and Trusts*, Health Services Management Centre, Birmingham.

Regen, E., Smith, J.A., Shapiro, J. (1999), *First Off The Starting Block: Lessons from GP Commissioning Pilots for Primary Care Groups*, Health Services Management Centre, Birmingham.

Richards, A., Carley, J., Jenkins-Clarke, S. and Richards, D. (2000), 'Skill Mix between Nurses and Doctors Working in Primary Care: Delegation or Allocation? A review of the literature', *International Journal of Nursing Studies*, Vol. 37, pp. 185-197.

Robinson, J. (2001), 'The End of Managed Care', *Journal of the American Medical Association*, Vol. 285(20), pp. 2622-2628.

Robinson, R. (2003), 'English Primary Care Organisations in an International Context', in B. Dowling and C. Glendinning (eds.), *The New Primary Care: Modern, Dependable, Successful?*, Open University Press, Maidenhead, pp. 40-53.

Robinson, R. and Exworthy, M. (1999), *Two at the Top: A Study of Working Relationships Between Chairs and Chief Executives at Health Authorities, Boards and Trusts in the NHS*, NHS Confederation/NHS Leadership Programme/IHSM, London.

Robinson, R. and Exworthy, M. (2001), *Three at the Top: Working Relationships Between Chairs and Chief Executives at First and Second Wave Primary Care Trusts. Final Report Submitted to the NHS Leadership Centre*, Unpublished report.

Robinson, R. and Steiner, A. (eds.) (1998), *Managed Health Care*, Open University

Press, Buckingham.

Roland, M. and Smith, J. (2003), 'The Role and Contribution of Primary Care Trusts in Quality Improvement', in S. Leatherman and K. Sutherland (eds.), *The Quest for Quality in the NHS: A Mid-Term Evaluation of the Ten-Year Quality Agenda*, The Stationery Office and the Nuffield Trust, London.

Rosleff, F. and Lister, G. (1995), *European Health Care Trends: Towards Managed Care in Europe*, Coopers and Lybrand Europe Ltd.

Rowe, R. and Shepherd, M. (2002), 'Public Participation in the New NHS: No Closer to Citizen Control?, *Social Policy and Administration*, Vol. 36(3), pp. 275-90.

Rummery, K. and Glendinning, C. (2000), *Primary Care and Social Services: Developing New Partnerships for Older People*, National Primary Care Research and Development Centre, Manchester.

Saltman, R., Figueras, J. and Sakellarides, C. (1998), *Critical Challenges for Health Care Reform in Europe*, Open University Press, Buckingham.

Saltman, R., Rico, A. and Boerma, W. (eds.) (2004), *Study Proposal: Primary Care in the Driver's Seat? Organizational Reform in European Primary Care*, The European Observatory on Health Care Systems, www.euro.who.int/observatory/ Studies.

Schoen, C. et al (2000), *Equity in Health Care Across Five Nations: Summary Findings from an International Policy Survey*, The Commonwealth Fund, New York.

Schoen, C., Osbon, R., Huynh, P-T., Doty, M., Davis, K., Zopert, K. and Peugh, J. (2004), 'Primary Care and Health Systems Performance: Adults' Experiences in Five Countries', *Health Affairs*, October 28th, EPublication, pp. 487-503.

Schut, F. (1995), 'Health Care Reform in the Netherlands: Balancing Corporatism, Etatism and Market Mechanisms', *Journal of Health Politics, Policy and Law*, Vol. 20, pp. 615-652.

Schut, F. and Dorslaer, E. (1999), 'Towards a Reinforced Agency Role of Health Insurers in Belgium and the Netherlands', *Health Policy*, Vol. 48, pp. 47-67.

Seale, C. (1999), *The Quality of Qualitative Research*, Sage, London.

Secretary of State for Health (1995), *Disability Discrimination Act 1995*, The Stationery Office, London.

Secretary of State for Health (1999), *Saving Lives: Our Healthier Nation*, The Stationery Office, London.

Secretary of State for Scotland (1997), *Designed to Care: Renewing the National Health Service in Scotland*, CMR 3811, TSO, Edinburgh.

Senge, P. (1990), *The Fifth Discipline: The Art and Practice of the Learning Organisation*, Doubleday/Century Business, London.

Shapiro, J. (2003), 'Lessons for the NHS from Kaiser Permanente', *BMJ*, Vol. 327, pp. 1242-1243.

Shapiro, J. and Goodwin, N. (2001), *Primary Health Care in Boston: Proceedings of a Study Tour*, HSMC, University of Birmingham.

Shapiro, J., Smith J. and Walsh, N. (1996), *Approaches to Commissioning: The*

Dynamics of Diversity, NAHAT, Birmingham.

Sheaff, R., Marshall, M., Rogers, A., Roland, M., Sibbald, B. and Pickard, S. (2004), 'Governmentality by Network in English Primary Healthcare', *Social Science and Administration*, Vol. 38(1), pp. 89-103.

Sheaff, R., Rogers, A., Pickard, S., Marshall, M., Campbell, S., Roland, M., Sibbald, B. and Halliwell, S. (2003), 'Medical Leadership in English Primary Care Networks', in S, Dopson and A. Mark (eds.), *Leading Health Care Organizations*, Palgrave-MacMillan, Basingstoke.

Shekele, P. (2002), 'Why Don't Physicians Enthusiastically Support Quality Improvement Programmes?', *Quality and Safety in Health Care*, Vol. 11(1), p. 6.

Sheldon, T. (2001), 'Dutch Government Plans to Reform Health Insurance System', *BMJ*, Vol. 323, p. 70.

Shepherd, M. (2000), *A Valuable Resource: Public Involvement in Primary Care Groups in the South West*, Avon Health Authority, Bristol.

Shum, C., Humphreys, A., Wheeler, D., Cochrane, M., Skoda, S. and Clement, S. (2000), 'Nurse Management of Patients with Minor Illnesses in General Practice: Multicentre, Randomised Controlled Trial', *British Medical Journal*, Vol. 320, pp. 1038-1043.

Sibbald, B. (2000), 'Primary Care: Background and Policy Issues', in A. Williams (ed.), *Nursing, Medicine and Primary Care*, Open University Press, Buckingham.

Sinha, S. (2005), *Care trusts: an English solution for integrated health and social care*, paper presented to the 6th Annual Conference of Integrated Care, Dublin Castle, Dublin, February 14th.

Smee, C. (1999), 'How can the UK best learn from other countries?' in N. Goodwin (ed.) *The new NHS: what can we learn from managed care in New Zealand and the US?*, Seminar briefing paper no.1, Office of Health Economics, pp. 8-10.

Smith, J. (1998), 'Managed Care: A Route Map for Exploring Health Policy Changes', in P. Spurgeon (ed.), *The New Face of the NHS*, The Royal Society of Medicine Press, London.

Smith, J, Bamford, M., Ham, C., Scrivens, E. and Shapiro, J. (1997), *Beyond Fundholding: A Mosaic of Primary Care Led Commissioning and Provision in the West Midlands*, Health Services Management Centre, Birmingham, Centre for Health Planning and Management, Keele, and West Midlands NHS Executive, Birmingham.

Smith, J., Barnes, M., Ham, C. and Martin, G. (1998), *Mapping Approaches to Commissioning: Extending the Mosaic*, King's Fund, London.

Smith, J. and Goodwin, N. (2002), *Developing Effective Commissioning by Primary Care Trusts: Lessons from the Research Evidence*, HSMC, University of Birmingham.

Smith, J.A., Goodwin, N., Peck, E. (2003), 'Building Bridges', *Health Service Journal*, Vol. 113(5856), pp. 24-26.

Smith, J., Mays, N., Dixon, J., Goodwin, N., Lewis, R., McLelland, S., McLeod, H. and Wyke, S. (2004), *A Review of the Effectiveness of Primary Care-Led*

Commissioning and its Place in the NHS, The Health Foundation, London, 2004.

Smith, J.A., Regen, E., Goodwin, N., McLeod, H., Shapiro, J. (2000), *Getting Into Their Stride: Interim Report of a National Evaluation of Primary Care Groups*, Health Services Management Centre, Birmingham.

Smith, J., Regen, E., Griffiths, R. and Kaur, B. (2000), 'Serving from the Shadows', *Health Service Journal*, 31 August, pp. 22-24.

Smith, J.A. and Shapiro, J. (1996), *Holding On While Letting Go: An Evaluation of Locality Commissioning in County Durham and Newcastle/North Tyneside*, HSMC, University of Birmingham.

Smith, J.A. and Shapiro, J. (1997), 'Local Call', in *Health Service Journal*, 9 January, Vol. 107, no. 5535, pp. 26-27.

Smith, J. and Walshe, K. (2004), 'Big Business: The Corporatization of Primary Care in the UK and the USA', *Public Money and Management*, Vol. 24(2), pp. 87-96.

Smith, P. (1999), 'Setting budgets for general practice in the new NHS', *British Medical Journal*, Vol. 318, pp. 776-779.

Smith, P. and York, N. (2004), 'Quality Incentives: The Case of General Practitioners', *Health Affairs*, Vol. 23(3), pp. 112-118.

Smith, R. (2001), 'Why are Doctors so Unhappy?', *British Medical Journal*, Vol. 322, pp. 1073-1074.

Spooner, A., Chapple, A. and Roland M. (2001), 'What Makes British General Practitioners Take Part in a Quality Improvement Scheme?', *Journal of Health Services Research and Policy*, Vol. 6(3), pp. 145-50.

Stake, R. (1995), *The Art of Case Study Research*, Sage, Thousand Oaks, California.

Starey, N. (2003), *The Challenge for Primary Care*, Radcliffe Medical Press, Abingdon.

Starfield, B. (1994), 'Is Primary Care Essential', *The Lancet*, Vol. 344(8930), pp. 1129-1133.

Starfield, B. (1998), *Primary Care: Balancing Health Needs, Services and Technology*, Oxford University Press, Oxford.

Stewart-Brown, S., Surender, R., Bradlow, J., Coulter, A. and Doll, H. (1995), 'The Effects of Fundholding in General Practices on Prescribing Habits Three Years After Introduction of the Scheme, *BMJ*, Vol. 311, pp. 1543-1547.

Strawderman T., Mays N. and Goodwin N. (1996), *Survey of NHSE Regional Total Purchasing Lead Officers*, Unpublished Report, King's Fund, London.

Street, A. and Place, M. (1998), *The Management Challenges for Primary Care Groups*, King's Fund, London.

Street, A., Place, A. and Posnett, J. (2001), 'The management and transaction costs of total purchasing', in N. Mays, S. Wyke, G. Malbon and N. Goodwin (eds.), *The Purchasing of Health Care by Primary Care Organisations: An Evaluation and Guide to Future Policy*, Open University Press, Buckingham, pp. 147-166.

Sweeney, G., Sweeney, K., Greco, M. and Stead, J. (2001), 'Moving Clinical

Governance Forward: Capturing the Experiences of Primary Care Group Leads', *Clinical Governance Bulletin*, Vol. 2(1), pp. 6-7.

Sweeney, G., Sweeney, K., Greco, M. and Stead, J. (2002), 'Softly, Softly, The Way Forward? A Qualitative Study of the First Year of Implementing Clinical Governance in Primary Care', *Primary Health Research and Development*, Vol. 3(1), pp. 53-64.

Swerrison, H. and Duckett, S. (2002), 'Health Policy and Financing', in H. Gardner and S. Barraclough (eds.), *Health Policy in Australia*, 2nd edition, Oxford University Press, Oxford, New York.

Taylor, G., Brown, K., Caldwell, K., Ghazi, F., Henshaw, L. and Vernon, L. (2004), 'User Involvement in Primary Care: A Case Study Examining The Work of One Patient Participation Group Attached to a Primary Care Practice in North London', *Research, Policy and Planning*, Vol. 22(1), pp. 21-30.

Taylor, P., Peckham, S. and Turton, P. (1998), *A Public Health Model of Primary Care: From Concept to Reality*, Public Health Alliance, Birmingham.

Thatcher, M. (1993), *The Downing Street Years*, HarperCollins, London.

The Shipman Inquiry (2004), *Fifth Report: Safeguarding Patients: Lessons from the Past – Proposals for the Future*, Cm 6394, HMSO, Norwich.

Timmins, N. (1995), *The Five Giants*, HarperCollins, London.

Titheridge, L. (2000), 'The Role of the Nurse Representative', in M. Dixon and K. Sweeney (eds.), *A Practical Guide to Primary Care Groups and Trusts*, Radcliffe Medical Press, Abingdon, pp. 143-148.

Van der Linden, B., Spreeuwenberg, C. and Schrijvers, G. (2001), 'Integration of Care in The Netherlands: The Development of Transmural Care Since 1994', *Health Policy*, Vol. 55, pp. 111-120.

Wade, E. (2004), *A Case Study Exploring the Conditions, Attractions and Simple Rules Shaping Professional Executive Committee Involvement in PCT Commissioning*, Health Services Management Centre, University of Birmingham.

Wagner, E. (1998), 'Chronic disease management: what will it take to improve care for chronic illness?', *Effective Clinical Practice*, Vol. 1, pp. 2-4.

Wall, A. (2003), 'Riding the Foundation Trust Hobby-Horse', *British Journal of Health Care Management*, Vol. 9(7), pp. 233-236.

Wall, A. and Baddeley, S. (1998), 'Chairman and Chief Executive Relations in the NHS', in A. Coulson (ed.), *Trust and Contracts*, The Policy Press, Bristol.

Walsh, N., Allen, L., Baines, D. and Barnes, M. (1999), *Taking Off: A First Year Report on the Personal Medical Services (PMS) Pilots in England*, HSMC, Birmingham.

Walsh, N., Andre, C., Barnes, M., Huntington, J., Rogers, H., Hendron, C. and McLeod, H. (2001), *First Wave PMS Pilots: Opening Pandora's Box*, Project report no. 18, Health Services Management Centre, University of Birmingham.

Walsh, N. and Huntington, J. (2003), 'From Parallel Policies to Integrated Practice: PMS and PCG/Ts', *Health Services Management Research*, Vol. 16(4), pp. 251-260.

Walshe, K. (1999), 'Baseline Assessment for Clinical Governance: Issues, Methods and Results', *Journal of Clinical Governance*, Vol. 7(4), pp. 166-171.

Walshe, K. (2003), 'Foundation Hospitals: A New Direction for NHS Reform?', *Journal of the Royal Society of Medicine*, 2003(96), pp. 106-110.

Walshe, K., Higgins, J. and Bradshaw, D. (2004), *Strategic Health Authorities: Researching their Developing Role and Function in the NHS in England – early findings*, Manchester Centre for Healthcare Management, Manchester.

Walshe, K. and Smith, J. (2001), 'Cause and Effect: How Do Chief Executives Feel About The Latest NHS Reorganisation?', *Health Services Journal*, 11 October, pp. 20-22.

Walt, G. (1994), *Health Policy: An Introduction to Process and Power*, Zed Books, London.

Weiner, J., Lewis, R. and Gillam, S. (2001), *US Managed Care and PCTs: Lessons to a Small Island from a Lost Continent*, King's Fund, London.

Wensing, M., Mainz, J., Ferreira, P., Hearnshaw, H., Hjortdahl, M., Olesen, F., Ribacke, S., Szecsenyi, J. and Grol, R. (1998), 'General Practice and Patients Priorities in Europe', *Health Policy*, Vol. 45, pp. 175-186.

White, K. (2000), 'The State, Market and General Practice: The Australian Case', *International Journal of Health Services*, Vol. 30(2), pp. 285-308.

White, K. and Collyer, F. (1998), 'Health Care Markets in Australia: Ownership of the Private Hospital Sector', *International Journal of Health Services*, Vol. 28(3), pp. 487-510.

Wicks, D. (1998), *Doctors and Nurses at Work: Rethinking Professional Boundaries*, Open University Press, Buckingham.

Wilkin, D and Coleman, A. (1999), 'Trusts and Mergers', in D. Wilkin, S. Gillam, and B. Leese (eds.), *The National Tracker Survey of Primary Care Groups and Trusts: Progress and Challenges 1999/2000*, The University of Manchester, Manchester.

Wilkin, D., Coleman, A., Dowling, B, and Smith, K. (eds.) (2002), *The National Tracker Survey of Primary Care Groups and Trusts 2001/2002: Taking Responsibility?*, National Primary Care Research and Development Centre, Manchester.

Wilkin, D. and Gillam, S. (2001), 'Progress and Challenges', in D. Wilkin, S. Gillam and A. Coleman (eds.) *The National Tracker Survey of Primary Care Groups and Trusts 2001/2002: Modernising the NHS?*, The University of Manchester, Manchester.

Wilkin, D., Gillam, S., Leese, B. (eds.) (2000), *The National Tracker Survey of Primary Care Groups and Trusts: Progress and Challenges 1999/2000*, National Primary Care Research and Development Centre, University of Manchester, Manchester.

Wilkin, D., Gillam, S., Coleman, A. (eds.) (2001), *The National Tracker Survey of Primary Care Groups and Trusts 2000/2001: Modernising the NHS?*, National Primary Care Research and Development Centre, University of Manchester, Manchester.

Williams, A. (ed.) (2000), *Nursing, Medicine and Primary Care*, Open University

Press, Buckingham.

Willis, A. (2002), *Making a Difference: Four Key Questions for PCTs*, NHS Alliance, London.

Wilson, A. (2000), 'The Changing Nature of Primary Health Care Teams and Interprofessional Relationships', in P. Tovey (ed.), *Contemporary Primary Care: The Challenge of Care*, Open University Press, Buckingham.

Woods, K. (2001), 'Sweden Today, Britain Tomorrow? Recent Policy Initiatives to Privatise Clinical Hospital Services in Stockholm', *British Journal of Health Care Management*, Vol. 7, p. 6.

Woolley, M., Ham, C., Harwood, A. and Patchett, S. (1995), *The Route to Total Care: Joint Commissioning of Community Care*, Institute for Health Services Management, London.

World Health Organisation (1978), *Declaration of Alma Ata. International Conference on Primary Health Care, Alma Ata, USSR, 6-12 September* 1978, WHO, Geneva.

Wyke, S., Gask, L,. Lee, J. and Scott, J. (2001), 'Purchasing Maternity Care, Mental Health Services and Community Care for Older People', in N. Mays, S. Wyke, G. Malbon, and N. Goodwin (eds.), *The Purchasing of Health Care by Primary Care Organisations: An Evaluation and Guide to Future Policy*, Open University Press, Buckingham, pp. 100-123.

Wyke, S., Mays, N., Abbott, S., Bevan, G., Goodwin, N., Killoran, A., Malbon, G., McLeod, H., Posnett, J., Raftery, J. and Robinson, R. (1999a), *Developing Primary Care in the New NHS: Lessons from Total Purchasing*, King's Fund Publishing, London.

Wyke, S., Hewison, J. and Posnett, J. (1999b), *General Practitioners Involvement in Commissioning Maternity Care. Does it make a Difference? Final report to the Department of Health*, Primary Care Research Group, University of Edinburgh.

Yin, R. (1994), *Case Study Research: Design and Methods*, 2nd Edition, Sage, Newbury Park, California.

Index